The Civil War in St. Louis

A Guided Tour

The Civil War in St. Louis
A Guided Tour

William C. Winter
for the
Civil War Round Table of St. Louis

Missouri Historical Society Press ■ St. Louis

Published in the United States of America by the Missouri Historical Society Press, P.O. Box 11940,
St. Louis, Missouri 63112-0040

Third Printing 1995

Library of Congress Cataloging-in-Publication Data
Winter, William C., 1947-
    The Civil War in St. Louis: a guided tour / by William C. Winter, for the Civil War Round
Table of St. Louis.
      p. cm.
      Includes bibliographical references and index.
      ISBN 1-883982-05-7 (cloth): $32.95 — ISBN 1-883982-06-5 (paper) $22.95
      1. Saint Louis (Mo.)-History-Civil War, 1861-1865. 2. Historic sites-Missouri-Saint
Louis-Guidebooks. 3. Saint Louis (Mo.)-Guidebooks. I. Civil War Round Table of St. Louis. II. Title.
III. Title: Civil War in Saint Louis.
      F474.S257W56 1994
      973.7'09778'65—dc20

94-22858
CIP

♾ ™ This publication meets the requirements of the American National Standard for Permanence of
Paper for Printed Library Materials, Z39.48, 1984.

Design: Robyn Morgan
Printed by: Walsworth Publishing Company
Cover: UK Paper Gleneagle Osprey Geo Dull recycled
Text: Simpson Evergreen Matte recycled
Fonts: Garamond, Garamond 3

Cover: Collision between the Federal Troops under Colonel M'Neil and the Citizens of St. Louis,
Mo.—The Fire of the Troops Taking Effect upon the Recorder's Court, Which Was Then in
Session. *The caption in the original erroneously identifies the unit's commander as M'Neil; the
commander was actually Colonel Kallmann. Wood engraving from* Frank Leslie's Illustrated
Newspaper, *June 29, 1861, p. 97. Missouri Historical Society Photograph and Print Collection.*

To the memory of the people of Civil War St. Louis,
men and women,
white and black,
blue and gray

Dedicated by the Civil War Round Table of St. Louis
on the occasion of its thirty-fifth anniversary, 1957-1992

Contents

Preface

The Civil War Round Table of St. Louis was organized in 1957 to promote the study of the American Civil War, with emphasis on Missouri's role in the conflict. Since its formation, the Round Table has expanded its membership to include more than 180 men and women who actively participate in its educational programs. The Round Table meets monthly from September to June, and its meetings are open to anyone interested in the Civil War period. To receive announcements of upcoming programs, send a stamped, self-addressed envelope to:

The Civil War Round Table of St. Louis
c/o 3930 Marietta Drive
Florissant, MO 63033

Over the years the Round Table has supported a variety of Civil War-related causes, ranging from battlefield preservation to scholarships for high school students to history conferences. In 1992 the Civil War Round Table of St. Louis celebrated its thirty-fifth anniversary, and to mark this occasion, the Round Table decided to undertake a project that would help citizens of St. Louis and Missouri understand the importance of the people and the places within our community during the Civil War years. This book is the result of that decision.

This tour guide is not intended to be a comprehensive history of St. Louis during the Civil War years; instead, it is intended to lead the reader to the sites of the most important events of that era. In some cases, the "site" may be no more than a street intersection, but such sites have been included because of the importance of the events that occurred at them.

Deciding what to include in the book was not easy. In fact, the process began by deciding what *not* to include. Because the book was not intended to be an architectural survey, buildings that still stand from the Civil War era are not included unless they have historical significance related to the Civil War. Even then, they may only be mentioned in the endnotes. On the other hand, numerous sites have been described at which nothing of the era still exists, for it is the event that is of importance. Without this distinction there would, for example, be no discussion of the Camp Jackson incident.

The identification and inclusion of burial places was also problematic. There are thousands of graves of Civil War veterans in the St. Louis area, but only the final resting places of the more prominent soldiers and politicians could be included if the guide was not to become a cemetery index. Officers below the rank of colonel and enlisted men have only been included when they made significant military contributions or had important connections to St. Louis. Winners of the Medal of Honor have been included wherever found, despite the occasionally questionable award of the Medal of Honor to Union veterans in the decades after the war.

The typical tour guide would divide the area under review into sections and describe the points of interest in each; as research began on this project, however, it soon became obvious that the geographical approach would not work. Instead, this tour guide is organized chronologically, giving the reader a better understanding of the chain of events, especially during the critical year of 1861. The best way to use this book is to study it before setting out to visit the sites it discusses. The reader will then have a better understanding of why it is necessary to begin the story at Jefferson Barracks County Park and to end it just a short distance away at Jefferson Barracks National Cemetery.

In preparing this book, members of the Civil War Round Table of St. Louis crossed paths with many who share our love of history. Frances Waldron of the Eugene Field House was gracious in her assistance with information about Eugene's father and Dred Scott's lawyer, Roswell Field. Charles Brown of the St. Louis Mercantile Library was always cooperative in our research. Candace O'Connor, then of the Missouri Historical Society, offered valuable suggestions on General Sherman's St. Louis years. The staff at the Missouri Historical Society's Library and Collections Center was also very helpful. James Mohan and M. Wells Huff, public affairs officers of the Defense Mapping Agency Aerospace Center (the modern tenants of the United States Arsenal), were forthcoming with materials about that facility's historical role. Douglas Harding, of the Jefferson National Expansion Memorial, willingly shared his compilation of newspaper articles and other firsthand accounts of the events of the military situation in St. Louis in early 1861. Charlene Gill, of the Alton Historical Society, answered many questions promptly and courteously. Carolyn Buckner, of the Ulysses S. Grant National Historic Site, and her former associate Kimberly Scott Little provided very useful insights into Grant's years in St. Louis and offered many suggestions on resources. Marjorie Ott, of the St. Louis County Library, often came to the rescue by her efforts to locate materials through interlibrary loan. Perhaps the most helpful contact of all was Michael Tiemann, the unofficial historian of the Bellefontaine Cemetery Association. Because of his personal interest—and a very thorough filing system—the stories of famous and obscure St. Louisans are kept alive.

As should be expected, thanks are owed to several individuals, past and present, associated with the Missouri Historical Society Press. Joseph Porter, then director of publications, read the manuscript and recommended its publication to Marsha Bray, who in turn had the courage to approve a major project dependent upon an unknown amateur historian. Director of Publications Lee Ann Schreiner came to the project shortly after its commissioning, and her commitment to a quality product certainly exceeded the Round Table's highest expectations. Duane Sneddeker's enthusiasm for the subject shows in his selection of images from the society's collection. Tim Fox, though the last to join the team, was in the end the most important. As editor, his expertise proved invaluable, and as project manager he demonstrated considerable ability in keeping everything on schedule.

Numerous members of the Civil War Round Table of St. Louis made contributions to this work. Included in the researchers and reviewers are Carolyn Buckner, Earl K. Dille, Jack Grothe, Douglas Harding, Henry C. Hartmann, Dennis Hermann, Hugh Johns, Vicki Vaughn Johnson, Jeffrey Leach, Phyllis McCauley, Hugh Mestres, Scott Nall, John F. Powell, William R. Piper, Oliver Sappington, Robert Sherrill, William F. Stoudt, William R. Vickroy, James Weir, and my elder son, William M. Winter. Robert Lauenstein performed invaluable detective work in a number of areas, especially in the case of Captain Constantin Blandowski. Dr. John Margreiter's long interest and ongoing research into the controversy surrounding Major James Wilson benefited us greatly. David Radcliffe's interest in Kirkwood's history and the fascination of William E. Winter, my father, with the history of the military prison at Alton also aided us beyond our expectations.

In this group of willing researchers, however, two stand out. Leonard E. "Gene" Dressel, Jr., is an authority on Confederate persons and places in Missouri. He graciously shared material from his own book, *A Self-Guided Tour of Confederate Graves at Bellefontaine Cemetery,* before its publication, and he answered my many questions promptly and with cheerful cooperation. Marshall D. Hier, past president of the Civil War Round Table and a major impetus behind this project, demonstrated his talents as a tenacious researcher with a particular specialty in newspaper archives. At times, he was an unstoppable wellspring of information. Marshall's most significant contribution, however, was as the person with whom I could argue the "facts" of the Civil War in St. Louis.

To my wife, Judy, go my thanks for note-taking assistance and advice during our numerous visits to the Civil War sites of St. Louis. She also deserves my appreciation for allowing the research to take over our home and for her unfailing encouragement to get this project done.

Despite all the research and all the reviews, errors may remain in this guide. If they do, they are my responsibility alone.

William C. Winter
Des Peres, Missouri

The Civil War in St. Louis

Chapter 1 Before

View of St. Louis. Wood engraving, ca. 1857. Missouri Historical Society Photograph and Print Collection.

Setting the Stage: St. Louis and Missouri, 1821-1861

Missouri was admitted to the Union in 1821 as a slave state, the result of Henry Clay's "Missouri Compromise." The decision maintained the balance of slave and free states while it prohibited slavery in the Louisiana Purchase outside of Missouri and north of Missouri's southern boundary. Slightly more than 10,000 slaves lived in Missouri in 1820; the number grew to 58,000 by 1840 and nearly doubled to 115,000 twenty years later. Despite this growth, Missouri was very different from the typical slave state. In 1860 only three slave states had fewer slaves than Missouri. Of those, only Delaware had a smaller percentage of slaves in its total population. The fact is that slave ownership was relatively uncommon in Missouri: only one family in eight held slaves, and of the slaveowning families, most owned fewer than five slaves. Only 540 families in Missouri held more than twenty slaves.[1]

St. Louis, being only a pleasant hour's drive from Jefferson Barracks, is the constant resort of the younger officers when not on duty. It is probably the greatest army place in the United States. The young ladies there are most accomplished coquettes and turn the heads and break the hearts of almost every Second Lieutenant who chances to come this way.

Journal of Army Life
1850

the War

If slavery was uncommon in Missouri, it was rare in St. Louis. While the city was a center for shipment of slaves to markets in the Deep South—thereby making slavery an important issue—only 3 percent of the state's slave population lived in St. Louis, used usually for domestic help or in tasks along the riverfront. Statistically, the city represented a relative haven for Missouri's free blacks. In 1840, more than a third of Missouri's free blacks lived in St. Louis; by 1850, more than half the state's free blacks lived there.[2]

In the forty years before the Civil War, the percentage of slaves in Missouri's population declined sharply, from 15.3 percent of the population in 1820 to only 9.7 percent in 1860. The reason for the decline, however, is less that slavery diminished in importance and more that the total population surged, particularly as a result of European immigration. Nowhere in the state was this more evident than in St. Louis.[3]

In the 1850s approximately three Missourians in four were of southern ancestry, but St. Louis was hit by a wave of immigrants. In 1840 its white population was less than 15,000 people. Ten years later the city's white population exceeded 73,000. By 1860, the population had more than doubled to 166,773, and 60 percent of St. Louis' residents were foreign-born, the highest percentage in any American city. Approximately 39,000 of these residents were Irish, and nearly 60,000 of them were German.[4]

Commercially, St. Louis rose remarkably in the decade before the Civil War. The railroad arrived in 1853, dramatically increasing the importance of the city relative to the rest of the state. In 1860 more than four thousand steamers with a capacity of more than 1.1 million tons loaded and unloaded at the city's wharves. Nearly two-thirds of the state's industrial output was produced there. In 1860 St. Louis was, in fact, the only urban area in Missouri worthy of being called a city. No other town in the state had as many as ten thousand inhabitants.[5]

St. Louis differed from the rest of the state politically, too. In November 1860 white male Missourians went to the polls to vote for a successor to President James Buchanan. Four candidates ran for the office. Stephen Douglas, the Democratic candidate from Illinois, received nearly 36 percent of Missouri's votes. John Bell, another centrist candidate running on the Constitutional Union ticket, drew 35 percent of the vote, only 429 votes fewer than Douglas. Slaveowners were represented by John Breckinridge, a "Southern Rights" Democrat. Breckinridge drew almost 19 percent of the vote. The candidate of the young Republican Party, Abraham Lincoln, received the endorsement of little more than 10 percent of the state's voters. Missourians had cast their votes squarely for the "status quo" as represented collectively by Douglas and Bell. Missouri was the only state in the Union that Senator Douglas carried in his national campaign.[6]

The situation was very different in St. Louis. St. Louis was one of only two counties in Missouri to be carried by Abraham Lincoln and the Republican Party. Breckenridge, the "slavery" candidate, received only 2.3 percent of the city's votes. In all the slave states combined, Lincoln received only twenty-seven thousand votes, but more than seventeen thousand of these votes came from the German-Americans of Missouri, and more than half of these came from St. Louis.[7]

A few months before the national election, Missourians elected Claiborne Fox Jackson, a scion of the planter class of central Missouri, as their governor. To gain wider support Jackson had run as a Douglas Democrat rather than as a Breckenridge Democrat, even though Breckenridge's pro-Southern positions were more consistent with Jackson's personal beliefs. Governor Jackson would soon be at odds with the growing political force of St. Louis.[8]

As historian Michael Fellman has described it, "By 1861 the St. Louis financial and industrial elite had become the new political force to challenge the dominance of the slave-holding elite of central Missouri. They made up in organization, discipline, and outside contacts what they lacked in numbers, tradition, or prior popular appeal." The stage was set for civil war in Missouri.[9]

Jefferson Barracks

Since 1950, part of Jefferson Barracks County Park, a unit of the St. Louis County Parks and Recreation Department, has been maintained as a historical area. From the intersection of Interstate 270 and Telegraph Road in south St. Louis County, proceed north on Telegraph Road. Do not follow the signs to Jefferson Barracks National Cemetery. Stay right on Kingston when Telegraph Road forks off to the west. Follow Kingston a short distance to South Broadway. Turn right (east) into the entrance of Jefferson Barracks County Park. Follow the signs to the Visitors' Center.

Four buildings still stand at Jefferson Barracks that saw service during the Civil War era. Near the Visitors' Center is the Laborers' House (erected 1851) and a stone stable of the same year. Follow the map to the Old Ordnance Room (1851), which houses temporary military exhibits from all eras. Past the Old Ordnance Room is the Powder Magazine (1857), which houses a standing exhibit concerned with the history of Jefferson Barracks.

The Visitors' Center and the exhibits in the historical area are open from 10:00 A.M. until 5:00 P.M., Tuesday through Saturday, and on Sunday from noon until 5:00 P.M. Closed in January. For more information, call 314-544-5714.

In the thirty-five years before the Civil War, many future leaders of both North and South were stationed at Jefferson Barracks during their military careers.

Jefferson Barracks was established on October 23, 1826, as a military post and training ground to replace Fort Bellefontaine, north of St. Louis. Its site had been selected by Colonel Henry Atkinson, commanding officer of the 6th U.S. Infantry, because of its fine natural position, its abundant nearby supply of building materials, and its proximity to a civilian population from which supplies and labor could be obtained at reasonable prices. The post was named in honor of former president Thomas Jefferson, who had died earlier that year.[10]

Lieutenant Philip St. George Cooke, just graduated from West Point, arrived at Jefferson Barracks in 1827 on his first assignment in a long and distinguished military career that would lead to the command of a division in the Union Army of the Potomac and the rank of brevet major general. Cooke remembered the infantrymen being crowded several to a room in stone barracks that were half-finished and uncomfortable.[11]

Jefferson Barracks. *Lithograph by J. C. Wild, 1840. From J. C. Wild,* The Valley of the Mississippi. *Lewis Thomas, ed., St. Louis, 1841. Missouri Historical Society Photograph and Print Collection.*

Below: Jefferson Barracks County Park. *Map by Pat Baer, 1994.*

The earliest role for Jefferson Barracks was to house soldiers protecting the growing population of settlers from the Indians. In June 1827 Captain William Selby Harney led two companies of infantry from Jefferson Barracks to Wisconsin in pursuit of two Indian leaders, Black Hawk of the Sauk and Red Bird of the Sioux. When the Civil War began, Harney was one of only four general officers of the line in the Regular Army. In 1861 he commanded the Union army's Department of the West, including Jefferson Barracks.[12]

In April 1832 elements of the 6th U.S. Infantry left Jefferson Barracks by steamer to participate in the Black Hawk War. Included in the expedition were two young lieutenants, Jefferson Davis and Albert Sidney Johnston. First Lieutenant Davis later became adjutant of the 1st Dragoons when the new cavalry regiment was organized at the post in 1833. Twenty-eight years later, he was elected president of the Confederate States of America. Johnston went on to a distinguished military career; he joined the Confederate army in 1861 and was appointed a full general.

In 1837 a promising engineering officer named Robert E. Lee arrived at Jefferson Barracks as superintending engineer for the St. Louis harbor. First Lieutenant Lee's assignment was to construct a pier to divert the current of the Mississippi River from the Illinois side back to Missouri.

In the autumn of 1842, the future commander of the First Corps of the Army of Northern Virginia, C.S.A., arrived at Jefferson

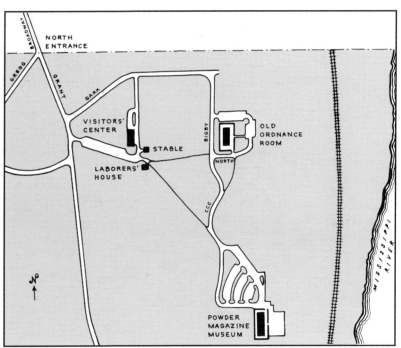

Barracks. Second Lieutenant James Longstreet was recently graduated from the United States Military Academy, and he took his post at Jefferson Barracks with the 4th U.S. Infantry. Longstreet enjoyed his assignment to "the hospitable city of St. Louis," recalling more than fifty years later that "the graceful step of its charming belles became a joy forever."[13]

On April 22, 1843, the 3d U.S. Infantry arrived at Jefferson Barracks, making the post temporarily the largest military establishment in the United States. The soldiers were commanded by Lieutenant Colonel Ethan Allen Hitchcock. He resigned from the army in 1855, but in February 1862, at age 61, Hitchcock was recalled to active duty as a major general of United States Volunteers. By accepting the appointment, Hitchcock became one of six West Point graduates born in the eighteenth century to serve as generals during the Civil War.[14]

Hitchcock was not the only future general to arrive at Jefferson Barracks in 1843. Fresh from West Point, Lieutenant Ulysses S. Grant arrived to begin his military career with the 4th U.S. Infantry. In Grant and Longstreet's regiment and in the 3d Infantry were many officers who would also reach high positions in the Civil War. The future generals included Don Carlos Buell, Richard Ewell, and George Sykes.[15]

With the outbreak of the war with Mexico in 1846, Jefferson Barracks gained even greater importance. It served as a training post for many of the leaders and troops going to Mexico, and it was instrumental in their supply. Colonel John C. Frémont, son-in-law of Missouri senator Thomas Hart Benton and future Union army leader in Missouri, was stationed at Jefferson Barracks briefly in 1847 after his victories in California.

Second Lieutenant Winfield Scott Hancock arrived at Jefferson Barracks with the 6th Infantry late in 1848. During the Civil War, Hancock would rise to the command of the II Corps of the Army of the Potomac and to the rank of major general in the Regular Army. In St. Louis he met Almira Russell, and on January 24, 1850, he married her. Buell and Orlando B. Willcox, who for his service in the Civil War would win the rank of brevet major general and the Medal of Honor, were among Hancock's groomsmen.[16]

In September 1849 future Confederate general Braxton Bragg and his wife arrived at Jefferson Barracks. His mission was to reorganize and reequip his horse artillery battery after its Mexican War service. In May 1850 Bragg requested additional officers to help with the task; in September of that year, Lieutenant William T. Sherman arrived in response to his request.[17]

Brevet Captain Nathaniel Lyon arrived at Jefferson Barracks on March 16, 1854. He found the post to be "a most unhealthy place, and the quarters are shockingly out of repair." Worried by a recent outbreak of cholera, Lyon was pleased when he and his unit were ordered west a month later.[18]

The 1st and 2d Cavalry were added to the organization of the United States Army in 1855 to meet the demands of the growing frontier. Both regiments served at Jefferson Barracks. Secretary of War Jefferson Davis was determined to have the best leadership possible in these regiments. As a result, the rosters read like a roll call of some of the most important Civil War generals.

The 1st Cavalry was commanded by Colonel Edwin V. Sumner. The second-in-command was Lieutenant Colonel Joseph E. Johnston. One of the regiment's majors was John Sedgwick; one of its captains was George B. McClellan. Sumner and Sedgwick would become corps commanders in the Federal Army of the Potomac. Johnston would command the Confederacy's Army of Tennessee. George McClellan would rise the highest, to the post of General in Chief of the Armies of the United States, and exercise command over both Sumner and Sedgwick.[19]

The 1855 roster of the 2d Cavalry is even more notable. Its colonel was Albert Sidney Johnston, its lieutenant colonel was Robert E.

Lee, and its majors were William J. Hardee and George H. Thomas. Among the captains and lieutenants were future Union generals Kenner Garrard, Richard W. Johnson, James Oakes, Innis N. Palmer, and George Stoneman. Future Confederate generals serving as company grade officers in the 2d Cavalry included George Anderson, George B. Cosby, Nathan G. Evans, Charles W. Field, John B. Hood, Edmund Kirby Smith, and Earl Van Dorn.[20]

The 2d Cavalry left Jefferson Barracks for Texas in late October 1855. On its way west, the regiment spent the night in Manchester, Missouri, where the regiment's first incident of stealing occurred. A farmer reported to Colonel Johnston that eight turkeys disappeared when the column passed his farm. A search of the camp ensued, and the culprits and three turkeys were apprehended.[21]

On April 13, 1861, Captain Albert Tracy and his company of recruits were ordered from the United States Arsenal to the magazine at the northern end of Jefferson Barracks to relieve the artillery company on guard there. Several of the buildings Tracy described in his diary still stand in Jefferson Barracks County Park: "Two immense stone buildings, enclosed each within an outer wall, beside its own—contain the stores to be guarded—consisting of many tons of rifle powder in barrels, in addition to ammunition fixed, for heavy guns, and a quantity of composition for rockets. A third stone building at the west side, by the gate of the grand enclosure, makes good quarters for the men, while a strong stone barn, suffices for stores and a guard house."[22]

A few weeks later, the 1st United States Volunteers and their commander, Colonel Frank Blair, arrived with orders to move forty thousand pounds of gunpowder, four hundred barrels, from Tracy's magazine to the arsenal. Tracy watched in horror as the volunteers, oblivious to their danger, handled the leaky barrels in a "perfectly wild and reckless manner" while loading them onto a waiting train. Tracy, however, was so in awe of Blair that he could not summon the courage to ask him to put out his cigar. Tracy confided to his diary that after the train pulled away and the soldiers departed, he felt as if he "had gotten safely through a battle."[23]

Jefferson Barracks played an important role in the early days of the Civil War in Missouri, providing housing and training for Missouri's Union volunteers in the days prior to the capture of Camp Jackson. The 13th United States Infantry, a Regular Army regiment that would attain an outstanding combat record, was organized there beginning in July 1861. After the initial flurry of organizational activity in 1861, however, the number of troops at Jefferson Barracks declined. Many soldiers were trained at Benton Barracks in north St. Louis instead of at Jefferson Barracks.[24]

The post's most important function during the war was as a military hospital. In March 1862 the buildings were turned over to the Medical Department for its use. The Western Sanitary Commission, a forebear of today's American Red Cross, organized a Sanitary Fair in 1862 to raise money for the construction of additional hospital facilities at the post. As crude as these facilities were by modern standards, they were a welcome sight to Civil War soldiers. Union physician John V. Lauderdale was aboard the steamer *D. A. January* when it landed at Jefferson Barracks on July 21, 1862. After helping his cargo of sick and wounded soldiers disembark, Dr. Lauderdale recorded his impressions: "How glad the poor fellows are to get here. How they crowd the way to the guards, and look out towards the beautiful grounds with shade trees with here and there long ranges of buildings which are the hospital barracks. Within these temporary asylums I am told every comfort is provided for the sick soldiers and we can hope that if our sick have any vitality left in them, it will be increased by a sojourn here."[25]

Unfortunately, with the need for medical care came the need for burial places. Jefferson Barracks National Cemetery was the result.

In April 1865 Jefferson Barracks was once again alive with military activity as soldiers of the victorious Union armies returned to St. Louis to be mustered out.

Hospital at Jefferson Barracks, Eight Miles below St. Louis. *Wood engraving, ca. 1863. Missouri Historical Society Photograph and Print Collection.*

Three Civil War Generals in St. Louis

Ulysses S. Grant

America's fratricidal war of 1861-1865 brought many individuals to national prominence who may have otherwise lived obscure, ordinary lives. There is no better example of this phenomenon than Ulysses S. Grant. When Grant first arrived in St. Louis, he was a bright-eyed graduate of the United States Military Academy with his entire military career ahead of him. Life in the army, however, proved hard for the young man, and he returned to St. Louis in 1854 to live as a civilian. Though he thoroughly enjoyed his family life, business conditions were difficult. When the Grants left St. Louis in 1860, they no doubt had very mixed emotions about their years there.

St. Louis has not been particularly kind to the memory of the Grants either. U. S. Grant is known to have resided at seven different locations in the city, and only two of them, Hardscrabble and White Haven, still exist in near-historical condition. Though Hardscrabble stands secure in the hands of Anheuser-Busch, the more significant White Haven was only recently rescued by the efforts of private citizens and the influence of the National Park Service. It is now a National Historic Site and is being preserved.

The Ulysses S. Grant National Historic Site, as White Haven is officially known, is located at 7400 Grant Road in St. Louis County.

From Interstate 44, take the Elm Avenue exit south to Pardee Road. Turn right (west) on Pardee. When Pardee forks to the right, continue straight ahead (south) on Grant Road. Cross the old railroad berm to enter the grounds. Alternatively, from Interstate 270 take the Gravois Road (Highway 30) exit east. Along Gravois Road, the visitor will see Hardscrabble on the west (left) side of the road. Pass Hardscrabble and then turn left on Grant Road.

The small, gray, one-story building is the office of the National Park Service. The Visitors' Center is open and tours are available on Tuesday and Thursday from 9:00 A.M. until 1:00 P.M. and at other times by appointment. Upon completion of the research, restoration, and preservation, the site will have more extended regular hours for visitation. For more information call 314-842-1867.

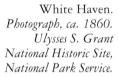

White Haven. *Photograph, ca. 1860. Ulysses S. Grant National Historic Site, National Park Service.*

1843-1844:
Jefferson Barracks and White Haven

Second Lieutenant "Sam" Grant reported to Jefferson Barracks in St. Louis on September 20, 1843. Fresh from West Point, he was an officer in the 4th United States Infantry. In his last year as a cadet, Grant's roommate had been St. Louisan Fred Dent. Dent had asked Grant to pay a call on his parents when he reached St. Louis, and after Grant settled in at Jefferson Barracks he set out to fulfill his promise. Five miles away, Grant found the Dent home called White Haven.[26]

When Grant first saw White Haven, it was beautifully situated in a long valley between wooded hills. The two-story farmhouse was surrounded by locust trees. Behind the house stood the barns, stables, and slave quarters. As Lieutenant Grant walked up to White Haven, he first encountered children and then Fred's father, Frederick Dent. What Grant did not know was that he was also meeting his future father-in-law.[27]

Frederick and Ellen Dent had moved to St. Louis from Maryland more than thirty years before. A lawyer and businessman, Dent was wealthy enough to buy the 925 acres on which White Haven stood and to own eighteen slaves. At White Haven the Dents raised eight children. The younger children were immediately taken with their brother's friend, and they soon had Grant coming twice a week for supper. He talked politics with Mr. Dent and took the girls on horseback rides. He also heard much talk about Julia, the eldest daughter, who was away at finishing school. After her return to the household in February 1844, it did not take long for everyone but Sam and Julia to recognize that they were in love.[28]

In May Grant learned that his regiment was being ordered to Louisiana. In his memoirs he summarized his new plan of attack: "Before I returned I mustered up courage to make known, in the most awkward manner imaginable, the discovery I had made on learning that the 4th Infantry had been ordered away from Jefferson Barracks." Julia accepted his proposal of marriage.[29]

1848:
Fourth and Cerre Streets

Military service took Grant to Mexico for two years beginning in 1846. On August 22, 1848, following his return to St. Louis, he and Julia Boggs Dent were married at the family's city home at Fourth and Cerre Streets, not far from the home of Roswell Field, now known as the Eugene Field House.[30] Nothing remains of this Dent home; the site is now a parking lot.

Not long after the wedding, the Grants left for Michigan, where Ulysses had been posted. In early 1850 Julia returned to St. Louis, on the advice of her physician, to live with her parents during her pregnancy. The Grants' first child, Frederick Dent Grant, was born in St. Louis on May 30, 1850. A second son, Ulysses S. Grant, Jr., was born on July 22, 1852.

Grant's military career in these years was far from promising. During a lengthy assignment in the Pacific Northwest, he became depressed over his absence from Julia and his two sons. Disappointed with his military prospects, he resigned his commission on the same day that he was promoted to captain, April 11, 1854.[31]

1854:
White Haven

Grant returned to St. Louis nearly penniless in late summer and immediately joined his wife, their two sons, and his in-laws at White Haven. The Grants stayed at White Haven with the Dents only until the following spring. Despite the tension of living with his wife's parents, Grant was not reluctant to suggest

2d Lieutenants U. S. Grant (right) and Alexander Hays in New Orleans, Waiting to Embark for Mexico. *Carte de visite copy photograph by Dana, New York, ca. 1880, of daguerreotype, 1846. Missouri Historical Society Photograph and Print Collection.*

Ulysses S. Grant. *Carte de visite photograph by G. Cramer, 1859. Missouri Historical Society Photograph and Print Collection.*

Below: Dent and Grant Holdings on the Gravois. *Map by Jennifer Ratcliffe-Tangney, 1994.*

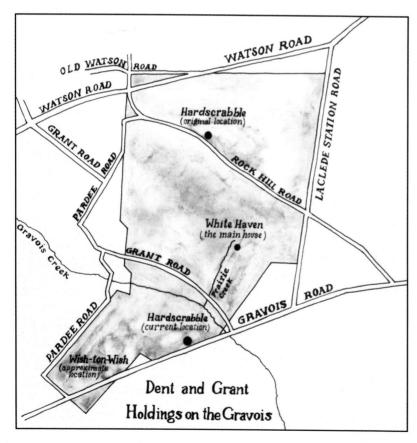

improvements in the management of the Dent household. When he observed that one slave was needed to constantly cut wood to keep the fireplaces in White Haven burning, Grant had an idea. He suggested that the slave stop cutting firewood and begin cutting timbers for a nearby coal mine; Grant then sold the timbers, the result of one day's work, to the mine for enough money to buy coal for a month. Two more days' cutting paid for a stove or grate in every room.[32]

Frederick Dent's White Haven was primarily a stock and dairy farm. A garden provided vegetables for the household, and fruit trees grew on the property. In the winter of 1854-1855, Grant harvested White Haven's first "cash crop," wood. Wood was in demand in St. Louis as fuel, and a wagonload could be expected to bring as much as six dollars. In addition to hauling timbers to the nearby mine, Grant sold wood at Jefferson Barracks and at the Twelfth Street Market in St. Louis.[33]

1855: Wish-ton-Wish

Wish-ton-Wish was located just a short distance southwest of the modern location of Hardscrabble, "Grant's Cabin," on property now belonging to Anheuser-Busch. To view the original location, follow Gravois Road south from White Haven to its intersection with Eddie and Park Roads. Wish-ton-Wish stood north of the two roads. The house burned to the ground in 1873.

In 1855 the Grants moved from White Haven to Wish-ton-Wish, a two-story brick house built in 1848-1849 on the southern portion of the White Haven acreage owned by Julia's absent brother, Louis. Wish-ton-Wish was about one and a half miles southeast of White Haven. In her memoirs Julia recalled that the "beautiful English villa" stood in "a magnificent forest of oaks."[34]

The Grants used Wish-ton-Wish while they farmed and prepared to build a house of their own. For her wedding, Frederick Dent had given Julia eighty acres and four slaves. The oldest of the slaves, however, was only fifteen, so Grant hired several free blacks to help him in the fields. Neighbors frequently saw Grant at work alongside his hired hands and slaves, and, though skeptical of his methods, they admired his honest work.[35]

Ellen "Nellie" Grant was born at Wish-ton-Wish on July 4, 1855, and the Grants lived there until October 1856.

1856: Hardscrabble

Hardscrabble originally stood on the northern portion of Frederick Dent's White Haven estate, about one mile from its present site. The location was east of Pardee Road on the north side of Rock Hill Road, within what is now a cemetery, St. Paul's Churchyard. To visit the site, follow Gravois Road north to Laclede Station Road. Turn left, following Laclede Station Road north to Rock Hill Road. Turn left at Rock Hill Road; St. Paul's Churchyard is a short distance ahead on the right (north). Drive past the cemetery's eastern entrance, entering instead at the gatehouse that marks the western entrance. After entering the cemetery, keep to the left. Stop 0.2 miles from the gatehouse. Walk approximately ninety paces across open ground toward Rock Hill Road into a widely spaced grove of seven trees. A small marker indicates the original site of Hardscrabble.

Hardscrabble is now part of the Grant's Farm tourist attraction of Anheuser-Busch Breweries. The building is not open to the public, but it can be seen on the north side of Gravois Road a short distance west of the intersection of Grant Road and Gravois Road.

In the fall of 1855 Grant made preparations to build a new house to a layout designed by Julia. He cut and notched logs, split shingles, and hauled stones for the cellar and foundation. After the cellar was dug and the foundation stones set in the summer of 1856, about seventy-five farmers, their hired hands, and their slaves came to help with the houseraising. The task was finished after two half-days of work, and the Grants moved into the new house, called Hardscrabble, in September.[36]

The two-story cabin had two rooms upstairs and two downstairs. A hall ran between the rooms on both floors. Both of the downstairs rooms had large log-burning fireplaces. Julia's slaves stayed at White Haven because there were no accommodations for them at Hardscrabble.[37]

Despite her husband's enthusiasm for the project, Julia thought the house crude and homely. According to her, the cabin's rough-hewn appearance was her father's idea; he thought a log house would be warmer than a frame house. The Hardscrabble name, she remembered, was a facetious joke because "the little house looked so unattractive," but there were other accounts of the name. A modern historian claims Grant gave his home the name because he had "scrabbled" (scratched and clawed) hard to build it. Grant's neighbors speculated that he was having some fun at the Dents' expense with their stately names of White Haven and Wishton-Wish.[38]

Hardscrabble may hold the record as "America's Most Dismantled Famous Log Cabin." From its original site on the northern portion of the Dent estate, it was dismantled and rebuilt at Old Orchard in Webster Groves. For the 1904 World's Fair, it was again dismantled and reassembled on Art Hill in Forest Park. A few years later, it was moved to the Busch estate along Gravois Road where it stands today. Anheuser-Busch restored the building in the 1970s.[39]

1857: Return to White Haven

No matter how Hardscrabble got its name, Julia hated it. Within five months the family had moved back to White Haven, with Julia using the death of her mother in January 1857 and the needs of her father as an excuse to return to the Dent family home. The Grants never again lived at Hardscrabble.[40]

Hardscrabble, Grant's Farmhouse, St. Louis County. *Photo by Emil Boehl, ca. 1880. Missouri Historical Society Photograph and Print Collection.*

One day in 1857, while Grant walked along a St. Louis street, he met someone he had not seen since his days as a cadet at West Point seventeen years earlier, William T. Sherman. Sherman had also left the army and fallen on hard times, but their casual conversation did not reveal the similarities of the two men's experiences. They soon parted, and Sherman remarked to himself, "West Point and the Regular Army were not good schools for farmers [and] bankers."[41]

The Grants' fourth and last child, Jesse Root Grant, Jr., arrived on February 6, 1858. U. S.

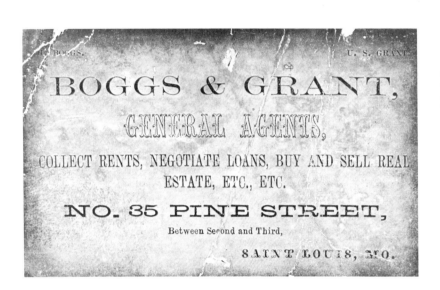

Grant barely made ends meet through the summer, and his hopes—and crops—were ruined by a severe freeze on June 5, 1858. By August Grant knew the farm was failing. Money troubles worsened in the fall, as sickness hit the family and the slaves. Young Freddy nearly died from chills and fever. Unwilling to leave her father and St. Louis, Julia convinced Ulysses to enter into a partnership with her cousin, Harry Boggs, a real estate agent and rent collector. "Boggs & Grant" operated from offices at 35 Pine Street (now under the pavement of Interstate 70).[42]

1859:
209 South Fifteenth Street

In order to eliminate the twelve-mile commute to White Haven, Grant moved into the back room of Harry and Louisa Boggs' house at 209 South Fifteenth Street in January 1859. His bare-floored room was without a stove and was furnished with only a bed and a washbowl on a chair.[43]

The location is now a parking lot.

1859:
632 Lynch Street

In March 1859 Julia and the children joined Grant in a rented house near the intersection of Lynch and Seventh Streets. The modern location is, like the home on South Fifteenth and too many other former Grant homes in St. Louis, a parking lot.

Although it was successful for a time, the real estate and rent collection business did not work out for Grant. Boggs had anticipated that Grant's military connections would work in their favor, but he soon learned that Grant's generosity with soldiers was a liability rather than an asset. In September 1859 Grant gave up on the real estate business.

1859:
1008 Barton Street

This former Grant home still stands at 1008 Barton Street, although it has been heavily modified from its prewar condition. The home is in private hands and is not open to visitors.

Over the summer, Grant had hoped to secure a job at Washington University teaching mathematics, a position for which he had prepared years before. However, when a position came open, Grant did not bother to apply, believing the quality of the competition was too high. In August Grant applied for the

Above:
Boggs and Grant, Real Estate Agents. *Business card, ca. 1859. Missouri Historical Society Archives.*

Right:
Major General U. S. Grant. *Carte de visite photograph by Peplow and Balch, Star Gallery, Memphis, Tennesee, 1863. Missouri Historical Society Photograph and Print Collection.*

position of county engineer but, despite numerous recommendations from prominent St. Louisans, he was not accepted. Out of work, Grant traded Hardscrabble for a frame cottage at the modern address of 1008 Barton Street and a note for three thousand dollars so that he could live with his family in the city. One historian calls the modern structure "hardly recognizable" when compared to its appearance when it was the Grant family home.[44]

Grant gained employment in November in the customs house but soon lost the patronage position after the collector of customs died. Although finances were certainly difficult for the Grants in 1859, the family was not apparently as poverty-stricken as it is often portrayed, for during this year Grant manumitted his only slave, the thirty-five-year-old William Jones. As one modern historian has pointed out, had Grant been in need of money, he could have sold Jones rather than freeing him. Ulysses and Julia Grant and their four children left St. Louis for Galena, Illinois, in the spring of 1860. After the Civil War, the Grants acquired the White Haven property from the Dents and made their home there in the summer of 1868. Although they would return to visit, this was the only time they lived in St. Louis after the war.[45]

The Grant Statue

A statue of General Grant stands near the southwest corner of Market Street and Tucker Boulevard in downtown St. Louis.

Robert Porter Bringhurst was born in Alton, Illinois, in 1858. He entered the St. Louis School of Art and Design at Washington University in 1880 for study under Howard Kretschmar; one of Kretschmar's other former students created the Francis Blair statue in Forest Park. In 1885 Bringhurst, back in St. Louis after studying in Paris, succeeded Kretschmar as instructor of sculpture at Washington University.[46]

Bringhurst's statue of General Ulysses Simpson Grant depicts Grant standing with a pair of field glasses in his right hand. On the base of the statue is a low-relief bronze entitled *Lookout Mountain,* which shows a mounted Grant with two other mounted figures, probably Generals Sherman and Thomas, in the background.

On its completion in 1888, the Grant statue was temporarily installed in the middle of Tucker Boulevard (then Twelfth Street) between Olive and Locust. In 1891 the statue

was decorated for the Fall Festivities, an ancestor of the Veiled Prophet parade, with an arch that held lights spelling "Let us have peace." When city hall was completed in 1898, the Grant statue was moved near its south entrance. A storm of protest arose over this "backdoor" treatment for the memorial to a St. Louisan who had led the Union armies to victory, been the only full general in the United States Army since George Washington, and served as president of the United States. In 1915 the statue was moved to its present site.[47]

Statue of Ulysses S. Grant Decorated for the Fall Festivities of 1891, Twelfth Street Looking South from Olive. *Photograph, 1891. Missouri Historical Society Photograph and Print Collection.*

William T. Sherman

In the constellation of Union generals, William Tecumseh Sherman is second in prominence only to Ulysses S. Grant. Though both Sherman and Grant had strong St. Louis ties in the years before the Civil War, Sherman's several periods of residence there both before and after the Civil War and his love for the city have generally escaped notice.

Tecumseh Sherman was born in Lancaster, Ohio, on February 8, 1820, the sixth of eleven children. His father died when he was only nine, and a home was found for the young "Cump," as the family called him, with the next-door neighbors, Thomas and Maria Boyle Ewing. The Ewings had children of their own, but they easily welcomed Sherman into the family. At Maria's insistence and with his mother's blessing, Cump was baptized into the Catholic Church and *William* was added to his name. The Ewings would exert powerful familial and political influence over Sherman for much of his adult life. In 1831 Ewing was elected to the United States Senate; in 1833 he told Sherman to begin preparing for an education at the United States Military Academy, which Sherman entered in 1836.[48]

Lieutenant General William T. Sherman. *Carte de visite photograph by E. and H. T. Anthony and Co., New York, ca. 1866. Missouri Historical Society Photograph and Print Collection.*

Sherman did well at West Point, graduating sixth in the class of 1840. While at West Point, he began a regular correspondence with Ellen Ewing, the daughter of his foster parents and his future wife.

Sherman's first visit to St. Louis was on November 24, 1843, when he was on his way to duty at Charleston, South Carolina, with the 3d Artillery Regiment. While in St. Louis he visited his former West Point classmate John McNutt at the United States Arsenal, called on future Mexican War hero Colonel Stephen W. Kearny, and visited Jefferson Barracks and "most places of interest" in the city. Sherman left St. Louis on a river steamer on December 4 and did not return for another seven years. More than three decades later, he wrote in his memoirs that it was during this brief visit to St. Louis that he "became impressed with its great future."[49]

1850:
The Planters' House and Jefferson Barracks

Like many visitors to St. Louis, Sherman's first stay was at the Planters' House. The magnificent hotel faced east along Fourth Street between Pine and Chestnut Streets in downtown St. Louis. His next residence was the officers' quarters at Jefferson Barracks. Some of the military buildings now a part of Jefferson Barracks County Park would have been under construction shortly after Sherman's arrival.

On May 1, 1850, Sherman married Ellen Boyle Ewing in a gala wedding at the Washington home of Thomas Ewing, then secretary of the interior, who invited all the right guests to the affair. President Zachary Taylor, members of his cabinet, Senator Thomas Hart Benton of Missouri, Senator Stephen A. Douglas of Illinois, and numerous other prominent political figures attended. When Sherman was subsequently ordered to St. Louis, Ellen remained with her parents at their home in Lancaster, Ohio, because she was pregnant.[50]

Sherman's first residence in St. Louis began on September 22, 1850. From the Planters' House Sherman wrote to his new wife to describe the adventures of his trip to St. Louis and what he saw upon his arrival.

The next day Lieutenant Sherman reported to Jefferson Barracks for duty with Company C, 3d United States Artillery. Captain Braxton Bragg, a future Confederate general, was the unit's commander. Because Bragg's battery was the only unit stationed at Jefferson Barracks at the time, Bragg had plenty of room and expected Sherman to live at the barracks. According to Bragg's modern biographer, Bragg and Sherman renewed their friendship during this period, and they remained friends for the rest of their lives.[51]

As soon as Sherman was settled in St. Louis, he began a campaign to encourage his wife and her parents to move from their "permanent" home in Lancaster to St. Louis. "I have walked about the city and at every step meet evidence of wealth and improvement that would seem miraculous in any country," he wrote. He also assured her that the private residences compared favorably even with those of New York. Hoping to persuade his mother-in-law, Sherman added, "The large Catholic population, with fine churches and well educated priests to her would be particularly pleasing."[52]

1850-1851:
Boarding House at Washington Street near Sixth Street

Now the northern edge of the St. Louis downtown business district, nothing remains of the pre–Civil War city in this area.

In October 1850 Sherman learned he had been promoted to captain and assigned to duty with the Commissary Department, whose office was located in downtown St. Louis on Washington Street between Second and Third Streets. It was too far from Jefferson Barracks for daily commuting, so Sherman moved back to the Planters' House. His experience with this luxury ended on October 21, 1850, when, for the first time in his life, he moved into a boarding house.

Sherman rented a room from the Widow Smith, who ran a boarding house on Washington Street near the corner of Sixth Street, only three blocks from the Commissary Department. "Fine pavements" lay between the boarding house and his office, which Sherman thought were "an excellent idea when snow and storms of winter make walking so disagreeable." Steps led up from the street to the front door of the two-story brick house. Just inside the front door was a parlor, complete with a piano. Opposite the parlor was the room of one of five young married couples boarding with Mrs. Smith. The hallway between the parlor and the rented room led to a porch, which in turn led to a "back building" with two rooms on its lower floor, one of which was Sherman's.

His room was carpeted and wallpapered, but after hanging his saber and other things, he still thought the walls looked bare. Sherman bought five framed pictures, which he hoped would later be used to decorate his and Ellen's home after her arrival in St. Louis. He also purchased bedroom furniture to use in addition to the wardrobe and washstand provided by Widow Smith. Sherman lived in the boarding house until March 1851.[53]

1851-1852:
Chouteau Avenue near Twelfth Street

There is no trace of the Sherman home on Chouteau Avenue near Tucker Boulevard, as Twelfth Street is now called.

Sherman visited Lancaster, Ohio, in December 1850 to be with his wife and her parents for Christmas. A few weeks after he returned to St. Louis, Ellen gave birth to their first child, Maria (called Minnie). In March Sherman brought Ellen and Minnie to St. Louis. At first the small family lived in a room on the second floor of the Planters' House, but Ellen found it "too confining." Sherman then bought a small house on Chouteau Avenue near Twelfth Street, which Ellen liked very much. The Shermans and their three servants lived in this house about a year before they were joined by Stewart Van Vliet, a West Point friend of Sherman's, and his wife. Van Vliet helped with the rent, and the wives shared household duties.[54]

During the summer of 1851, Sherman represented his father-in-law and his cousin Henry Stoddard in securing several tracts of land in St. Louis, which came to them as the result of litigation over the titles. Sherman bought some of this property and visited Illinois to acquire additional land near Edwardsville. Ellen, pregnant again, left St. Louis in May 1852 for Lancaster. Their second daughter, Mary Elizabeth (Lizzie), was born there in November. After Ellen left St. Louis, Sherman rented a room on Market Street across from the courthouse. He lived there until October 1852, when he received orders transferring him to New Orleans.[55]

1861:
226 Locust Street

No evidence remains of the home in which the Shermans lived for several months in 1861.

William and his pregnant wife, Ellen, their five children, and two servants returned to St. Louis on March 27, 1861. On April 1 they occupied a house rented from James H. Lucas, a three-story brick home at 226 Locust Street between Tenth and Eleventh Streets. To help defray their $50 monthly rent (against Sherman's monthly salary of $160), Ellen's brother Charles Ewing and his friend John Hunter moved in as boarders on the third floor.[56]

The eight years since the Shermans last lived in St. Louis had been difficult ones. In 1853 Sherman had resigned his commission in the army in order to manage the San Francisco branch of the St. Louis-based Lucas and Turner Bank. The Shermans' third child, William Ewing, was born in San Francisco in June 1854. Sherman was less impressed with the joys of fatherhood than he was with the increased financial responsibility. To a friend he wrote that his growing family would mean that he would have to give up his "dream" of living in St. Louis with a steady income and a farm in Illinois to spend it on.[57]

Sherman's banking experience in San Francisco was generally good, but after closing the bank and moving to New York to operate another branch, his St. Louis partners were caught in the Panic of 1857 and driven out of business. Sherman then turned to the practice of law in Leavenworth, Kansas, where he was admitted to the bar "on the ground of general intelligence." This career, too, ended abruptly. He applied for reinstatement with the army but was turned down. In 1859 he accepted the position of superintendent and professor of engineering, architecture, and drawing at the Louisiana Seminary of Learning and Military Academy near Alexandria, the predecessor of Louisiana State University at Baton Rouge. That position, too, came to a disappointing conclusion in January 1861, when Sherman felt compelled to resign rather than accept weapons seized by secessionist sympathizers from the United States Arsenal in Baton Rouge.[58]

Sherman returned to St. Louis to accept the presidency of the St. Louis Railroad Company, an opportunity offered by his former banking compatriot, Henry S. Turner. The events of the secession crisis of early 1861 soon had a major impact on Sherman. Not long after Sherman's arrival in St. Louis, Postmaster General Montgomery Blair wrote to him asking if he would accept the chief clerkship in the War Department, with the promise of soon becoming an assistant secretary of war. A former soldier more politically adept than Sherman would have thought twice about declining an offer from the powerful Blair family, but Sherman refused the offer immediately, citing his obligations to his new

employer and the demands of his large family. Late one evening after the fall of Fort Sumter to the Confederates in April, Sherman was summoned to the home of Francis P. Blair, Jr., Montgomery's brother and St. Louis' representative in the United States House of Representatives. Blair indicated the government's distrust of Brigadier General William S. Harney, then commander of the Department of the West in St. Louis, and offered Sherman an appointment as brigadier general of volunteers and duty as Harney's replacement. Sherman declined this offer too, again citing his St. Louis obligations. Blair's attention turned next to Captain Nathaniel Lyon.[59]

Sherman's friends began to wonder about his relative inaction during this period of national crisis. Feeling the pressure of family, friends, and his own patriotism, in May 1861 he wrote to the secretary of war to explain that he had been unwilling to accept a position as a three-month volunteer because of the hardship and disruption it would cause his family. Now that three-year volunteers were required, however, he was anxious to serve. In early October he was appointed colonel of the 13th United States Infantry, a new Regular Army regiment being mustered at Jefferson Barracks. A few days later, Sherman was ordered to Washington, D.C., to report to the War Department. There he was told that he would remain in the capital while his regiment's lieutenant colonel supervised its organization in St. Louis. Sherman informed Ellen of the situation and asked her to pack up their household and move to Lancaster.

1861-1862:
Benton Barracks

Benton Barracks was located along Natural Bridge Road near Grand Avenue in north St. Louis. There is no remaining evidence of this Civil War-era structure.

Sherman came back to St. Louis twice in 1861, once as a visiting emissary and once in disgrace.

Brigadier General Sherman arrived in St. Louis in late August 1861 to confer with Major General John C. Frémont concerning the availability of reinforcements for Kentucky, Sherman's new assignment. In the first battle at Bull Run, Virginia, Sherman had led an infantry brigade with distinction, resulting in his promotion. He spent the night at the Planters' House, and on the next morning visited Frémont at the Brant mansion, 806 Chouteau Avenue. Sherman later remembered, "Our conversation took a wide turn about the character of the principal citizens of St. Louis, with whom I was well acquainted." He left the city the same afternoon for Louisville.[60]

Despite his request to remain in a subordinate position, his Kentucky assignment was to a command position. In Louisville the strains of working with volunteer soldiers, having too few supplies, and facing the constant annoyance of newspaper correspondents nearly overwhelmed him. In a meeting with Secretary of War Simon Cameron, Sherman was asked how many men would be required to subdue the Mississippi Valley. Without hesitation he responded, "Two hundred thousand." Cameron was aghast at this preposterous—although ultimately prophetic—estimation. To both military and civilian authorities, Sherman seemed deranged. He was relieved of command and sent to St. Louis, where in November 1861 he reported for duty with Major General Henry W. Halleck, commander of the Department of Missouri.[61]

Sherman was soon sent to inspect the troops at Sedalia, where he ordered the dispersed units to concentrate in anticipation of a Confederate attack. This rash action was too much for Halleck, who recalled Sherman to St. Louis. On December 2, 1861, Halleck wrote General in Chief George McClellan that Sherman was unfit for duty and was being sent to Ohio for a twenty-day furlough. On December 11 a headline in a Cincinnati newspaper declared, "General William T. Sherman Insane."[62]

Two days before Christmas, Sherman returned to St. Louis to take command of Benton Barracks, a camp of instruction for the thousands of volunteer soldiers arriving in the city. While in the east with the Army of the Potomac, Sherman had developed a reputation as a "hard man" and one who "seems to have had something to learn about the way to handle volunteer troops." During his assignment at Benton Barracks, he must have demonstrated that he had learned from his mistakes. On March 1, 1862, he left the city to command a division in the Army of the Tennessee under another sometime St. Louisan, Ulysses S. Grant.[63]

The Postwar Years: 912 North Garrison Avenue

The Shermans lived in St. Louis for two years or more in each of the three decades following the Civil War. On each occasion they lived at their house at 912 North Garrison Avenue. No trace of the building remains.

To visit the site, take U.S. 40 to the Grand Boulevard exit. Go north on Grand approximately 0.7 miles to Franklin Avenue. Turn right (east) on Franklin and go 0.5 miles to its intersection with Garrison. The Sherman home stood near the northeast corner of the intersection, opposite the modern U.S. Post Office at 901 Garrison.

William T. Sherman Residence, 912 North Garrison Avenue. *Photograph, 1910. Missouri Historical Society Photograph and Print Collection.*

On August 15, 1865, a committee of St. Louisans presented General Sherman with thirty thousand dollars to use to purchase a home in St. Louis. In his first postwar assignment as commander of the Military Division of the Mississippi, Sherman's headquarters were in the city, so he and Mrs. Sherman were only too happy to accept the offer. In his letter of acceptance, Sherman pointed out that the generosity of his St. Louis friends exceeded all that he had "received from the government of the United States for four years of labor in the midst of danger and trouble."[64]

Sherman had already been investigating homes in St. Louis, but he did not want to make a selection before Ellen's arrival. In the first week of September, the Shermans ventured forth from their temporary quarters at the Planters' House to visit "the Nicholson place" located at 912 North Garrison Avenue. Ellen was immediately pleased with her husband's recommendation.[65]

The front doors of the large red-brick mansion opened on a wide entrance hall and a broad stairway. On one side of the hall were large "double parlors"; on the other side of the hall were the library and the dining room. Upstairs were four large, airy bedrooms and the servants' quarters. The finished attic and the ample cellar offered room for storage. A fine front porch and an enclosed porch at the back completed the house.[66]

The Shermans were very happy in their new home. On only one occasion during their first postwar stay in St. Louis did a period of gloom fall over the house. A few months after they settled in, General Sherman decided that they should acquire a family plot in Calvary Cemetery so their sons, Willie and Charley, could be buried there. When the boys' coffins arrived from Ohio and Indiana, they rested for a night in the Sherman parlor before their burial in Calvary Cemetery the next day.[67]

The last child of William and Ellen Sherman, Philemon Tecumseh, was born in St. Louis on January 9, 1867. He was sickly at birth, so his older sister Minnie took him to be baptized the day he was born. On April 6, 1867, General Sherman and his friend Father De Smet took Philemon to the "shabby little old church" of St. Bridget Parish, then located on Pratt Avenue at the northeast corner of Carr Street, for a more proper baptism.[68]

In February 1869 Sherman moved to Washington, D.C., to accept a promotion to full general and command of the United States Army. Ellen and the children moved from St. Louis in April, but the Shermans retained possession of their St. Louis home.

Sherman's years in the nation's capital were difficult ones. Congress worked to cut not only the size of the army but also the pay of those remaining with the colors. Increasing activity against the Indians and constant skirmishing with the civilians of the War Department over the rights of the commanding general added to the tension. Above all, Sherman disliked the growing distance between himself and President Grant. Tired of the constant political battles, Sherman asked for permission to move his headquarters to St. Louis.

In October 1874 the Shermans returned to the house on Garrison Avenue. In its library, Sherman completed his memoirs, one of the most important books on the Civil War. Published in two volumes in early 1875, *Memoirs of General W. T. Sherman by Himself* sold ten thousand copies in its first month of publication. Sherman's self-initiated "exile" in St. Louis came to an end in 1879. In April of that year, Secretary of War Alphonso Taft issued orders requiring Sherman to return to Washington, D.C. To soothe Sherman's feeling about the move, Taft clarified and strengthened the authority of the commanding general in relation to the staff departments and the War Department.[69]

In June 1883 increasing concern over his wife's health caused Sherman to turn over command of the army to General Philip Sheridan and move his family back to their Garrison Avenue home.

After his retirement, Sherman was increasingly pressured to seek political office. The scene of one of the most often told stories of Sherman's indifference to politics occurred in St. Louis. One evening during the first week of June 1884, Sherman and his son Tom were talking in the library of their home when a telegram was delivered to General Sherman from the Republican Convention in Chicago urging him to accept the presidential nomination. Tom watched in awe as his father quickly wrote out his response: "I will not accept if nominated and will not serve if elected." As the messenger left, Tom was amazed that his father resumed their conversation as if they had not been interrupted.[70]

Despite their love for St. Louis, General and Mrs. Sherman decided to move to New York City, where their youngest child, Philemon, was attending school. They left St. Louis in September 1886.

1891:
To Calvary Cemetery

After leaving St. Louis, Ellen Sherman's health began to deteriorate. In November 1888 she suffered two heart attacks, the second one fatal. General Sherman returned to St. Louis for her burial in Calvary Cemetery, home of the family plot, on December 1, 1888.[71]

William T. Sherman's life came to an end on February 14, 1891, six days after his seventy-first birthday. Demands were made on the family to bury the national hero at Arlington or at West Point, but, anticipating this move, Sherman himself had issued "positive orders" that he was to be buried next to his wife in St. Louis.[72]

Sherman's funeral in New York City was the occasion for an outpouring of national admiration. After Grant's death Sherman had become the prominent symbol of Union victory and national reconciliation. President Benjamin Harrison attended the funeral, chief among many dignitaries, citizens, and old soldiers who came to pay their last respects. Former Confederate general Joseph E. Johnston, Sherman's adversary in the campaign for Atlanta in 1864 and again in the final days of the war in North Carolina in 1865, stood bare-headed in cold, raw weather as Sherman's casket passed. His insistence on honoring his old enemy contributed to his own death by pneumonia a month later.[73]

If Sherman's funeral in New York City was his official one, then his funeral in St. Louis was his "homecoming." Never before had the city's residents turned out in such strength to do honor to one of their own.

The weather on February 20, 1891, was beautiful. At 8:45 A.M. minute guns along Poplar Street began firing to announce the arrival of Sherman's funeral train. Crowds had begun assembling three hours earlier in order to view the event. A timely rain had washed the streets, making the city appear "as clean as though it had been scrubbed."[74]

Funeral Procession of General Sherman Passing the Corner of Grand and Pine. *Photograph by Emil Boehl, 1891. Missouri Historical Society Photograph and Print Collection.*

Just after 11:00 A.M., the funeral procession began the seven-mile march from the railroad station near Eleventh and Poplar Streets to Calvary Cemetery. Units were deployed along the route so the column gained strength as it moved through the city. At the corner of Twelfth (now Tucker) and Pine Streets, a bugler from the 7th U.S. Cavalry sounded "Forward" to alert the divisions of the procession. The procession moved west on Pine Street to Grand Avenue, where it turned north. From Grand Avenue the column turned northwest on Florissant Road (now called West Florissant Road) and completed the march to the entrance of Calvary Cemetery.

Sherman's funeral cortege was organized in six divisions. The first division was led by the city's mounted police, who frequently had difficulty forcing back the crowd so the column could pass. The buglers of the 7th Cavalry came next, preceding Brigadier General Wesley Merritt and his staff. Six troops of the 7th Cavalry, Battery F of the 2d Artillery, and Battery F of the 4th Artillery came next. They were followed by eight companies representing the 7th, 10th, 12th, 13th, and 14th Infantry Regiments.[75]

The honor of guarding Sherman's casket and the caisson on which it rode went to St. Louis' Ransom Post of the Grand Army of the Republic, the veterans' organization to which Sherman belonged. Former members of the 13th U.S. Infantry, Sherman's first Civil War command, marched with the old soldiers of Ransom Post. Sixteen carriages carrying family members and five carriages bearing the official funeral party followed the caisson and its honor guard. Former president Rutherford B. Hayes and Generals John Schofield, Oliver O. Howard, and Henry Slocum were among the dignitaries present.[76]

The second division included members of the Missouri Commandery of the Military Order of the Loyal Legion of the United States and members of various societies of the Army of the Tennessee, including delegations from Colorado, Illinois, Indiana, Iowa, Kansas, Nebraska, and Ohio. The third division was composed of twelve hundred members of the Grand Army of the Republic, Sons of Union Veterans, and other veterans' groups.

The fourth division comprised several Missouri delegations. Governor David R. Francis and his staff rode at the head of twelve hundred Missouri militia, followed by fourteen hundred soldiers of the Ohio militia representing Sherman's native state. The Missouri judiciary and members of the Missouri, Illinois, and Ohio legislatures followed. Confederate veterans marched in the fifth division with members of several civil societies. The sixth division included organizations representing a variety of civic, mercantile, and industrial interests.[77]

The funeral procession began arriving at Calvary Cemetery just before 2:00 P.M. The police and U.S. soldiers detailed specifically for the task held the crowd at bay while the caisson and members of the Sherman family entered the cemetery.

After Sherman's coffin was lowered into his grave, Father Thomas Sherman, the general's eldest son, stepped forward to conduct the brief funeral service. Following his prayer, a battalion of infantry standing just thirty feet away fired three volleys in salute. As the smoke drifted across the crowd, an artillery battery on a hillside just one hundred yards away fired three salvos in quick succession. The echoes dying away, the chief bugler of the 7th Cavalry took position at grave side and sounded taps. With the first note, the crowd fell silent.[78]

John S. Bowen

1853:
Jefferson Barracks

John Stevens Bowen graduated from the United States Military Academy in July 1853 and was commissioned as a brevet second lieutenant in the Regiment of Mounted Rifles. After a brief assignment at the Cavalry School for Practice at Carlisle, Pennsylvania, Bowen was sent to join his regiment at Jefferson Barracks in St. Louis.

Bowen, a native of Liberty County, Georgia, was the sixth of thirteen children born to William Parker Bowen and Ann Elizabeth Wilkins. He was admitted to West Point on July 1, 1848, three months before his nineteenth birthday, and graduated thirteenth in the class of 1853. West Point had been difficult for Bowen, not for academic reasons but because of his apparently contentious, combative nature. On Christmas Day, 1851, the cadets were allowed to leave the post, and many went directly to the infamous Benny Haven's tavern or other favorite haunts. Later that night, Bowen watched as one of the cadets, visibly drunk, gave Cadets Jerome Bonaparte and John Forney an inebriated embrace. When the cadet moved toward Bowen, Bowen knocked him down.[79]

A week later, on New Year's Day, Cadet Lieutenant Bowen was responsible for the roll call of his company. Finding that his friend Henry Davidson had not yet returned from an unauthorized visit to New York City, Bowen ordered the cadet first sergeant not to report Davidson's absence. For this offense, Bowen was tried in February 1852 by general court martial, found guilty of "conduct grossly unsoldierlike," and sentenced to be dismissed from the service. A subsequent review by Secretary of War C. M. Conrad and President Millard Fillmore mitigated the punishment on the grounds that Bowen, as a cadet officer, thought he had the power to grant a leave of absence, a power that others before him may have assumed. "Nothing but youth and a want of reflection" could have caused such an understanding, Conrad wrote. This circumstance, in addition to Bowen's high class standing, caused his punishment to be reduced to a suspension from West Point until July 1852. Classmate Cyrus Comstock commented that "few out of his own class care to have him back" because "he is unpopular as an officer." Sectional pride may well have played a role in Comstock's evaluation.[80]

John Bowen in Uniform of Missouri Volunteer Militia. *Photograph, ca. 1860. Missouri Historical Society Photograph and Print Collection.*

On arriving at Jefferson Barracks, Bowen found more than the United States Army; he found romance. On May 8, 1854, he married Mary Lucretia Preston Kennerly. Mary Kennerly was the daughter of George Hancock Kennerly, a veteran of both the War of 1812 and the Mexican War, and Alzire Menard, daughter of Lieutenant Governor Pierre Menard and Therese Godin. Through marriage, John Bowen united with a family whose states' rights sympathies were as strong as his own. Mary gave birth to their first son, Menard Kennerly, at her parents' home at Jefferson Barracks on September 10, 1855, several months after Bowen had departed for Fort McIntosh, Texas, where he served with his regiment until his resignation from the service on May 1, 1856.[81]

1857:
A Boarding House on Fifth Street

After returning to St. Louis in 1857, the Bowens lived in a boarding house on Fifth Street (the modern Broadway) between Chestnut and Pine Streets, now in the center of the St. Louis business district.

After leaving the army, the Bowens first went to Savannah, Georgia, his parents' home, to see if Bowen could earn a living as an architect. While there, he was active in the local militia and held the rank of lieutenant colonel. In 1857 the Bowens returned to

St. Louis, where he took up the profession of "engineer and architect" with offices along Pine Street between Third and Fourth Streets. On their return to the city, the Bowens probably first moved in with Mary's parents at Jefferson Barracks.[82]

On March 14, 1858, Bowen became one of the twelve charter members of the St. Louis Architectural Association, organized "to protect and assist each other in the elevation of its members and the profession." That year, Bowen entered into partnership with Charles C. Miller and conducted business from 97 Chestnut Street. The Bowens lived nearby in a boarding house on modern Broadway between Chestnut and Pine Streets.[83]

1859:
6727 Michigan Avenue

On September 21, 1981, the Carondelet Historical Society placed a marker on the prewar home of General and Mrs. John Bowen. An honor guard was provided by the 1st Missouri Infantry, a Confederate reenactment unit. The home is privately owned and not open to visitors.

From downtown St. Louis, take Interstate 55 south approximately 5.0 miles to the South Broadway exit. Take Broadway south 1.5 miles to its intersection with Holly Hills Road. Turn right (west) at Holly Hills Road and proceed three blocks to the intersection with Michigan Street. Drive south to 6727 Michigan, the last house on the right before Krauss Street. The house's number is not readily visible; it is shown only in the glass above the front entrance. The nearby Bowen Street is named in honor of General Bowen.

The Bowens built a two-story brick house with basement on the northwest corner of what were then Fourth and Olive Streets in Carondelet, a growing community between Jefferson Barracks and St. Louis. There the Bowens' first daughter, Annie Beauregard, was born on May 22, 1860. Mrs. Bowen's younger sister, Abbie Frances Kennerly, lived with them to help with the growing family.[84]

While living in the new house, John Bowen became increasingly active in Missouri's militia. In June 1859 he served as a captain in the 1st Regiment, Missouri Volunteer Militia, and by May of the next year he had been promoted to lieutenant colonel. Increasing flare-ups along the Missouri-Kansas border and incursions into Missouri by Kansan "free-soilers" caused Governor R. M. Stewart to order the militia in St. Louis and Jefferson City to the state's western border for defense. Bowen,

who told an acquaintance that he would "follow the western bandits home if they pollute the soil of Missouri," was one of the senior officers in what became known as the Southwest Expedition. William Clark Kennerly, Bowen's brother-in-law, was an officer in the cavalry with the force. Over the winter of 1860-1861, the campaign slowly dissolved, and after the first of the year, Bowen was left in command of a much reduced force, elements of which remained in the field until May.[85]

Bowen's prominence in the Southwest Expedition no doubt contributed to his election as colonel of the 2d Regiment, Missouri Volunteer Militia, in March 1861. Bowen was among the Missouri militia taken prisoner by the United States forces at Camp Jackson on May 10, 1861, and with the others he was paroled the next day. Despite the fact that he was still under the conditions of his parole, Bowen went almost immediately to the Confederate War Department in Richmond, Virginia, where he received a commission as colonel on May 19, 1861. Bowen then proceeded to Memphis, Tennessee, where he organized the 1st Missouri Infantry Regiment, C.S.A., the first Missouri unit to be organized for the service of the Confederacy. The ranks of the 1st Missouri Infantry contained more than a few Camp Jackson veterans.[86]

Bowen's military talents won him rapid promotion and recognition as one of the better combat commanders in the Confederacy's western forces. Bowen was promoted to brigadier general in March 1862 and led a brigade at the battle of Shiloh, where he was wounded. He also led a brigade consisting of his own 1st Missouri and three Mississippi regiments at the battle of Corinth in October 1862, and he subsequently brought charges against his commanding officer, Major General Earl Van Dorn, for a number of offenses related to the mismanagement of the Confederate offensive. A sympathetic court of inquiry cleared Van Dorn, but the event did not seem to reflect unfavorably on Bowen. He was given command of a two-brigade division, including most of the Missourians serving east of the Mississippi River, to serve under Lieutenant General John C. Pemberton in the defense of Vicksburg. At Grand Gulf, Mississippi, on April 29, 1863, Bowen's well-placed artillery—only thirteen guns—punished seven Union ironclads in "the most impressive victory of land guns over river vessels since Fort Donelson in February 1862." Despite the efforts of his gunners, Bowen was unable to prevent the landing of General Grant's Union army at Bruinsburg, Mississippi, the next day. In the subsequent campaign for

Camp Lewis. *Bowen was a lieutenant colonel in the Missouri Volunteer Militia here in 1860. Missouri Historical Society Photograph and Print Collection.*

Vicksburg, Bowen and his division were heavily engaged in three of the five battles Grant's forces won as they drove the Confederates inside the city in May. Bowen repeatedly won commendations for his skill and bravery, attributes which were recognized by his promotion to major general on May 25, 1863. During the siege, Bowen commanded Pemberton's reserve force inside Vicksburg, an assignment which put Bowen and his men repeatedly at the point of danger as they counterattacked to repel Union assaults against the entrenchments.[87]

On July 3, 1863, General Pemberton turned to General Bowen to perform the distasteful task of asking Grant to discuss the conditions of surrender. Bowen, despite his failing health, was dressed in full uniform as he rode through the Confederate lines. A staff officer rode beside him carrying a white flag. Grant refused to see Bowen, but Bowen and Grant's staff arranged a meeting between Pemberton and Grant. Vicksburg was surrendered the next day.[88]

A number of reasons have been proposed as to why Pemberton chose Bowen to open discussions with Grant, but the St. Louis connection is often overlooked. As Grant explained in his memoirs, he "had been a neighbor of Bowen's in Missouri, and knew him well and favorably before the war." The Confederates had tried this tactic with Grant before; at Fort Donelson, Confederate general

Simon Buckner had hoped that his past acquaintance with Grant would soften the terms of surrender. The tactic of appealing to antebellum friendships had not worked then, and it did not work now for the two former St. Louisans at Vicksburg.[89]

After the surrender, General and Mrs. Bowen left Vicksburg in an army ambulance, traveling as far as Raymond, Mississippi, before he weakened and had to stop for treatment. Bowen died of dysentery on July 13, 1863. Ephraim Anderson, a member of the 1st Missouri Brigade under Bowen's command, remembered the fallen leader with pride: "His generalship was admired and applauded throughout the army, and he was held in the very highest personal esteem by the soldiers of his division, and by all who knew any thing of his character."[90]

Mary Bowen would remain in exile from St. Louis until the war's end. She had given birth to their third child and second son, John Sidney, at Camp Sterling Price, Mississippi, on September 6, 1862. After her husband's burial, she moved to Atlanta until she and her three children were driven out with many other civilians by the order of General William T. Sherman. After the war, "Mrs. General" Bowen, as she was known, returned to her home in Carondelet until she sold it in 1867. The house has been in private hands since that time.[91]

Chapter 2 The Coming

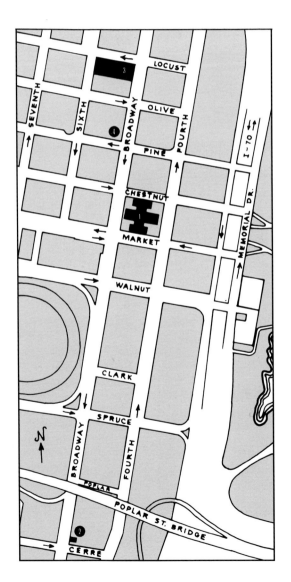

Downtown
St. Louis. *Map by Pat
Baer, 1994.*

Our creed is that slavery is a sin—now, heretofore, hereafter, and forever—a sin. Consequently it follows that whoever has participated, or does now participate, in that sin, ought to repent without a moment's delay.

Elijah P. Lovejoy
St. Louis Observer
1836

# of War

Fortunately for students of the Civil War in St. Louis, three sites remain that symbolize the political struggles of the city, state, and nation in the years before reason failed and a divided nation went to war. Nearby, a fourth site no longer in existence was the gathering place for pro-Southern sympathizers.

The Old Courthouse, which stood at the center of antebellum St. Louis, witnessed both the first stage of the long and famous Dred Scott lawsuit against slavery and the last instance of a slave auction in St. Louis. It stands a few minutes north of the home of Scott's lawyer, Roswell M. Field. Known as the Eugene Field House in honor of Roswell Field's famous poet son, this building predates the Civil War. To the north of the courthouse is the Mercantile Library, located exactly where it stood at the time of the Civil War, within whose walls echoed debates over the political future of the state in 1861 and in 1865. The Berthold mansion, headquarters first for the Democratic supporters of Stephen A. Douglas in the 1860 presidential election and then for St. Louis' Southern partisans, stood north and across the street from the courthouse.

1. The Old Courthouse

The Old Courthouse occupies the city block bounded by Fourth Street and Broadway on the east and west and by Chestnut and Market Streets on the north and south. It is part of the Jefferson National Expansion Memorial and is administered by the National Park Service. It is open from 8:00 A.M. to 4:30 P.M. daily except New Year's Day,

Thanksgiving, and Christmas Day. Enter the courthouse from the Fourth Street side.

While standing on the front steps of the Old Courthouse and looking east to the Mississippi River, it takes only a small amount of imagination to picture the center of St. Louis in the Civil War era.

One block north on Fourth Street, the famous Planters' House Hotel faced the river and stretched from Chestnut Street to Pine. Just one block west of the courthouse at Broadway (then called Fifth Street) and Pine stood the stately Berthold mansion, headquarters of St. Louis' "Minute Men" and where a flag proclaiming Southern sympathies proudly flew in the early months of 1861. Between Fourth and Broadway along Chestnut, architect and engineer John S. Bowen had his office. Bowen would become one of only four Confederate major generals from Missouri.

Ulysses S. Grant, Bowen's future adversary at Vicksburg, freed his only slave on March 29, 1859, by filing a signed document of manumission at the courthouse. Behind the courthouse on Broadway ran the tracks of a horse-drawn trolley line of the St. Louis Railroad Company, whose president in early 1861 was William T. Sherman.[1]

Lynch's Slave Pen stood two blocks south of the courthouse at Fifth and Myrtle Streets, as Broadway and Clark Avenue are now known. Not far away at the southeast corner of Third and Market Streets stood the Old National Hotel, where "A. Lincoln and family, Illinois" once registered.[2]

In the 1850s the importance of these people and places was yet to be established. In fact, what is now the Old Courthouse was then the new courthouse. The first courthouse to

St. Louis Courthouse.
*Daguerreotype by
Thomas M. Easterly,
1862. Missouri
Historical Society
Photograph and Print
Collection.*

*Walk through the rotunda to the west
wing, where an exhibit gives brief details of
the Dred Scott case. On the second floor of the
west wing is a courtroom restored to appear
as it did in the 1860s.*

Unfortunately for Scott, Mrs. Emerson
appealed the decision to the Missouri Supreme
Court. In 1852 the court reversed the earlier
decision and returned the Scotts to slavery.
Justice Hamilton R. Gamble, a fellow
St. Louisan, was the only one of the three
Missouri Supreme Court judges to favor giving
Scott his freedom. In ruling against Scott, the
Missouri Supreme Court reacted to proslavery
pressure and overturned its own precedents in
similar cases, cases that had resulted in
freedom for slaves.[6]

By this time Mrs. Emerson had remarried
and left the city for New York, leaving Scott in
St. Louis. On November 2, 1853, Roswell M.
Field brought a new suit in the Federal circuit
court under the diverse-citizenship clause of
the United States Constitution. In 1854 the
United States Circuit Court in St. Louis
accepted Scott's case and upheld the
previous decision against him. Roswell Field
appealed to the United States Supreme Court
with the hope of forcing a ruling on the
constitutionality of the Missouri Compromise.
Field enlisted the support of one of the most
powerful political families in the United States,
the Blairs. Attorney Montgomery Blair, brother
of Francis P. Blair, Jr., and future postmaster
general in Abraham Lincoln's cabinet, practiced
law in Washington, D.C., where his father ran a
newspaper. Blair, who still considered himself a
Missourian, agreed to help by representing
Scott before the Supreme Court; he had been
moved by Field's integrity. Blair explained: "I
received a letter from Mr. Field (who is a
distinguished lawyer in Missouri, and one who
never during the fifteen years I have known
him, manifested any interest in politics),
requesting me to present the case to the
court."[7]

Though the case of Dred Scott had moved
to Washington, the situation was no calmer in
Missouri. In August 1856 citizens gathered in
the courthouse rotunda to debate the question
of slavery in Kansas. The assembly was
dominated by Southern sympathizers, who
passed resolutions supporting the proslavery
position in Kansas and asking the Federal
government for help.[8]

Dred Scott's case returned to public
attention, with the Supreme Court hearing
arguments on the case in late 1856 and again
in 1857. Dominated by justices sympathetic to
Southern interests, the court bypassed the

stand at this site was completed in 1828, but
construction began on an expansion in 1839.
The rotunda and west wing of today's Old
Courthouse were completed in 1845, and the
rotunda quickly became the gathering place for
public forums. The cast- and wrought-iron
dome was begun in 1859, and, with the
completion of the dome and the rotunda
murals in 1862, the courthouse was dedicated
and declared officially complete.[3]

As early as 1846, slaveholders assembled in
the rotunda to demand protection from "the
evil designs of abolitionists," for they believed
they had reason to worry. In that year a slave
named Dred Scott sued for freedom and set off
a series of court battles that would not end for
a decade and then only with a decision by the
United States Supreme Court.[4]

In 1833 Dr. John Emerson, Scott's owner,
had taken him to Illinois and then to the
Wisconsin Territory, areas in which slavery was
prohibited. While there, Scott married another
slave, Harriet Robinson. A daughter was born to
them on free soil. Dr. and Mrs. Emerson and the
Scotts returned to St. Louis in 1842, and after
Dr. Emerson's death white friends of Scott
advised him to sue for freedom. In 1846 Scott,
represented by local attorney Francis Murdoch,
brought suit against Mrs. Irene Emerson in the
circuit court of St. Louis in the Old Courthouse.
The basis of his argument was that he had
been taken to live in territory in which slavery
was prohibited; therefore, he must be free.
Scott lost his initial suit in St. Louis County
Circuit Court but in 1850 won it on retrial.[5]

opportunity to reject the case by pointing out that Scott had voluntarily returned from free to slave territory. The court went instead to the larger question. In the process of denying Scott his claim for freedom, the court ruled the Missouri Compromise to be unconstitutional, thus seemingly guaranteeing slavery in all the territories. The Dred Scott case further divided political opinion and helped move the nation closer to civil war.[9]

Ownership of Scott and his family was passed to St. Louisan Taylor Blow, who set the Scotts free on May 26, 1857. After more than ten years of court battles, Dred Scott was a free man for little more than a year; he died in St. Louis on September 17, 1858. He is buried in Calvary Cemetery.

Return to the east entrance of the Old Courthouse.

The last public slave auction was held here on New Year's Day of 1861.

When estates in St. Louis were being settled, it was often necessary to dispose of the slaves at auction. If there was no immediate demand, the slaves were hired out or put into the county jail to prevent them from running away. The custom had developed of selling these imprisoned slaves from the steps of the courthouse on New Year's Day.[10]

More than two thousand people assembled for the event on January 1, 1861. As the auctioneer led seven slaves to the courthouse, he must have been confident that the large crowd of potential bidders assured top prices. The onlookers stood silent as the auctioneer cried out, "What will you bid for this able-bodied boy? There's not a blemish on him."[11]

At the top of their lungs, the people in the crowd roared back, "Three dollars, three dollars," and they kept up their cry for another twenty minutes. Unknown to the auctioneer, many of those present that morning had attended to stop what one St. Louis resident called "this annual disgrace."[12]

Finally the yelling died down. The auctioneer decided to try again. This time his offer was met by the response, "Four dollars, four dollars." Two hours later, the price had reached only eight dollars. The exhausted and bewildered auctioneer gave up and returned the slaves to the jail.[13]

A great rally was held in the east yard of the courthouse on January 12, 1861, as states were leaving the Union to join the infant Southern Confederacy. Encouraged by speeches from Hamilton Gamble and others, the citizens approved resolutions calling for support of the Union by decrying the use of force by the

Dred Scott.
Photographic copy of daguerreotype, 1858. Missouri Historical Society Photograph and Print Collection.

Federal government or the seceding states. As the meeting prepared to adjourn, the crowd demanded a speech from attorney Uriel Wright. No one in the city had a higher reputation as an orator, and his remarks in favor of keeping Missouri in the Union were received with "irrepressible thunders of applause."[14]

During the days of the Civil War, the courthouse was the scene of many patriotic events. In June 1862 citizens gathered there to persuade the Federal government to build a navy yard in St. Louis. The next month a crowd filled the rotunda, the first-floor hallways, and the yard on the Fourth Street side to hear Frank Blair, now a general in the Union army, as he encouraged enlistments to fill Missouri's regiments. On July 4, 1862, ceremonies were held to mark the official completion of the courthouse.

The courthouse was again decorated in April 1865 to celebrate the surrender of Robert E. Lee's army in Virginia. The assassination of President Lincoln, however, caused black funeral streamers to be woven in with the victorious red, white, and blue bunting. A memorial monument to the slain president was erected in the rotunda where it remained for thirty days, guarded by soldiers of the 41st Missouri Infantry Regiment, a regiment raised in St. Louis.[15]

2. The Roswell Field House

Not far south from the Old Courthouse is the home of Roswell M. Field, Dred Scott's principal legal defender in St. Louis. The home is known locally as the Eugene Field House, and it predates the Civil War. It is typical of the city's middle-class homes of the period. The Field House is maintained by the Eugene Field House Foundation, Inc., a not-for-profit corporation. Hours of operation are 10:00 A.M. to 4:00 P.M. Tuesday through Saturday and noon to 4:00 P.M. on Sunday. A small admission fee is charged. For information call 314-421-4689.

From the Old Courthouse, take Broadway south to 634 South Broadway. The Field House is on the east (left) side of the one-way street. Turn left on Cerre Street and park behind the house.

The Field House is the only remaining structure of a row of twelve brick homes built on the east side of Broadway in 1845. The owner of the homes, a Mr. Walsh, lived in the corner unit at Broadway and Cerre, which shared a wall with the Field home. The other eleven units in "Walsh's Row" were rented, including the Field House. All the houses in the row had separate kitchen buildings attached to the main house by outside wooden staircases. Carriage houses and privies were also located behind the houses.[16]

The Field House was saved from destruction in the 1930s by "spirited editorials" in the *St. Louis Post-Dispatch*. By this time, the Walsh home south of the Field House had been heavily modified for use as a store. Funds could not be raised to undo the damage and in 1935 it was torn down. The Field House now stood alone. Its firebrick was exposed on either side and required covering in order to make the building waterproof. A brick wall was added around the property in 1936.[17]

Roswell Martin Field was born in Vermont on February 22, 1807. At the age of eleven, he entered Middlebury College, Vermont, and graduated four years later. He then studied law and was admitted to the bar at age eighteen. In 1826 he was appointed postmaster of Newfane, Vermont, and was the state's attorney for his county from 1832 to 1835. In 1832 a significant emotional event occurred that resulted in his decision to leave Vermont and move west.[18]

In August 1832 Field met Miss Mary Ann Phelps when she visited Vermont. Miss Phelps was engaged to Mr. James Clark, a fact that Field knew. During her visit, however, Miss Phelps became enamored of Field, and in October they agreed to marry. As she began her trip home, she and Field were married in Putney, Vermont, with an understanding that she could change her mind as she continued on her journey to

Walsh's Row. *Photograph, ca. 1910. Missouri Historical Society Photograph and Print Collection.*

her family. At the end of the month, she met with Clark and her family and informed them of her marriage to Field. That same evening, she wrote to Field disavowing their marriage agreement; on November 6 she sent a second letter confirming the sentiments of the first letter; on November 27 the erstwhile "Mrs. Field" married Mr. Clark.

Clark went to court to nullify his new wife's "marriage" to Field, arguing that Miss Phelps' contract was conditional and not ratified by her. The matter made its way on appeal to the Supreme Court of Vermont, which upheld the lower court decision: Phelps was married to Clark, not Field.[19]

Field was incensed. He vowed never again to practice law in Vermont and left the state. He arrived in St. Louis in 1839 but was so withdrawn that his law practice suffered. During his first six years in the city he was supported by financial assistance from his father.[20]

A stroke of good fortune came to Field in 1846. He married Miss Frances Reed, also a Vermonter. Miss Reed had gone west to Iowa in response to a minister's plea for more teachers. A graduate of Mount Holyoke College, Massachusetts, she found Iowa to be too desolate to her liking and traveled to St. Louis to obtain transportation home. There she met the aspiring lawyer. The Fields had six children, but only two, Eugene and Roswell, Jr., lived past infancy. An acquaintance of Field's recalled his fondness for children and how he would sit on the steps of the house in the evening to play his violin for them.[21]

In 1853 Field took on the Dred Scott suit in the Circuit Court of the United States for the Eastern District of Missouri, a case that over the next four years would help him gain a national reputation. On the appeal to the United States Supreme Court, Field turned the case over to Montgomery Blair, then living in Washington.

Frances Field died in 1856 at age thirty. Eugene and his younger brother were sent to Massachusetts for schooling, returning to St. Louis to be with their father for the summers until the Civil War prevented the visits. During the Civil War, Field was a staunch supporter of the Union cause. In 1865 he was offered a position on the Supreme Court of Missouri but declined for "the freedom and independence of private citizenship." Roswell Field died from a cancer of the stomach in 1869 and was buried in Bellefontaine Cemetery next to his wife.[22]

A bronze plaque on the Field House honors not the father but his more famous son. It reads: "Here was born Eugene Field, the Poet, 1850-1895." The plaque was dedicated on June 6, 1902, by one of Missouri's Confederate veterans, Mark Twain.[23]

3. The St. Louis Mercantile Library

The St. Louis Mercantile Library at 510 Locust, Sixth Floor, is a short walk north of the Old Courthouse. Founded in 1845, the Mercantile Library is the oldest subscription library west of the Mississippi. At the time of the Civil War, its patrons included prominent members of St. Louis society on both sides of the conflict. Though a membership organization, the St. Louis Mercantile Library is open to the public. The library is open on Monday through Friday from 8:30 A.M. to 5:00 P.M. For information call 314-621-0670.

The St. Louis Mercantile Library occupies the exact location it did during the Civil War, except that the building in which it is housed is now three stories taller.

After its organization in 1845, the St. Louis Mercantile Library moved several times before settling in a building of its own on the corner of Broadway and Locust Street. The first floor of the three-story building was rented to retail firms. The second and third floors housed the library. Its lecture hall on the third floor seated two thousand people, the largest assembly hall in St. Louis at that time. The library hosted some of the most important speakers and entertainers of the day.[24]

The library's director at the outbreak of the Civil War was Edward William Johnston. Johnston's loyalties to the Union were much suspected because his younger brother was Joseph E. Johnston, who in 1861 was named the commanding general of the Confederate army in Virginia. Johnston was first employed by the library in June 1858 to prepare a printed catalog of its seventeen thousand books. The skill he demonstrated in this task led to his selection as librarian in April 1859. In 1861 the tight economy resulted in only one novel being added that year to the library's holdings: *Great Expectations*, by Charles Dickens.[25]

Despite his superb services on behalf of the library, Edward Johnston was forced to resign in early 1862 when he refused to take a "test oath" to support the Union, required of all persons in public positions by Mayor Daniel Taylor and the Union military authorities. Admiring friends discreetly managed to engage Johnston's valuable services to continue to catalog library

collections, but before long he retired to a cottage on the Meramec River near Glencoe, Missouri. He was kept on the library's payroll for a small amount under the thin disguise of "Edward Johnson."[26]

The Mercantile Library was host to various Union patriotic gatherings during the Civil War, served as a drill hall for a Union militia unit, and was the meeting place for two state conventions that shaped Missouri's participation in the Civil War.

In March 1861 the state convention meeting in Jefferson City, called by Governor Claiborne Fox Jackson to decide whether Missouri would join the states seceding from the Union, accepted the offer by the library of the free use of its facilities and adjourned to St. Louis. Though the presiding officer of the convention was former Missouri governor and future Confederate general Sterling Price, the most influential participant was aging lawyer and former Missouri Supreme Court judge Hamilton Gamble. Under Gamble's leadership, a committee of the convention issued a report that was adopted by the delegates, most of whom, like Gamble, had been born in slave states. The report stated that there was "at present no adequate cause to impel Missouri to dissolve her connections with the Federal Union."[27]

Indicative of Union hostility toward citizens of Southern sentiment in St. Louis was an incident involving the wife of the former librarian of the Mercantile Library. On August 16, 1862, Mrs. Edward Johnston was arrested in her home at Eureka, Missouri, for refusing to allow a Union officer to enter it and search for weapons. Though the officer was reported to be courteous, Mrs. Johnston assaulted him "in terms of violent abuse." As reported in the *Missouri Democrat*, Mrs. Johnston "defiantly avowed the rankest hostility to the National Government . . . and took pains to make her remarks personally offensive to the officer." For her resistance, she was taken away and confined in the Gratiot Street Prison at Eighth and Gratiot Streets.[28]

Mr. Johnston arrived at the prison to visit his wife, but when forbidden to do so, he announced his intention to commit an act that would cause his arrest. Based on the sincerity with which he delivered this threat, he too was arrested and committed to the prison. Mr. and Mrs. Johnston were released on August 19, 1862.[29]

A second state convention met in the lecture hall of the Mercantile Library on January 6, 1865. Only three of the sixty-six members had been present at the state convention four years earlier. One of the most important acts of the new convention was the passage of the Emancipation Ordinance on January 11, nearly eleven months in advance of the adoption of the Thirteenth Amendment to the United States Constitution. Although many Missourians regarded the Constitutional Convention as a radical body whose views did not represent most Missourians, St. Louisans welcomed the Emancipation Ordinance with great enthusiasm. Three days after its adoption, sixty cannon roared in salute as church bells rang and thousands celebrated in the streets.[30]

In the 1880s the library's board decided it could do better with its property and temporarily moved the library collections to another site while a new building, six stories tall, was built to replace the original one. After the building's completion the library moved into its present location on the Sixth Floor of 512 Locust. Though the lecture hall did not survive the move, the library is a delightful civic attraction that will transport the visitor back to the 1880s.[31]

The St. Louis Mercantile Library currently houses a fine collection of Civil War related books, papers, and artifacts, including an outstanding collection of books printed in Confederate cities during the Civil War. Among the library's holdings are military atlases "borrowed" from the United States Military Academy by one of the library's postwar patrons, General William T. Sherman (whose portrait hangs in the main reading room), and a collection of letters between a St. Louis family and its son/brother, Edward Robbins, an artilleryman in a Missouri Confederate battery serving east of the Mississippi River.

4. The Berthold Mansion

Just a short walk away from the Old Courthouse, the Berthold mansion stood at the northwest corner of modern Broadway and Pine Street, fronting along Broadway and facing east.

The Berthold mansion, as the two-story brick home was always known, was originally the residence of Bartholomew Berthold and his wife, Pelagie Chouteau. When the Bertholds began to build the home in 1829, "his friends were amazed at first and then horrified" that the house was being built so far out in the country, and it was several years before the Bertholds had neighbors. Berthold was a partner of Pierre Chouteau, Jr., his wife's brother, in the fur trade, and he later joined John Jacob Astor and others in operating the American Fur Company. Berthold's home, "one of the best in St. Louis of that day," became a social center for the city's Creole families. The mansion had wide verandas on both the lower and upper levels, supported by four large pillars. The property was surrounded by a low stone wall topped by an iron fence, the style at the time. The Bertholds lived there until 1859 when Broadway (then called Fifth Street) began to become part of the city's business district.[32]

In 1859 the Berthold mansion became the headquarters of the Democratic Party in St. Louis, and after presidential aspirant Stephen A. Douglas failed in the 1860 election, the mansion became the stronghold of the "Minute Men," as the paramilitary organization of the city's Southern sympathizers was known. The Minute Men were organized by eight St. Louisans, all of them future soldiers for the Confederacy, to offset the "exceedingly insolent and aggressive" followers of Republican congressman Frank Blair. Blair's "Wide Awakes," predominantly German-Americans, were often called on to keep order at Republican rallies. Five companies of Minute Men, about four hundred strong, were eventually organized.[33]

On the evening of March 3, 1861, the night before the state Constitutional Convention convened a few blocks north at the Mercantile Library, the officers of the Minute Men met at the Berthold mansion to plan a demonstration. They created two secessionist flags and the next morning flew one of them from the front porch of the mansion. The other flag, by the predawn daring and agility

Berthold Mansion,
Northwest Corner of
Fifth and Pine.
*Photograph, ca. 1859.
Missouri Historical
Society Photograph and
Print Collection.*

of J. R. "Rock" Champion and James Quinlan, flew from the flagstaff atop the dome of the courthouse.[34]

The flag flying from the courthouse was an "American ensign" with only one star and bearing the Missouri coat of arms. What the other flag looked like is a matter of disagreement. Basil Duke, a leader of the Minute Men and a principal in the event, remembered that since the South had not yet adopted a flag, it was necessary to "exercise our imagination to a rather painful extent in order to devise a fit emblem." Duke and his friends added to each flag "every conceivable thing that was suggestive of a Southern meaning." The flag flying from the Berthold mansion was described in unflattering terms by one newspaper as "an ugly, doleful, uninspiring piece of cloth, consistent of a 'yaller' cross, crescent and star arranged in an angle in a deep indigo-blue field." Another newspaper described the flag's color as nearly black. A crescent was on one corner, a

cross turned upside down occupied its center, and the other corner was occupied by a single star. This "singular piece of patchwork," the newspaper editorialized, "reminded one very strikingly of a fancy patchwork quilt manufactured by a young miss of thirteen summers for the premium at a country fair. This quilt, however, we judge would not even be entered as a competitor for the second premium."[35]

The two flags, probably the first pro-Southern flags to fly in Missouri, created a near riot at the Berthold mansion. The flag over the courthouse was brought down as soon as it was discovered, but the flag at the Minute Men's headquarters proved more problematic. An angry crowd gathered in the street to demand the flag's removal, but the belief that the Minute Men kept state arms and ammunition in the building caused the crowd to be cautious about physical force. An armed guard could be seen at the door, and fifteen armed Minute Men patrolled the property. Piles of bricks lay on the veranda outside the windows of the second floor, ready to be used to throw at the "damned Dutch" should they try to force the issue. Several prominent citizens made unsuccessful appeals not only to the Minute Men to remove the flag but also to the crowd to disperse. The flag still flew the next morning.[36]

On April 26, 1861, the Berthold mansion was again involved in the increasing tensions between the Minute Men and the Wide Awakes. As a group of German volunteers were moving by the street railway from the U.S. Arsenal to the north side of the city, they were stopped near Broadway and Pine Street by an armed crowd and pulled from the cars. As the men were sent walking toward their homes, cheers for "Jeff Davis" rose behind them. Direction of these activities seemed to come from officers in uniform congregating at the Berthold mansion.[37]

After the war, the Berthold mansion yielded to the advance of progress. On May 23, 1866, Mrs. Berthold leased the property to a confectioner, who demolished the mansion to replace it with a building more suited to his business.[38]

Basil Duke. *Carte de visite photograph by E. & H. T. Anthony and Co., ca. 1861. Missouri Historical Society Photograph and Print Collection.*

Chapter 3 The Camp

Camp Jackson (Night View of Encampment). *Ink wash on paper by Mat Hastings, ca. 1861. Missouri Historical Society Art Collection.*

No incident is more important to an understanding of the Civil War in St. Louis than the events at Camp Jackson. On May 10, 1861, Union forces under the command of Captain Nathaniel Lyon marched to the city's western outskirts to surround and capture the Missouri Volunteer Militia drilling at Camp Jackson in Lindell Grove, ostensibly because of the threat those troops posed to the United States Arsenal. The Federal troops prepared to march their prisoners and their prisoners' commander, Missouri militia general Daniel M. Frost, to the U.S. Arsenal as an angry crowd collected around the column. Shots were fired, but whether a gunman in the crowd or an anxious soldier began the firing may never be known. The Union volunteers reacted spontaneously and fired into the crowd. Nearly three dozen people died, most of them civilians, and many more were wounded.

Measured against subsequent events, the casualty list at Camp Jackson seems short, but at the time the high number of civilian casualties caught the attention of a divided nation. By comparison, the better remembered "Baltimore Massacre," which occurred a few weeks earlier when soldiers in a Union regiment marching between trains were assaulted by a Baltimore crowd, resulted in the deaths of only thirteen people.

If Unionism means such atrocious deeds as have been witnessed in St. Louis, I am no longer a Union man.

Uriel Wright
May 1861

Jackson Affair

The capture of Camp Jackson came after weeks of tension in the city over the control of its military resources, the ambitions of Missouri's pro-Confederate governor Claiborne Fox Jackson, and the sentiment of the pro-Union Constitutional Convention. States' rights adherents and Southern sympathizers saw the Camp Jackson affair as an illegal act of aggression by the United States against Missouri, arguing that the militia had been assembled by a lawful order of the governor. Ardent Unionists, led by Frank Blair and Lyon, were unwilling to allow the military resources of the U.S. Arsenal to fall into "traitorous" hands. Despite the storm of criticism from both secessionists and moderates, Lyon's action held St. Louis, and therefore Missouri, in the Union.

Even after the passage of 130 years and the dissipation of the deep passions then aroused, many of the critical elements and their exact sequence in the Camp Jackson story are unclear. The surviving eyewitness accounts often conflict with each other on major points. What can be said with certainty is that Camp Jackson was a watershed event. Pro-Confederate citizens in St. Louis, though enraged by the turn of events, were either cowed into acceptance of Union control of the city or forced to flee to other areas. Pro-Union elements in St. Louis were heartened by this Union show of force after months of inaction. For those St. Louisans caught in the middle, perhaps the majority of the city's citizens, the time had come to choose sides. There would be no safe middle ground.

The following tour traces the events of May 10, 1861, and the impact they had not only on the citizens of St. Louis but also on the citizens of Missouri. Unfortunately, little remains of the sites as they existed on that day.

Nathaniel Lyon as Brigadier General, U.S.A. *Carte de visite photograph by Webster's Photographic Gallery, 1861. Missouri Historical Society Photograph and Print Collection.*

1. Captain Lyon Takes Command

The beginning point of the tour is Lyon Park, located at the corner of South Broadway and Utah Streets, just south of the city's center. Parking is most convenient on the east side of Lyon Park.

The Eight Sites Discussed in the Text as They Were Positioned in the Mid-Nineteenth Century. Base Map, Lithograph by Alexander McLean for the R. V. Kennedy Co., 1859. Missouri Historical Society Map Collection.

Nathaniel Lyon was born in Connecticut on July 14, 1818. He graduated from the United States Military Academy in 1841 and was commissioned in the infantry. By the time of the Civil War, he was a combat veteran, having served in the Seminole War, on the frontier, in the Mexican War, in Indian fighting, and in the vicious disputes along the Missouri and Kansas border during Kansas' bid for statehood.

In early 1861 Lyon, a captain in the 2d U.S. Infantry, and his company arrived in St. Louis to increase the garrison of the United States Arsenal. Lyon's ardent antisecessionist sympathies were soon recognized by Frank

Blair and other leading citizens of the city, and Lyon quickly became a leader in the fight to "save" Missouri for the Union. Blair, noted for his strong antislavery sentiment, was St. Louis city and county's representative in the United States Congress. He was also the brother of Montgomery Blair, a member of President Lincoln's cabinet. Frank Blair played an important role in seeing that Lyon's cautious, conciliatory superior, Brigadier General William S. Harney, was removed from influence in St. Louis, thus allowing Lyon to execute the plan to capture Camp Jackson. One week after the incident, Lyon was commissioned a brigadier general of U.S. Volunteers.[1]

Over the following summer, Lyon organized a campaign to drive the pro-Confederate Missouri State Guard from the state. On August 10, 1861, Lyon and his Union army attacked the soldiers of Generals Ben McCulloch and Sterling Price south of Springfield, Missouri, at Wilson's Creek. Lyon's forces were defeated and forced to withdraw. General Lyon was killed in the battle.[2]

Follow the footpath to the center of the park and the first Lyon monument.

Slightly more than ten acres are included in Lyon Park. The site, once part of the grounds of the U.S. Arsenal, was granted to St. Louis by an act of Congress in March 1869 on condition that a monument to Lyon be erected there within three years of the transfer; the secretary of war transferred the ground to St. Louis in September 1871. Lyon's first monument was dedicated on September 13, 1874.

The red granite obelisk is twenty-eight feet high and sits on a mound about fifteen feet above the footpath. The obelisk rests on a square base. Midway up the shaft is a bronze medallion, which in relief depicts the face of General Lyon. Beneath it is the date "August 10, 1861," the date of Lyon's death at Wilson's Creek. Lower down toward the base is inscribed the name *Lyon*. On the eastern side of the monument is another medallion representing an allegorical scene: a female with a club and behind her the figure of a lion. The monument was designed by local architect Adolphus Druiding, and the medallion's sculptor was James Wilson Alexander MacDonald, brother of one of the Missouri militia officers taken prisoner by Lyon in May 1861.[3]

Lyon's monument is reportedly on the spot where he organized the troops to carry out his operations against Camp Jackson. For many years ceremonies were held there on the anniversary of Lyon's death. After a parade and the placing of flags and flowers around the

Lyon Monument, Lyon Park. *Postcard, ca. 1908. Missouri Historical Society Photograph and Print Collection.*

monument, two orations would be given: one in German and one in English.[4]

Continue along the footpath to the northwest corner of Lyon Park and the statue of General Lyon.

At the northwest corner of the park stands a mounted statue of General Lyon. Its history is as curious as the life of the man it honors.

In the late 1920s, the Camp Jackson Union Soldiers Monument Association conducted a fund-raising campaign to erect a monument to General Lyon. The group selected sculptor Erhardt Siebert, the Swiss-born son of a St. Louis physician. Siebert had grown up in St. Louis and studied art at Washington University. He left the city to pursue further study but later returned to St. Louis.

The Lyon monument was originally designed to occupy a street triangle within the Camp Jackson site across from St. Louis University at Grand Avenue and West Pine Boulevard. Siebert's concept included ornamental walls along two sides of the triangle with an opening at the apex for an equestrian statue. But before the plan could be carried out, things began to go wrong.

First, the fund ran short of money. Siebert cut back his design to consist of the mounted general with an orderly crowded on a narrow ledge against a rock background. The mass of bronze rested on a limestone pedestal. The horse's hindquarters were done in high relief; the forward part of the animal and its rider were elongated and swung about to emerge in the round. As a result, the elements of the sculpture were badly out of scale with each

other. Simply put, the figures and the pedestal relief were crudely done.

Even before the statue could be installed at Grand and West Pine in 1929, the criticism began. Among the critics were no less than Edmund H. Wuerpel, director of the Washington University School of Fine Arts, and Victor S. Holm, instructor in sculpture. St. Louis mayor Victor Miller directed the members of the Municipal Art Commission, whose review of projects for civic sites was required by ordinance, to take no position on the statue or risk losing their appointments. In the words of a recent critic, "Siebert was not equal to the demands of his new composition."[5]

The final indignity came nearly thirty years later. In 1959 Harriet Frost Fordyce, the daughter of General Frost, gave St. Louis University more than one million dollars to purchase 22.5 acres in the Mill Creek Redevelopment Area. Mrs. Fordyce's gift came with only one condition: that the entire campus be renamed after her father. The administration at St. Louis University saw only one problem— the statue of Frost's adversary, General Nathaniel Lyon, stood in this tract. Working with local politicians, St. Louis University managed to get the statue removed to the northwest corner of Lyon Park in 1960. It now stands on the approximate location of one of the U.S. Arsenal's Civil War–era powder magazines.[6]

Lyon Park is in the shadow of Anheuser-Busch, Inc., one of the world's largest breweries. Ironically, Corporal Adolphus Busch and Private Eberhard Anheuser, his father-in-law, the founders of the brewery, marched in Companies E and C of the 3d Regiment, United States Reserve Corps, under Lyon's command.[7]

2. The U.S. Arsenal a Coveted Prize

Walk to the east side of Lyon Park and observe the U.S. Air Force Installation that now occupies the grounds of the U.S. Arsenal. Access to these grounds is restricted. For more information contact the Public Affairs Officer, Defense Mapping Agency Aerospace Center,

3200 South Second Street, St. Louis, MO 63118-3399. Telephone: 314-263-4142.

In May 1826 the secretary of war authorized the purchase of land for an arsenal in St. Louis to replace the dilapidated Fort Bellefontaine on the Missouri River north of the city. In August 1827 a forty-acre tract of mixed timbered and cultivated land was selected three miles south of St. Louis. The first building was completed in 1827. The main arsenal building, a three-story structure, was completed the following year. The first shipment of ordnance arrived in 1829: twelve thousand six-pounder and three thousand twelve-pounder cannonballs. One hundred tons of stores were also received from Fort Bellefontaine, abandoned that same year.[8]

During the Mexican War the U.S. Arsenal was the site of frenzied activity. At the time, the arsenal employed more than five hundred workers. A new building program began in the late 1840s, and throughout the next decade the arsenal sold arms and ammunition to settlers traveling west as well as arming and equipping military expeditions, including forces for the Utah Expedition in 1857.[9]

Between the arsenal's establishment and the time of the Civil War, the population of St. Louis increased nearly twenty-fold. By 1860 lots around the arsenal had been sold for development. The arsenal, once isolated from the city, was slowly surrounded by it. In 1861 it housed sixty thousand muskets, ninety

Above:
The Arsenal at St. Louis, Missouri. *Wood engraving after Alexander Simplot.* Harper's Weekly, *August 31, 1861, p. 555. Missouri Historical Society Photograph and Print Collection.*

Right:
Entrance to the Arsenal at St. Louis. *Wood engraving, ca. 1861. Missouri Historical Society Photograph and Print Collection.*

thousand pounds of powder, one-and-a-half million cartridges, forty cannon, and equipment for the manufacture of arms. Despite its importance, the arsenal was guarded by only forty soldiers.[10]

Early in 1861 the U.S. Arsenal had been identified as a coveted prize. In January General Daniel Marsh Frost sent out secret instructions to his subordinates informing them of his scheme to summon the Missouri militia "upon the bells of the churches sounding a continuous peal, interrupted by a pause of five minutes." A copy of these instructions, implicating the Catholic churches and their Irish parishioners, fell into the hands of Union authorities. Blair successfully pressured Archbishop Peter Richard Kenrick to stop the plan.[11]

On January 24 Missouri militia general Frost wrote to Governor Jackson to inform him of a conversation he had had with Major William H. Bell, the Federal officer commanding the arsenal. Frost repeated to Jackson the assurances he received from Bell. Missouri had the right, said Bell, to claim the contents of the arsenal because they were on Missouri soil. He further assured Frost that he would not attempt any defense against the proper state authorities. Bell also gave Frost permission to quarter soldiers at the arsenal to protect it if necessary. Bell was "everything that you and I could desire," Frost asserted to Jackson.[12]

Bell quickly found himself at the center of powerful forces. After Bell refused to allow St. Louis congressman Frank Blair's Unionist volunteers to guard the arsenal to prevent an anticipated attack, Frank telegraphed his brother, Montgomery, recently appointed to Lincoln's cabinet as postmaster general. Together, the Blairs quickly brought about Bell's transfer. Bell chose instead to retire to his farm near St. Charles, Missouri. He was replaced by Brevet Major Peter Hagner. Montgomery Blair then used his influence to assure that more Federal troops were sent to St. Louis.[13]

Captain Nathaniel Lyon, 2d U.S. Infantry, and his company arrived soon after. Then came Captain Rufus Saxton, 4th U.S. Artillery, and a small detachment. Later Captain James Totten and Company F of the 2d U.S. Artillery arrived. The arsenal's garrison had increased to 9 officers and 484 men. One of Lyon's first actions was to make contact with Frank Blair. From that time forward Lyon and Blair would work together closely to assure that the arsenal remained safely in Federal hands.[14]

Concern for the arsenal was real. Even Brigadier General Harney, though criticized unmercifully by Blair and his followers for his conciliatory approach toward Governor Jackson and General Frost, wrote to army headquarters in Washington, D.C., as early as April 16 to express his concern for the arsenal's security. Harney explained that the buildings and grounds were commanded by hills, placing them within easy range of artillery. He further explained that reliable sources informed him that "it is the intention of the executive of this State to cause batteries to be erected on these hills, and also upon the island opposite to the arsenal." Harney, who commanded the Department of the West, also asked for "an officer of rank" to command the arsenal, an attempt to limit the authority of the upstart Captain Lyon.[15]

Unfortunately for his career, Harney sided with the Board of Police Commissioners, all of whom were Democrats and most of whom were states' rights men, in a dispute over who would patrol the streets around the arsenal. On April 18 Harney ordered Lyon to cease interfering with the police by confining his patrols to inside the arsenal's grounds. He also ordered Lyon to cease issuing arms from the arsenal without his prior consent. Through the influence of the Blair family, Harney was removed from command a few days later.[16]

Harney's departure allowed Lyon to begin enrolling volunteers in the service of the United States, an order from the War Department that Harney had been obstructing. Anxious to prove their patriotism and their loyalty to the Union, St. Louis' German citizens responded to the call; more than 80 percent of the volunteers who quickly filled the four infantry regiments authorized by the War Department were of German ancestry. Lyon was quick to realize the opportunity created by this ethnic enthusiasm, and in April and May he enrolled five regiments of the United States Reserve Corps (the "Home Guards") and a fifth regiment of U.S. Volunteers.

The arsenal, rather than Jefferson Barracks, was the organization point for Lyon's volunteers. John Buegel and his friend H. Hinzman decided to enlist in Colonel Franz Sigel's 3d U.S. Volunteers because "Germans at that time were looked upon as belonging to an unworthy nation" and were held in contempt and disdain by "Americans." After "a good lunch with fine beer" at Washington Hall, the recruiting center on Second and Elm Streets, Buegel and Hinzman were marched with other recruits to the arsenal. As soon as they were sworn in, they were issued rifles, but no uniforms were available. The next morning the new soldiers fell in for drill, each wearing the civilian clothes he had enlisted in. The wide assortment of caps, straw hats, and even silk hats gave the regiment "a very funny appearance," but Buegel noted that "the main thing . . . was that each one was eager to teach the German-haters a never-to-be-forgotten lesson." St. Louis' Southern sympathizers lost no time in comparing these "damned Dutch" to the Hessians of the American Revolution.[17]

In the early morning hours of April 25, 1861, Captain Lyon removed twenty thousand muskets and more than one hundred thousand cartridges from the arsenal and sent them by steamboat to Alton, Illinois. Approximately ten thousand muskets remained, which he used to arm the Union volunteers and Home Guards. A much smaller arsenal at Liberty, Missouri, had been taken by prosecession Missourians just a few days earlier, so Lyon and Blair had good reason to fear the loss of the U.S. Arsenal.

Early on May 9, a mysterious shipment arrived at Camp Jackson. Rumor had it that the boxes, marked "Tamaroa marble," actually contained weapons for those with secessionist sympathies. These reinforcements were the result of an appeal for siege guns sent by Governor Jackson to Confederate president Jefferson Davis earlier in the month. Two captains of the Missouri Volunteer Militia, Colton Greene and Basil Duke, carried the request to Davis in Montgomery, Alabama.[18]

Later that same day, a low, open carriage arrived at the arsenal. It was driven by William Roberts, a black driver, and carried J. J. Witzig, a member of the Committee of Public Safety and prominent engineer, and an old woman dressed in black and wearing a heavy veil and an oversized bonnet, presumably Mrs. Mira Alexander, Frank Blair's blind mother-in-law. In fact, the old woman was Nathaniel Lyon in disguise. He and Witzig were returning from a surreptitious firsthand reconnaissance of Camp Jackson.[19]

During the Civil War, the arsenal's activities were greatly expanded. By 1863 Captain F. D. Callender, the arsenal's commander, employed 700 civilians at the facility, including 150 children; the children were used to make cartridges. After the war most of the arsenal's functions were assumed by the Rock Island Arsenal, and in 1868 it was recommended that the arsenal be moved to Jefferson Barracks. No land was sold, though the six acres now constituting Lyon Park were given to the City of St. Louis that year. By the time the arsenal was officially moved to Jefferson Barracks in 1870, most of the ordnance stores had been removed; only fifty soldiers remained at the site. Since then, the "old" arsenal grounds have remained under military jurisdiction and have served a variety of purposes, ranging from a cavalry camp to its present use by the United States Air Force.[20]

3. Union Troops Converge on Camp Jackson

From Lyon Park, follow one of the routes of Lyon's columns to the Camp Jackson area. Changes in street names and the city's layout may cause some confusion between contemporary accounts and the current landscape. In 1859, for example, the street at the north side of Lyon Park was called the Carondelet Road. As it went north it became Fourth Street, and still farther north was labeled Broadway. The modern Broadway through downtown St. Louis would have been Fifth Street in the Civil War era.

Daybreak on May 10, 1861, arrived under a threatening sky, but before the day's end, the temperature would reach 72 degrees. Before dawn Lyon had sent orders to the commanders of the Union units located throughout the city to prepare to converge on Camp Jackson.[21]

Just as Lyon prepared to leave the arsenal, he was sought by St. Louisan John S. Bowen, General Frost's chief of staff and one of his two regimental commanders. Bowen bore a message from Frost, which read in part as follows: "Sir: I am constantly in receipt of information that you contemplate an attack upon my camp; whilst I understand you are impressed with the idea that an attack upon the arsenal and United States troops is intended on the part of the militia of Missouri, I am greatly at a loss to know what could justify you in attacking citizens of the United States, who are in the lawful performance of duties devolving upon them, under the Constitution."[22]

If Frost chose Bowen to be a peacemaker, he made a wrong decision. Like Captain Lyon, John Bowen was a graduate of the United States Military Academy. After Bowen's graduation in 1853, he served in the Mounted Rifles, first at Jefferson Barracks and then on the Texas frontier. While at Jefferson Barracks, Bowen met and later married Mary Kennerly, one of the daughters of a prominent pro-Southern St. Louis family.

Bowen left the United States Army after less than three years of service to pursue a career as an architect, first in Savannah, Georgia, his native state, and then in St. Louis. In both cities he was active in the local militia. In the fall of 1860, Bowen was a lieutenant colonel in the Missouri Volunteer

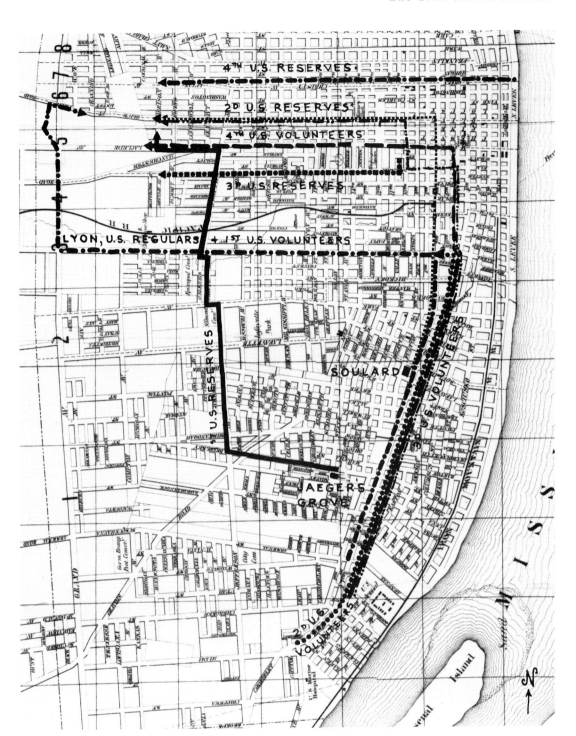

United States Troops
Move to Surround
Camp Jackson. *Base
Map, Lithograph by
Alexander McLean for
the R. V. Kennedy Co.,
1859. Missouri
Historical Society Map
Collection. Overlays by
Pat Baer, 1994.*

Militia and Brigadier General Daniel Frost's assistant adjutant general when the St. Louis Militia was called out by Governor Stewart to defend the western borders of the state from "free-soilers" and "jayhawkers" led by Kansan James Montgomery. The threat having passed, the militia returned to St. Louis except for a few companies known as the Southwest Expedition. Bowen was left in command of this unit.

Now Bowen held the rank of colonel and commanded Frost's 2d Regiment of Missouri Volunteer Militia. The 2d Regiment consisted primarily of militia companies formed in 1861. It attracted the city's most ardent young Southern sympathizers. Several of the companies began their existence as "Minute Men," organizations which sprouted in reaction to Frank Blair's "Wide Awake" companies. Whether by his military competence or his politics, John Bowen was second in rank only to General Frost at the Missouri militia encampment in May 1861.

A much better choice for Frost's messenger might have been his other regimental commander, Lieutenant Colonel John Knapp. Knapp had served in the Missouri militia since the early 1840s. When the militia was called on for service in the war with Mexico in 1846, Knapp commanded a company. By the time of the Civil War, John and his brother George, also a distinguished militia officer, were prominent in the St. Louis community. George Knapp was the owner and editor of the *Missouri Republican*, St. Louis' influential Democratic newspaper.

Perhaps John Knapp was too conciliatory for Frost to trust with carrying his message. Two days before Lyon surrounded Camp Jackson, Knapp had reportedly met with some of the Regular Army officers at Jefferson Barracks and told them that his regiment would break camp as scheduled on May 11, 1861. The companies would be dismissed and the militiamen sent to their homes.[23]

John Bowen's and John Knapp's later actions are indicators of their political leanings in the spring of 1861. After Camp Jackson Bowen formed the 1st Missouri Infantry, C.S.A. He would rise to the rank of major general before his death to illness in July 1863. Knapp, however, chose to remain in the service of the Union. During Governor Hamilton Gamble's administration, Knapp helped develop plans for enrollment of the Missouri militia to aid in local defense. Knapp would be appointed to command the 8th Regiment, Enrolled Missouri Militia, U.S.A., and in 1864 would be involved in the pursuit of General Sterling Price and his Confederate column in the last Missouri raid.[24]

For whatever reason, Frost chose the young, Southern-born, Southern-sympathizing West Point graduate Bowen to carry his message. The choice of messenger may not have mattered. Lyon refused to receive Bowen. Worse, when Bowen's message was finally delivered by one of Lyon's aides, Lyon refused to read it. He had already decided what action he would take.

Around 1:00 P.M., seven columns of Union soldiers, perhaps as many as eight thousand men, began moving toward the confrontation with the Missouri militia. Lyon's troops were certainly more impressive because of their number than their appearance. Fifteen-year-old Philip D. Stephenson and his classmate Harry Newman left the St. Louis High School around 2:00 P.M. and walked directly into the path of the oncoming Union soldiers. The boys joined the throng of excited citizens walking alongside the soldiers. Forty years later, Stephenson could still clearly recall the impression Lyon's volunteers made: "The troops were formed in a peculiar way for marching, not in 'fours' but in 'platoons,' filling the street from curb to curb and massed closely. They were Germans . . . [and] had no uniforms, were not very orderly, were very much excited and frightened, held their arms 'at a ready' many of them, at the people on the pavement. There was no music and everything was oppressively silent, nothing being heard but the shuffling of feet, or now and then an officer's command, or a taunt from the dogging crowd."[25]

The routes of march for Lyon's forces were as follows:[26]

Lyon, the U.S. Regulars, and the 1st U.S. Volunteers

The 1st U.S. Volunteers, commanded by Colonel Frank Blair, and two companies of U.S. Regulars left Jefferson Barracks for the arsenal eight miles away around 8:00 A.M. From the arsenal Lyon led the column north on Seventh Street to Chouteau Avenue and westward on Chouteau until Lindell Grove came into view. The troops turned north on an unnamed narrow lane about a block west of Grand Avenue, cutting through the western end of Lindell Grove and passing along the western edge of Camp Jackson. Striking Olive Street (at the time also called the Central Plank Road), the column turned right (east).

Part of the 1st U.S. Volunteers was still in the western lane when the head of the column, moving east on Olive, met the 3d U.S. Volunteers coming westward from the city.

Riding with General Lyon was a young officer named John M. Schofield. Though now on leave from the army to teach physics at Washington University, Schofield would later achieve fame as a major general and commander of the Union's XXIII Corps during Sherman's campaign through Georgia and at the Union victories of Franklin and Nashville in the war's last winter.

2d U.S. Volunteers

The fifty-six-year-old Heinrich "Henry" Boernstein, an elderly man by military standards, led the 2d U.S. Volunteers, a regiment more than 85 percent German. A veteran of five years in the Austrian army, Boernstein arrived in the United States in 1849 as a successful publisher with special interests in culture and politics. Boernstein took over *Anzeiger des Westens,* one of St. Louis' several German-language newspapers, and he used it aggressively to promote his antislavery, anti-Temperance, and anti-Catholic views. Boernstein was proof that not all the "fire-eaters" were in Dixie.[27]

The 2d U.S. Volunteers started their march from the U.S. Marine Hospital, located along Marine Avenue six blocks south of the arsenal's main buildings. The regiment followed Broadway (also called the Carondelet Road at the time) north to Chouteau Avenue. They then followed the route of the 1st U.S. Volunteers.

The Marine Hospital had been established to care for sick and disabled boatmen. The boatmen, whose only home was their river craft, paid a regular fee or "hospital money" to the Collector of the Port of St. Louis.

3d U.S. Volunteers

Franz Sigel came to the United States as one of the "Forty-Eighters," refugees from the failed republican revolutions in central Europe in 1848-1849. Sigel had led the revolutionary military forces of the Grand Duchy of Baden, only to be overcome by Prussian troops. Despite his failure, Sigel was considered a military hero and was a popular figure with German-Americans, not just in St. Louis but across the North. Sigel's regiment, the 3d U.S. Volunteers, was proudly accounted as nearly all German and carried a United States flag onto which the words *Lyoner Fahnenwacht* were embroidered to announce the regiment as "Lyon's Colorguard."

Franz Sigel as Brigadier General, U.S.A. *Carte de visite photograph by J. A. Scholten, 1861. Missouri Historical Society Photograph and Print Collection.*

Francis Hassendeubel as Colonel, 17th Missouri Infantry, U.S.A. *Carte de visite photograph by J. A. Scholten, 1861. Missouri Historical Society Photograph and Print Collection.*

Colonel Sigel, the 3d U.S. Volunteers, and six pieces of artillery began at the arsenal and marched north on Broadway. A few blocks north of the arsenal, Sigel tried to move to the head of his regiment in the crowded street, but his galloping horse slipped on the pavement and fell, injuring Sigel's leg. Lieutenant Colonel Francis Hassendeubel took command, Sigel following along later in a carriage. The column moved north on the Carondelet Road and Fifth Street (modern Broadway) to Elm Street (Elm Street no longer exists; it was parallel and close to modern Clark Avenue). The column turned left on Elm and marched west to Tenth Street. At Tenth Street, the 3d U.S. Volunteers went north to Olive. Turning west, they stayed on Olive until it reached Garrison Avenue, the eastern edge of Lindell Grove. The artillery took position on elevated ground northeast of the camp.[28]

Those attempting to follow the route of the 3d U.S. Volunteers will discover that it passes through the grounds of Busch Memorial Stadium, home of the St. Louis Baseball Cardinals.

4th U.S. Volunteers

The 4th U.S. Volunteers, commanded by Colonel Nicholas Schuettner, also started from the arsenal. They marched north up Broadway behind Sigel's column. When the 4th U.S. Volunteers reached Market Street, they turned left (west) and followed it toward the camp. When Market Street crossed Jefferson Avenue it became Laclede Avenue, the southern edge of Lindell Grove. The 4th U.S. Volunteers stopped along Laclede at the southern side of the camp but near its east end.

The United States Reserve Corps: The Home Guard

Though the Home Guard regiments were not called on to play a major role in the events of May 10, 1861, their presence gave added weight to Lyon's military force.

St. Louis' Home Guard began its unofficial existence in early 1861 in response to the organization of the pro-Southern Minute Men within the city. Among the German immigrants were a number with military experience in Europe's armies, so drillmasters were readily available. To facilitate recruiting, the Home Guards aligned their organization with the political organization of St. Louis. Recruits for the 1st Home Guard Regiment came from the city's First Ward. The members of the 2d Home Guard lived between Soulard and Chouteau and from the river to Jefferson Avenue, the approximate boundaries of the Second Ward; Soulard Market Hall became their headquarters and place of assembly. The 3d Home Guard recruited from the territory north of Chouteau to Market and west to Rock Spring and Cheltenham. The 4th Home Guard recruited along Franklin Avenue but was somewhat isolated in 1861 by the "Americans" on the south and the Irish residential area to the north. The 5th Home Guard recruited from the Tenth Ward on the north side of the city. One of the results of recruiting by political division was homogeneity of livelihood or occupation. The 1st and 5th Home Guards contained the largest number of laborers, the 2d and 4th members of the retail trade, and the 3d Home Guards professional men and others from the central business district.[29]

Technically, these five regiments were regiments of the United States Reserve Corps, an organization created specifically for St. Louis to accommodate the overabundance of volunteers. In official reports or other military correspondence, these units are referred to as "1st U.S.R.C." or "1st Reserves." In the contemporary press and in other civilian accounts, they are almost always called "Home Guards."

1st Reserves

The 1st Battalion of the 1st Regiment, United States Reserve Corps, marched from Jaeger's Garden on Tenth and Sidney Streets across the commons to Jefferson Avenue. Once on Jefferson it moved north. From Jefferson Avenue, the column probably went west on Laclede until it reached Garrison Avenue at the east end of Camp Jackson. Its final position along Garrison Avenue was south of the artillery of Sigel's column.

2d Reserves

Colonel Herman Kallmann commanded the 2d Reserves. Only the 1st Battalion, under Lieutenant Colonel J. T. Fiala, made the march to Camp Jackson. Beginning at Soulard Market, the troops moved north to Olive Street and then west on Olive to the camp. The 2d Reserves took position northwest of the 1st Reserves.

Order of Battle
The Camp Jackson Affair
May 10, 1861
United States Forces

Captain Nathaniel Lyon, 2d U.S. Infantry, Commanding

2d U.S. Infantry, two companies	Captain Thomas Sweeny
Artillery Battery, Missouri Volunteers	Major Francis Backoff

U.S. Volunteers

1st Regiment	Colonel Francis P. Blair, Jr.
2d Regiment	Colonel Henry Boernstein
3d Regiment	Colonel Franz Sigel
4th Regiment	Colonel Nicholas Schuettner
5th Regiment	Colonel Charles E. Salomon

U.S. Reserve Corps

1st Regiment	Colonel Henry Almstedt
1st Battalion	Lt. Col. Robert J. Rombauer
2d Battalion	Major Philip Brimmer
2d Regiment	Colonel Herman Kallmann
1st Battalion	Lt. Col. John T. Fiala
2d Battalion	Major Julius Rapp
3d Regiment, U.S. Reserve Corps	Colonel John McNeil
4th Regiment, U.S. Reserve Corps	Colonel B. Gratz Brown
5th Regiment, U.S. Reserve Corps	Colonel Charles G. Stifel

Sources: Rombauer, *Union Cause in St. Louis,* 200-205, 226-30. Dyer, *Compendium of the War of the Rebellion,* 1699, 1710. *Missouri Democrat,* April 27, 1861. The name of the artillery commander, Major Backoff, is also spelled "Backof" and "Backhof" in contemporary accounts.

3d Reserves

The 3d Reserves, commanded by Colonel John McNeil, formed at the St. Louis Turner Hall on Tenth and Walnut Streets. Leaving Turner Hall, the regiment probably marched south one block to Clark Street. It then followed Clark west to Jefferson, stopping near the southeast corner of the camp.

4th Reserves

The 4th Reserves, under Colonel B. Gratz Brown, marched west on what was then called Morgan Street (following the approximate course of the modern Convention Center Drive) to near the northeast corner of the camp. As with the 3d Reserves, the 4th Reserves guarded the approaches to town and formed a reserve for Lyon's command.

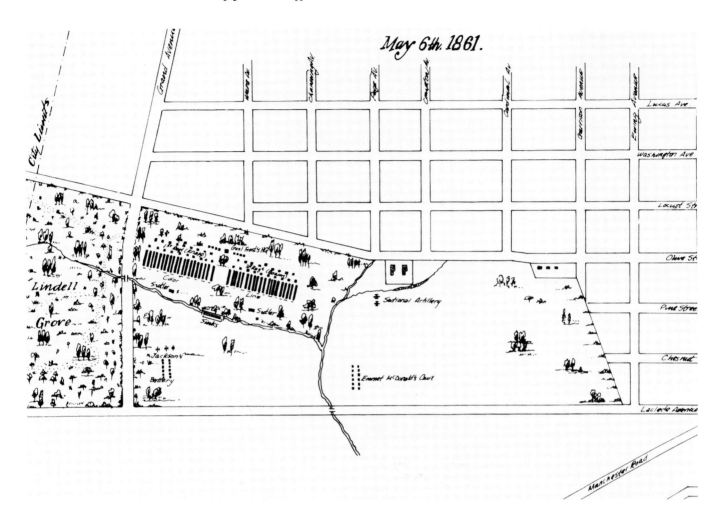

May 6th. 1861.

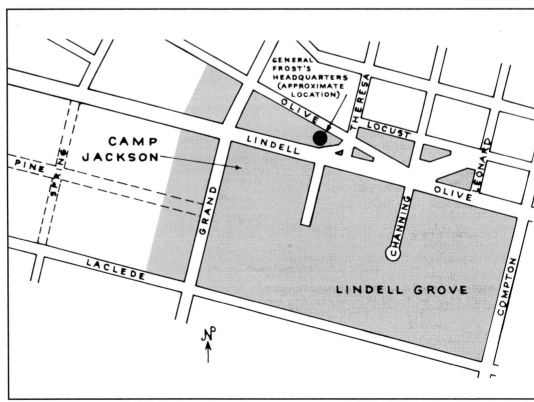

Above:
Camp Jackson, after Survey of Edward B. Sayers, Missouri Volunteer Militia. *The original Sayers survey is in the Collections of the St. Louis Mercantile Library.*

Right:
Modern Location of Camp Jackson. *Site now occupied by the Frost Campus of St. Louis University. Map by Pat Baer, 1994.*

On Guard at the Arsenal

The organized companies of the 5th Volunteers under Colonel C. E. Salomon and two companies of U.S. Regulars held the arsenal. The 2d Battalions of the 1st and 2d Reserves occupied the streets and guarded the arsenal's approaches. The 5th Reserves, though unarmed and not yet organized for service, was assembled at Stifel's Brewery, its headquarters.

4. The Missouri Volunteer Militia Takes the Field

Lindell Grove, at the city's western edge, was the site of the militia encampment in May 1861. The modern streets that roughly outline Lindell Grove are Garrison Avenue on the east, Olive Street on the north, Grand Avenue on the west, and Laclede Avenue on the south. The militia camp was located in the northwest corner of Lindell Grove.

Nothing remains of Camp Jackson, not even a marker at the site. Camp Jackson was lost forever in the Grand Avenue Redevelopment Project of the 1960s. It is now part of the Frost Campus of St. Louis University.

Concerned by the buildup of Unionist strength in St. Louis, Governor Jackson had used the Militia Act of 1858 to call the militia into camp for its annual week of drill. The militia district commander in St. Louis, General Frost, originally intended to have his troops camp on the heights around the U.S. Arsenal, but Captain Lyon had anticipated this move and placed Federal troops there. Frost then asked permission from city officials to use Lindell Grove.[30]

On Monday, May 6, 1861, the First Brigade of Missouri Volunteer Militia, the state's largest and best militia organization, assembled in full uniform at 9:30 A.M. in downtown St. Louis. Large crowds assembled to watch the military evolutions of the militiamen. The 1st Regiment of Missouri Volunteer Militia formed facing west along Eighth Street with its right wing resting on Locust Street. The 2d Regiment formed along Sixth Street with its right on Olive Street. At 10:30 A.M. the 1st Regiment moved to Washington Avenue, the 2d Regiment following soon after. On Washington Avenue a brigade line was formed facing south with its right resting on Eleventh Street. From here the troops marched to Camp Jackson, arriving around 11:30 A.M.[31]

Most of the members of the Missouri Volunteer Militia were present because of the governor's proclamation, but one of them, Elihu Hotchkiss Shepard, was present by personal invitation. Born in 1795 and a combat veteran of the War of 1812, Shepard had enlisted in the Missouri Volunteer Militia in May 1846 in order to fight in the war with Mexico. Officers of his former company, the St. Louis Grays, invited him to leave his home in Washington County, Missouri, to join them at the 1861 militia encampment. As the company now prepared to march to Camp Jackson, Shepard was told that a seat had been provided for him in an ambulance so he could ride to the camp. At sixty-five years of age, Shepard was treated as "the patriarch of the brigade." Later in the week, Shepard would be taken prisoner with all the rest.[32]

The encampment at Lindell Grove was named Camp Jackson in honor of the governor. Edward Brydges Sayers, engineer for the State of Missouri, surveyed the site on May 6. Sayers showed the camp's position in the northwest corner of Lindell Grove with its northern edge following the course of Olive Street. The militia's four artillery pieces faced the city in a north-south line slightly west of and parallel to the modern Channing Avenue. Two "company streets" intersected the tent rows. Frost's headquarters was located at the intersection of the two streets.[33]

The *Missouri Democrat* of May 7, 1861, described the camp as if it were a holiday attraction for the city's citizens. In the newspaper's words, "The camp ground selected is a few hundred yards south of the suburban terminus of the Olive street railway. It is a beautifully shaded grove, the trees standing well apart, and with a nearly level extent of open field around. The site is near the termini of both the Olive and Market street cars, and is one of both convenience and taste." Young Philip Stephenson and his adventurous friends had slipped in and out of Camp Jackson several times during the week-long encampment. On one occasion he was bold enough to peek into the tent of General Frost, and he saw that it was carpeted and furnished with a bureau, a bedstead, and other comforts. "This struck me, young as I was, as over luxurious, and my hero fell somewhat in my admiration," he recorded in his memoirs.[34]

The movements around the arsenal in the early hours of May 10, 1861, were quickly reported to General Frost by spies. Rumors of a potential attack on the camp had been flying since its organization, so Frost was likely not

William Bull in the
Uniform of the
Engineer Corps, 2d
Regiment, Missouri
Volunteer Militia.
*Photograph by J.
Sidney Brown, 1861.
Missouri Historical
Society Photograph and
Print Collection.*

very surprised. Captain Basil Duke, one of
Frost's militia officers, also served on the city's
Board of Police Commissioners. As a result, he
received immediate reports of the Federal
movements from the chief of police. Duke told
Frost on the evening of May 9 that "movement
against the camp was imminent" and urged
preparation for an attack to come the next
morning. Frost's own scouts provided further
confirmation of Lyon's activity.[35]

Sometime during the morning of May 10,
John Knapp, commanding officer of the 1st
Regiment, Missouri Volunteer Militia, took time
to write his wife a prescient note: "We have
reliable information that there is a large force
on the way here. We await their arrival when
we will make no reaction to their demands. If
they come I will be home to-night. Do not
speak of this."[36]

General Frost did not act on these warnings
other than to send the message to Lyon
carried by Bowen around midday. Lyon's men
began appearing at Camp Jackson around 3:15
P.M. Lyon sent Major Bernard G. Farrar to
General Frost with the surrender demand.[37]

Farrar waited while Frost drafted the
following reply to Captain Lyon: "I never for a
moment conceived the idea that so illegal and
unconstitutional a demand as I have just
received from you would be made by an
officer of the United States army. I am wholly
unprepared to defend my command from this
unwarranted attack, and shall therefore be
forced to comply with your demand."[38]

Shortly after Lyon received Frost's surrender
note, he dismounted from his horse onto Olive
Street. Concentrating on the many details that
now faced him, Lyon failed to realize how
close he was walking to the horse of one of his
artillery officers. The horse kicked backward,
hitting Lyon in the stomach and knocking him
unconscious. Some of his aides feared he was
dead. A regimental physician was called, and
after about thirty minutes Lyon was able to
return to command.[39]

The captains of the militia companies were
summoned to Frost's tent, where they learned
of their surrender. The actions of Captain
George West, commanding Company G of the
1st Regiment, must have been typical of what
was occurring throughout the camp. He
hurriedly returned to his men and informed
them that their private property was not to be
taken from them but would be guarded by
Captain Sweeny and the U.S. Regulars. Orders
were given to pack and then to fall in on the
parade ground as quickly as possible.[40]

Once his company was formed, Captain
West decided to show off the soldierly bearing
of his men by putting them through the
manual of arms. This completed, West's
militiamen were then ordered to stack arms.
As the color company, they took their place at
the head of the column of prisoners.

Major Farrar rode on General Frost's left as
Frost led the column of prisoners out of the
camp. Colonel Bowen and Lieutenant Colonel
Knapp rode immediately behind Farrar and
Frost. As the knot of officers passed through a
gap in the fence along Olive Street, Knapp
drew his sword and, "wild with excitement,"
flourished it over his head before breaking it
over the fence.[41]

5. Civilians and Soldiers Clash Violently

Twentieth-century urban development has eliminated all but the most basic features of Lindell Grove and Camp Jackson. A topographical map drawn during the Civil War and now in the collections of the Missouri Historical Society shows that Camp Jackson was in a valley and dominated by higher ground to its north and west. There was a difference in elevation of at least forty feet between the lowest point in Lindell Grove and the crest of what Lyon described as "the bluff" north of Olive Street. Olive Street, also called the Central Plank Road, cut across the base of the bluff. The effect of the high ground to its north and the lower ground of Camp Jackson to its south was to give Olive Street a raised surface. William T. Sherman, one of the many civilian visitors to the camp on May 10, 1861, viewed Olive Street from the south and described it as having "an embankment about eight feet high." The street was bordered on its south side by a rail fence. The official "entrance" to Camp Jackson was through this fence at a point just east of Channing Avenue.[42]

The military movements ordered by Lyon were successful in surrounding Camp Jackson while bringing the best-trained troops in closest contact with the Missouri militia. The column led personally by Lyon was now along Olive Street with its head to the east. Leading the column were the U.S. Regulars. Before requesting General Frost's surrender, Lyon showed concern for the group of men congregating around Lieutenant Guibor's four Missouri artillery pieces. He ordered Captain Sweeny to watch the militia artillerymen and, if they moved to work their guns, to deploy the leading company of Regulars as skirmishers and charge the cannon. For Lyon to have ordered this movement, Sweeny's men must have been at least as far east on Olive Street as the intersection with Channing.[43]

While the militia made itself ready to surrender with dignity, the Federal commanders worked to receive their prisoners. Lyon ordered the 1st U.S. Volunteers, Blair's regiment, to open its ranks in Olive Street to form a long hollow column with two files of soldiers on each side of the roadway. Into the center of this column were marched the prisoners. The column made its way along Olive Street nearly to Cardinal Avenue before

Order of Battle
The Camp Jackson Affair
May 10, 1861
Missouri Volunteer Militia
Brigadier General Daniel M. Frost, Commanding

1st Regiment: Lieutenant Colonel John Knapp, Commanding

Company A, St. Louis Grays	Captain Martin Burke
Company B, Sarsfield Guards	Captain Charles S. Rogers
Company C, Washington Guards	Captain Patrick Gorman
Company D, Emmett Guards	Captain Philip Coyne
Company E, Washington Blues	Captain Joseph Kelly
Company F, Laclede Guards	Captain William H. Fraser
Company G, Missouri Guard	Captain George W. West
Company H, Jackson Guard	Captain George W. Thatcher
Company I, Grimsley Guards	Captain B. Newton Hart
Company K, Davis Guard	Captain Emile "Charles" Longuemare

2d Regiment: Colonel John S. Bowen, Commanding

Engineer Corps, National Guards	Captain William B. Hazeltine
Company A, Independent Guards	Captain Charles H. Frederick
Company B, Missouri Videttes	Captain Overton W. Barrett
Company C, Missouri Videttes	Captain Basil W. Duke
Company D, McLaren Guards	Captain W. W. Sanford
Company E, Minute Men	Captain Colton Greene
Company F, Jackson Grays	Captain Hugh A. Garland
Company G, Dixie Guards	Captain Given Campbell
Company H, Southern Guard	Captain James T. Shackleford
Company I, Carondelet Guards	Captain James M. Loughborough

Southwest Battalion: Major W. Clark Kennerly, Commanding

Cavalry, Troop A	Captain Staples
Cavalry, Troop B	Lieutenant Archibald McFarlane
Cavalry, Troop C	Captain Emmett MacDonald
Artillery	First Lieutenant Henry Guibor

Sources: Scharf, *History of St. Louis City and County*, 493. Hyde and Conard, *Encyclopedia of the History of St. Louis*, 2432-33. *St. Louis Post-Dispatch*, "These Men Answered the Camp Jackson Roll Call," undated clip in Missouri Historical Society. Hopewell, *Camp Jackson*, 11-13. Peckham, *General Nathaniel Lyon and Missouri in 1861*, 132-35. *Official Records*, ser. 2, vol. 1, 553-58. The colonel of the 1st Regiment was Alton R. Easton, but he was absent during the militia encampment because of a "serious indisposition" (Hopewell, *Camp Jackson*, 28).

coming to a halt to allow the remainder of the prisoners to enter between the ranks of the 2d Volunteers, the hollow column of one regiment proving too small to contain the militia's 50 officers and 639 men. While halted, Captain George West of the Missouri militia made sure the National flag was brought to the van of the column of prisoners.[44]

Before the 1st and 2d U.S. Volunteers could move further east, something had to be done with the 3d U.S. Volunteers, Colonel Franz Sigel's regiment. The 3d U.S. Volunteers were also in Olive Street, blocking the path of the return march through St. Louis. Sergeant Otto Lademann, Company E, 3d U.S. Volunteers, recalled that his regiment was ordered forward along the south side of Olive Street, passing the militia prisoners on their right. After crossing the creek that ran through Lindell Grove, the regiment turned left and formed a line along the western side of the creek. In this position, the troops were nearly at a right angle to the 1st and 2d U.S. Volunteers in Olive Street. They faced east toward the city.[45]

One of the unanticipated problems of the delay in marching the prisoners away from Camp Jackson was the behavior of the large crowd of spectators that had assembled. Like many others, William Chauvenet and his young son, Samuel, had come from home to see what was happening. To the youthful Samuel, "it seemed as though the whole population of the city was there in carriages, wagons, on horseback, and on foot." Chauvenet took hold of his son and pushed through the crowd until he reached John Schofield, a fellow professor in the mathematics department at Washington University. Schofield told him abruptly, "This is

no place for citizens and I advise you to go home at once." Father and son immediately started back along Olive Street away from Camp Jackson.[46]

The crowd was becoming abusive. Some prisoners were recognized, their names called out, and cheers delivered in their honor. Some citizens brandished revolvers. Others were content with cheers for "Jeff Davis" and shouts of "Damn the Dutch." Numerous militiamen and civilians would later attest that no shots were fired from the crowd at this time.[47]

From his position in the column of prisoners, Captain West could see troops on the north side of Olive standing in ranks four deep. Behind them, in a more elevated position, was stationed the artillery of Major Backoff's battery, a part of Sigel's original column. The infantry West saw was most likely the 4th Reserves. A large group of civilians had crowded into the level space between the troops and artillery north of Olive Street and Lyon's column in Olive Street. Federal, militia, and civilian accounts agree that the first serious incident occurred there.[48]

A Federal officer north of Olive Street tried to stop the insults from the crowd but was mocked for his efforts. He ordered his men to fix bayonets and clear the ground in front of the battery. In the course of this activity, at least six and perhaps as many as thirty shots were fired by the soldiers. A reporter for one of the city's German-language newspapers saw the soldiers become "so upset that they fired their weapons, admittedly over the heads of the onlookers." The soldiers guilty of the firing were immediately "arrested."[49]

By now, the crowd swelled around Lyon's troops on all sides. Incidents were occurring all along the line of march. One person in the crowd stepped forward, drew his revolver, and fired at Captain Rufus Saxton, an officer in the U.S. Army commanding Company A, 1st Volunteers. Having missed with his first three shots, the would-be assailant laid his pistol across his arm to steady his aim. Before he could fire again, a soldier lunged and thrust him through with his bayonet, killing the man instantly.[50]

Three citizens standing on Olive Street watched the soldiers who stood in front of them facing south into Camp Jackson in ranks two deep, probably Henry Boernstein's 2d U.S. Volunteers. Though people in the crowd threatened the soldiers, these observers saw no one in the crowd fire. When one man made particularly strenuous efforts to taunt the soldiers, one soldier bayoneted him just as another soldier shot him. An irregular volley

Otto Lademann as Captain, Company F, 3d Missouri Infantry, U.S.A. *Carte de visite photograph by Hoelke and Benecke, ca. 1863. Missouri Historical Society Photograph and Print Collection.*

then began, which the three eyewitnesses described as being aimed "right into the densest of the crowd."[51]

William T. Sherman walked through Lindell Grove with his seven-year-old son. He saw the 1st U.S. Volunteers standing in Olive Street with the prisoners inside their column. As he continued on, he met his brother-in-law, Charles Ewing, and another friend. Together they stood looking north toward the troops heading back toward the city. Sherman watched as a "drunken fellow" tried to cross Olive Street from south to north by forcing his way through the military column. A sergeant of the Regulars pushed him back, forcing him down the slope in front of Sherman. By the time the man collected himself and recovered his hat, the column had moved forward. Volunteers now occupied the place in Olive Street formerly held by the Regulars. The drunken man produced a pistol and fired. Sherman watched in disbelief as the U.S. Volunteers stopped and fired into the crowd in response. The quick-thinking Ewing grabbed Sherman's small son, threw him to the ground, and covered him with his body. Sherman too

hit the ground. As soon as he saw the soldiers begin to reload, he grabbed his son and ran back to a gully for protection. There they stayed until the firing stopped.[52]

A reporter from the *Westliche Post*, one of the city's German newspapers, stood only seventy or eighty paces from where he claimed the first shot was fired. He watched as the last prisoner left Camp Jackson and marched into Olive Street. He saw a revolver shot come from the crowd, accompanied by flying rocks. The soldiers returned fire at once. More shots issued from the crowd. Some of the prisoners pulled previously hidden revolvers from their clothing. Others tried to use the confusion to escape. A "platoon volley" that "probably spread more rapidly than the officer giving the command wished" followed. A man fell dead next to the German reporter. Another fell nearby with a knee shattered by the gunfire.[53]

After all the prisoners were out of Camp Jackson and standing in Olive Street, Henry Milne watched as a crowd of two or three hundred people cursed and insulted the United States troops. One member of the

"Terrible Tragedy at St. Louis." *A popular but inaccurate view of the Federal troops at Camp Jackson. Wood engraving,* New York Illustrated News, *May 25, 1861. Missouri Historical Society Photograph and Print Collection.*

The Civilian Casualties of Camp Jackson

As is shown by the fatalities, people from all over St. Louis had come to see the action at Camp Jackson. These onlookers were the first victims of civil war in Missouri.

Victim	Description	Residence
Thomas Ahearn (Hahren)	tinman	Sixth St. between O'Fallon and Cass
Frank D. Allen	shoe dealer	
Charles Bodsen (Bodson)	bartender	
Jacob Carter	boatman	319 North Sixth Street
Christian Dean	machinist	
Benjamin D. Dunn	carpenter	109 North Third Street
John English	age 12	
Patrick Enright		
Caspar H. Glencoe		
William Harmon	age 14	
John J. Jones		Portage County, Ohio
William Juenhower		
Henry Jungel (Jungle)	gardener	Grand Avenue near Market Street
Armand Latour	carpenter	
Philip Leister (Lester)		24th St. between Morgan, Franklin
Rebecca Ann McAuliff		Eleventh St. between Carr, Biddle
James McDonald	driver, age 15	Olive St. between Seventh, Eighth
Walter McDowell		Elizabeth Street
William Sheffield	stone cutter	
Emma (Emily) Somers	age 14	Carr and Seventeenth Streets
William Patton Summers	bank cashier	Newark, New Jersey
John Sweikhardt	laborer	Fifteenth between Washington, Carr
John Underwood	age 18	Brooklyn St. near Twelfth St.
Unknown	"about 14 years of age"	
John Waters		
Francis Wheelan (Whelan)	quarryman	266 North Fourteenth Street
Erie Wright	carpenter	Bernard St. near Pratt
Jacques Yerdi (Gerdy)		

Sources: *Missouri Republican,* May 11, 15, and 18, 1861. *Missouri Democrat,* May 20, 1861. Scharf, *History of St. Louis City and County,* 499-500. *St. Louis City Directory for 1860.* The casualty lists conflict in numerous cases.

crowd suggested attacking the soldiers, and a man nearby offered to do so with the Colt revolver he was holding. Others prepared to join in, some picking up stones to use as missiles. As the crowd moved to attack, Milne saw the man with the pistol shoot a soldier, knocking him down. Another fired and hit Dr. Roepke, a military surgeon, and then turned and ran. The first gunman fired again and hit a Union officer, almost certainly Captain Constantin Blandowski of Company F, 3d Volunteers. Milne then saw gunfire come from the crowd on both sides of Olive Street into the soldiers. The wounded captain, by Milne's account, commanded "fire" while he lay on the ground. Milne turned and ran for his life.[54]

Teenagers Philip D. Stephenson and Harry Newman arrived at Camp Jackson just after the militia surrendered. They passed through the gaps in the Union units surrounding the camp and stood with a thousand or more citizens who had done the same. Stephenson saw the delays in moving the Missouri militia into Olive Street Road as the cause of the trouble that followed. "The masses of people and the troops themselves grew more and more into a ferment of ill-suppressed excitement," he remembered.[55]

Stephenson believed he had seen the act that precipitated the shooting. A boy his own age, standing nearby and only thirty feet from the soldiers, tossed a dirt clod at Captain Blandowski, hitting him in the leg. Blandowski released "a smothered exclamation of some kind," and his "exclamation" was interpreted by his troops as an order to fire. In an instant, a wild volley crashed into the crowd.[56]

Colonel Boernstein, commanding the 2d U.S. Volunteers, reported seeing the U.S. Regulars and soldiers of the 3d U.S. Volunteers fire before his regiment began firing in "instinctive self-defense." He and Lieutenant Colonel Friedrich Schaefer rode into the ranks demanding that the firing stop immediately. Boernstein called to his prisoners to throw themselves on the ground to avoid the gunfire, but two of them tried to take advantage of the confusion by drawing concealed pistols.[57]

Sergeant Lademann believed that the first shots fired at the crowd came from the 2d Volunteers, not the U.S. Regulars or the 3d Volunteers, as the regiment stood along Olive Street. The shooting was conducted as a "fire by file" rather than as a full volley. The fire moved rapidly along the line, and because of the position of the 2d U.S. Volunteers, it fell on both civilians and the 3d U.S. Volunteers in the confusion. The height of the Olive Street roadbed caused most, but not all, of the fire of the 2d Volunteers to pass over the 3d

Volunteers. As the fire of the 2d Volunteers neared the left flank of the 3d Volunteers, the 3d Volunteers too began firing. From its position facing east, it created a crossfire for the civilians in Lindell Grove. Colonel Sigel rushed down the line of his regiment, ordering his men to cease firing, but he was too late to stop the tragedy.[58]

In a letter written only two days after these events, First Lieutenant William S. Stewart of Company F, 1st Volunteers, described to his father and mother what he saw and felt:

> The mob began first by insulting our men, without retaliation then they threw stones hurting some of the soldiers, yet the soldiers stood it till the mob began firing pistols killing one or two and wounding others. Then our men opened a fire mowing down about 30, between 15 and 20 of whom were killed on the spot. The firing lasted several minutes and the bullets whistled around us in a perfect shower, most of them going over our heads. Our Company stood it bravely, ready all the time to engage in the firing but it did not become necessary.[59]

A reporter for the *Missouri Republican* was shocked by the results. "We went over the grove immediately after the occurrence," he wrote, "and a more fearful and ghastly site is seldom seen." Nearly three dozen civilians, Missouri militiamen, and Union soldiers were dead or mortally wounded. The crowd paid the heaviest toll: at least twenty-seven citizens were dead or dying. One of them was a boy of twelve, another a girl of fourteen. Three members of the Missouri militia, William E. Icenhower, P. Doan, and Nicholas Knobloch, were killed. Colonel Boernstein reported two soldiers of the 2d U.S. Volunteers killed and six wounded. Captain George Weckerlin, Company B, narrowly escaped death when a bullet passed through his hat, grazing his scalp. In the 3d U.S. Volunteers, four men were wounded. One soldier of Company H was killed immediately, and Captain Blandowski's wound proved to be fatal.[60]

Lyon and his officers stopped the firing as quickly as it began, but civil war had come to St. Louis.

6. Lyon and His Prisoners Return to the U.S. Arsenal

Following the route of the prisoners and their captors will return you to Lyon Park and the U.S. Arsenal.

Around 5:30 P.M. soldiers and prisoners began the march back to the arsenal. The Union artillery at the northeast corner of the camp led the column. As the guns pulled out of their position on Garrison Avenue and turned east on Olive, they were followed by the 1st Battalion, 1st Reserves. The 1st U.S. Volunteers in their extended hollow column were already on Olive Street. They began moving east after the 1st Reserves had passed. The 2d U.S. Volunteers followed the 1st Volunteers. The 1st Battalion, 2d Reserves, followed the 2d U.S. Volunteers and formed the rear of the column.

Sweeny's U.S. Regulars and the 3d and 4th U.S. Volunteers were left at Camp Jackson overnight to secure the military stores gathered there. The soldiers spent the night in the tents of the Missouri militia, and the next day they cleaned up the camp, burned what was not of value, and moved the rest to the arsenal. In his official report, Lyon calculated the spoils as "1200 rifle muskets of United States manufacture, late model, .58 caliber; 6 field pieces, brass; 25 kegs of powder; from 30 to 40 horses, and several arm chests of arms understood to be like the 1,200 muskets mentioned." More than forty years later, Sergeant Lademann of the 3d U.S. Volunteers remembered the militia armament differently, calling it "a lot of old junk—guns without cartridges, shot and shells unfitted for service, the whole outfit thoroughly worthless, good only to adorn a military museum."[61]

As Lyon's column passed along Olive Street, doors and windows were slammed shut, if they were not already closed. At Fourteenth Street, the column turned right, marched south to Chouteau Avenue, and then turned east to Seventh Street. The sympathies of the bystanders had changed markedly by the time Chouteau was reached. National flags appeared as increasing numbers of spectators turned out to cheer the returning regiments.[62]

It was well after 8:00 P.M. before the column of prisoners reached the U.S. Arsenal. There they were ushered into the various stone buildings where straw had been spread on the floor for their "comfort." Soon after the men were crowded into their quarters, a light rain began to fall. The prisoners were guarded by the 1st U.S. Volunteers. The 2d U.S. Volunteers returned to the U.S. Marine Hospital south of the arsenal. The Reserve Regiments each detailed one company to guard their armories, and the rest of the men dispersed to their homes.[63]

7. A Rebel Rebuffed at Fourth and Pine

Near the corner of Fourth and Pine Streets, two of the city's citizens confronted each other over the issues of the day. Though there must have been many encounters like this throughout the city that day, this one was different: one of the civilians was the future commanding general of the Armies of the United States.

Earlier in the day, Ulysses S. Grant had been at the arsenal to watch the troops leave for Camp Jackson. By late afternoon, he had heard the news of the surrender and decided to go to the arsenal to congratulate the returning soldiers. He got on a streetcar at the corner of Fourth and Pine Streets just in time to see a crowd taking down a secessionist flag from the Berthold mansion on Pine Street. Not all the crowd was sympathetic to the move. Only one other passenger was in the car with Grant when another man bounded in. He "was in a great state of excitement and used adjectives freely to express his contempt for the Union and for those who had just perpetrated such an outrage upon the rights of a free people."

Believing Grant to be sympathetic to his plight, he turned to him and said, "Things have come to a — pretty pass when a free people can't choose their own flag. Where I came from if a man dares to say a word in favor of the Union we hang him to a limb of the first tree we come to."

Grant's reply was a quiet one. He observed that "after all we were not so intolerant in St. Louis as we might be," and remarked that he "had not seen a single rebel hung yet, nor heard of one." Grant added, "There are plenty of them who ought to be, however."

With this opposition, the young man quieted down. The remainder of Grant's ride to the arsenal was without incident.[64]

8. The Prisoners Are Released

On the riverfront, near where the Jefferson National Expansion Memorial and the Arch now stand, the Missouri Volunteer Militia made its last appearance in St. Louis during the Civil War years.

The militiamen were roused around 7:00 A.M. on Saturday, May 11, 1861, and marched to another building inside the arsenal where they were served a breakfast of two hardtack biscuits and a cup of water. About 9:00 A.M. the prisoners were informed that they would be released at once if they took an oath of allegiance to the United States. The prisoners reacted with indignation, claiming they had performed no acts that would cause their allegiance to the United States to be in question. After negotiations, the prisoners agreed to a parole, which included a pledge not to take up arms against the United States.

A crowd had assembled outside, and Federal authorities, concerned about sparking another incident, decided not to release the militia directly from the arsenal. Instead, around 5:00 P.M. the prisoners were taken from the arsenal by steamer to the foot of Chestnut Street. There the men were released and allowed to make their way home.[65]

The propriety of the detention of the militia members arrested at Camp Jackson was indirectly challenged by the Federal District Judge for the Eastern District of Missouri in a legal proceeding brought by Captain Emmett MacDonald, the only Camp Jackson prisoner who refused to give his parole. MacDonald's case was argued by Uriel Wright, the preeminent St. Louis criminal lawyer of his day, member of the Constitutional Convention, and future Confederate army officer. Judge Samuel Treat, a New Englander and graduate of Harvard College whose distinguished thirty-year tenure on the Federal bench would continue until 1887, rendered a well-reasoned opinion upholding the court's jurisdiction to issue a writ of habeas corpus to the Union military authorities to release MacDonald. Although circumstances (including his removal to Illinois) would make MacDonald's legal victory rather meaningless to MacDonald's own situation, Judge Treat's opinion remains a shining defense of the right of an American citizen to freedom from arbitrary detention, even in times of crisis: "Every one who is illegally restrained of his liberty, under color of United States authority, has the fullest redress in the United States courts."[66]

CAMP JACKSON MO.

George G. Friedlein 1st Lieut of Topogr. Engineer. del.   Ch. Robyn & Co. Lith. cor. 3d & Chesnut St. St. Louis

Camp Jackson.
*Lithograph by
E. Robyn, ca. 1862.
Missouri Historical
Society Photograph and
Print Collection.*

Obverse of the Flag of the 1st Regiment, Missouri Volunteer Militia, Company G, "Missouri Guard," Captured at Camp Jackson. *The flag measures approximately 42 inches on the staff and 66 inches on the fly edge. Missouri Historical Society Museum Collection. Photograph by David Schultz.*

Reverse. *Missouri Historical Society Museum Collection. Photograph by David Schultz.*

Right:
John Stevens Bowen as Cadet, United States Military Academy. *Locket daguerreotype, ca. 1852. Gift of Estate of Marion Bowen. Missouri Historical Society Photograph and Print Collection.*

Far Right:
Lieutenant Colonel John Knapp's Broken Sword with Its Scabbard, Presented to Him by the St. Louis Grays, 1860. *Missouri Historical Society Museum Collections. Photograph by David Schultz.*

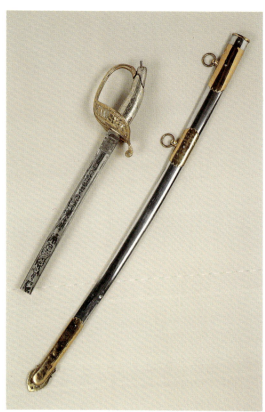

Eagle from Flagstaff of the 1st Regiment, Missouri Infantry, U.S.A. *Collection of David V. Radcliffe. Photograph by David Schultz.*

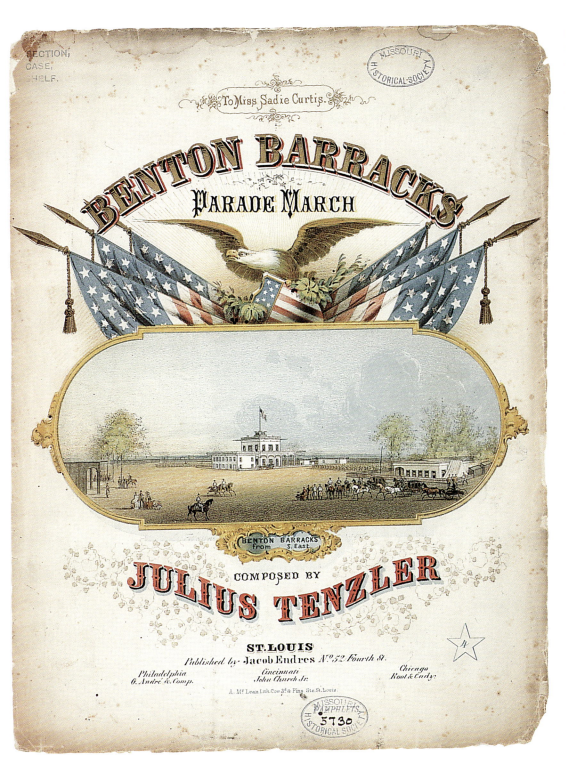

Benton Barracks
Parade March.
*Lithograph by
Alexander McLean.
Published by Jacob
Endres, 1862.
Missouri Historical
Society Library.*

Small Wooden Chain
Made by Prisoner in
Gratiot Street
Military Prison.
*Missouri Historical
Society Museum
Collections. Photograph
by David Schultz.*

Gunboats Being
Built at Carondelet,
Missouri. *Hand-
colored wood engraving
after Alexander
Simplot, from* Harper's
Weekly, *October 5,
1861, p. 630.
Missouri Historical
Society Photograph and
Print Collection.*

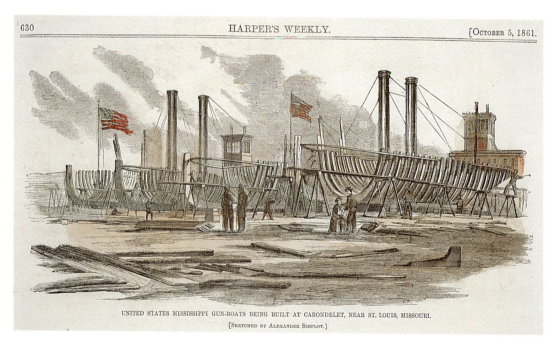

UNITED STATES MISSISSIPPI GUN-BOATS BEING BUILT AT CARONDELET, NEAR ST. LOUIS, MISSOURI.
[SKETCHED BY ALEXANDER SIMPLOT.]

An Ordinance
Abolishing Slavery in
Missouri, January 11,
1865. *Lithograph by
the* Westliche Post
*and Theo Schrader after
E. Knobel, 1865.
Missouri Historical
Society Photograph and
Print Collection.*

We look anxiously and hopefully forward for the day when the star of Missouri shall be added to the constellation of the Confederate States of America.

President Jefferson Davis
to Governor Claiborne Fox Jackson
April 1861

Chapter 4 At War in

The President of the United States directs that you enroll in the
military service of the United States the loyal citizens of St. Louis
and vicinity . . . for the purpose of maintaining the authority of the
United States [and] for the protection of the peaceable inhabitants of
Missouri.

It is revolutionary times.

General Winfield Scott
to Captain Nathaniel Lyon
April 1861

Earnest

After the events of Camp Jackson, there was never a serious military threat to Union control of St. Louis. Clashes between soldiers and civilians occurred in May and June of 1861, but as the city grew rapidly in importance as a troop and supply staging area for the Union army, the overwhelming might of the Federal government made secessionist sympathizers very cautious.

Taking no chances, Federal military authorities ringed the city with fortifications in the war's first summer. Thousands of troops were quartered at Jefferson Barracks, Benton Barracks, and other sites throughout the city. By fall gunboats were being launched from the boatyards in south St. Louis, further deterring any thoughts of advance on the city by Confederate forces.

In the fall of 1864, General Sterling Price's Confederate forces at first appeared to hold St. Louis as an objective of their great raid into Missouri. After they realized how great a citadel the city had become—and how rapidly it was being reinforced—they turned west to meet their eventual defeat near Kansas City.

St. Louis saw the human spirit at its best and at its worst. The lofty goals and the magnificent achievements of the Grand Mississippi Valley Sanitary Fair created succor for all victims of the war, Union or Confederate, slave or free. Within a few months of the fair's closing, the retaliatory executions of Confederate prisoners of war were a brutal reminder of the darker side of war in Missouri.

1861

May 11:
Home Guards Ambushed
from Church Steps

An incident at Fifth and Walnut Streets on the day after Camp Jackson showed that tensions were still high in the city.

During the events at Camp Jackson the day before, the members of the 5th United States Reserve Corps (called the 5th Reserves) met at Stifel's brewery in south St. Louis, an establishment owned by their regimental commander, Colonel Charles G. Stifel. Not having completed its organization, the regiment did not take part in the march to capture the Missouri militia.

On Saturday, May 11, 1861, the men of the 5th Reserves enlisted for three months' service and became soldiers of the United States Army. At twilight, after being armed at the arsenal, the new soldiers were ambushed when marching back to their north St. Louis homes.[1]

The column of one thousand volunteers moved west on Walnut Street between Fifth and Sixth Streets as angry secessionists first jeered the predominantly German recruits, then threw dirt and stones at them. Suddenly, a pistol shot rang out. Some witnesses thought it was fired from the steps of the

Facing:
Corner Scene during the Excitement at St. Louis, Missouri. *Wood engraving after Mat Hastings,* Harper's Weekly, *June 1, 1861, p. 349. Missouri Historical Society Photograph and Print Collection.*

Second Presbyterian Church at the corner of Fifth and Walnut, but another witness thought it came from a citizen standing on the north sidewalk. More shots followed from the windows of the houses opposite the church. An eyewitness described the event: "My attention was drawn to a crowd of persons collected at the corner of Fifth and Walnut, many of whom I could see standing on the south end of the church steps on the northwest corner of Fifth and Walnut; there was at this time considerable hooting and abusive language used, and a pistol shot fired from the steps of the church, as I supposed from the flash and smoke."[2]

The surprised recruits returned fire wildly, firing at the church, at the houses, at bystanders, and even into their own ranks. When the firing stopped, eight people were dead and a ninth lay mortally wounded. Four soldiers had been killed: William Hollinghast, Conrad Lappe, Bernard Miller, and John Shaukbeer. Citizens William Cody, John Dick, Patrick Enright, and Jacob Lawrence were also dead. Charles Rebstock died several days later. Those seriously wounded included Jeremiah Godfrey, Charles H. Woodward, James F. Welsh, Michael Davy, and John Nelus. Several others were injured slightly, including the daughter of a Mr. Mathews, who was struck by a spent ball after three shots entered the Mathews home.[3]

The soldiers eventually regained their composure and continued their march, but the situation remained tense. After the incident, Mayor Daniel G. Taylor made an address from the steps of the Second Presbyterian Church and urged the onlookers to disperse peacefully. As Reverend Galusha Anderson, pastor of nearby Second Baptist Church, remembered that evening: "Feeling on both sides ran high. It was intense, bitter, hot. Portentous rumors filled the air. Apprehension of something awful pervaded many minds. Disaster seemed impending. On a city thus agitated and torn midnight darkness at last graciously fell. A merciful Providence had at least held the contending multitudes back from general riot."[4]

May 27: Captain Constantin Blandowski Buried with Military Honors

Gatewood Gardens Cemetery is located in south St. Louis County at 7133 Gravois Road. It was formerly known as New Picker Cemetery and then St. Louis Memorial Gardens. The cemetery has been a source of local controversy because of the lack of maintenance of both grounds and records caused by a succession of ownership changes. The cemetery is located on both sides of Gravois. The section in which Blandowski is believed to be buried is on the east side of Gravois just south of Sts. Peter and Paul Cemetery.

From downtown St. Louis, take I-55 south to the Loughborough exit. Turn right (east) and follow Loughborough for 1.7 miles to its intersection with Gravois Road. Turn left (south) on Gravois and proceed ahead for about 0.5 miles. The entrance to the Old Picker Cemetery, an unmarked gravel road, is on the left (east) side of Gravois. Follow the gravel road straight ahead to the far end of the cemetery and around to the right as the road turns parallel to Stolle Street just outside the cemetery fence. The unmarked Blandowski gravestone is on the right about halfway between Primm and Tesson Streets. Local tradition has it that the two unidentified, stacked rectangular blocks (apparently once the base of an obelisk) not far from the Stughl family monument mark Blandowski's gravesite.

Captain Constantin Blandowski, commanding Company F, 3d U.S. Volunteers, was shot in the leg at Camp Jackson on May 10, 1861. Most accounts claim he was struck by a shot from a pistol wielded

United States Volunteers Attacked by the Mob from the Steps of the Second Presbyterian Church, Corner of Fifth and Walnut Streets, on May 11, 1861. *Wood engraving after Mat Hastings,* Harper's Weekly, *June 1, 1861, p. 349. Missouri Historical Society Photograph and Print Collection.*

by a member of the crowd. With one of his soldiers already dead and uncertain of the threat of mob action, the wounded Blandowski gave the order that began the deadly firing on the crowd of civilians at Camp Jackson.[5]

Blandowski was born on October 8, 1828, near Tornwitz in Silesia, Prussia, near the border with Poland. Because of their participation in the Polish revolution of 1830, the Blandowski family moved to a town near Dresden in Saxony. Young Constantin received his literary and military education at Dresden's Polish Institute before the continuing problems of the Polish émigrés took him to France. From there, Blandowski made his way to Algiers where he served until 1846 with France's recently formed "Legion Étrangere," the Foreign Legion. In 1846 a Polish uprising against Austria brought Blandowski back to Poland. Austrian troops crushed the rebellion, and Blandowski fled again to France. In 1848 he took part in another Polish revolution with similar results. This time, Blandowski went to Italy, where he took part in Sardinia's War of Independence against Austria in 1848-1849 as a member of the Polish Legion under General Albert Chrzanowski, King Charles Albert's chief of staff. Austrian marshal Josef Radetzky crushed Charles Albert's army at the Battle of Novara on March 23, 1849.[6]

After Novara, Blandowski made his way through Turkey to Hungary to join fellow Polish officers who had enlisted in the cause of Hungarian independence from Austria. He joined the forces of General Jozef Bem, himself a Pole in Hungarian service. Blandowski arrived to be present at the Battle of Temesvar on August 9, 1849, after which the defeated Hungarians recognized the hopelessness of their position and surrendered. Blandowski fled to America.[7]

Arriving in the United States in 1850, he made his way west through New York, Philadelphia, and Cincinnati to St. Louis, probably making his living by giving lessons in fencing and in other arms. Precisely when Blandowski arrived in St. Louis is not known, but by early 1858 he had met and befriended German-American artist Carl Wimar.

On the morning of May 23, 1858, Wimar and Blandowski left St. Louis on the steamboat *Twilight* to follow the Missouri River to the mouth of the Yellowstone River and Fort Union. Wimar was making the trip to observe Indian life and culture to help him with his painting. Blandowski apparently went along for the adventure. After reaching Fort Union in mid-summer, Wimar, Blandowski, and six

Constantin Blandowski. *Oil on canvas by Carl Wimar, 1861. St. Louis Art Museum, gift of Mrs. F. W. Schneider.*

others in their party remained three weeks before deciding to return to St. Louis. At some point during the trip, Wimar did a pencil sketch of his friend. This sketch was the basis for his 1861 portrait of Captain Constantin Blandowski, now in the collection of the St. Louis Art Museum.[8]

Blandowski, Wimar, and the others left Fort Union in a small boat on September 1. They took turns rowing, often traveling at night to avoid uncertain tribes, until they arrived below Sioux City on October 12, 1858. There the tired travelers boarded the steamer *Omaha*, the last boat of the season to be heading downriver. After five months on the Missouri River frontier, Wimar and Blandowski arrived in St. Louis on October 23.[9]

By June 6, 1859, Constantin Blandowski had conducted another whirlwind campaign. On that date, he wed Miss Sophie Steinhauser, a native of Prussia. By the time the census-taker arrived at the Blandowski residence in 1860, the newlyweds had a son and a daughter. Constantin's occupation was listed as "dancing master."[10]

On May 12, 1860, the dashing European revolutionary was the subject of an announcement by the *Missouri Democrat* to the citizens of St. Louis:

Tournament of Arms at Turner's Hall on Twelfth Street between Market and Walnut Streets—Given by the justly renowned Polish fencer and teacher, Mr. Constantine Blandowsky, on this Saturday evening, at eight o'clock. . . . Four of the best French fencers in this city have also volunteered to exhibit their skill on this occasion.

To this we will add that the members of Mr. Blandowsky's fencing class will also go through their drill and evolutions without arms, and afterward they will arm and show their dexterity in the use of rapiers and broadswords.

We have on several occasions witnessed the masterly skill with which Mr. Blandowsky wields a rapier, broadsword or gun and bayonet. In the battle fields of liberty-loving Hungary and in the terrible Crimean battles, his gleaming blade is said to have done great execution upon the enemies of his country.[11]

After receiving the gunshot wound at Camp Jackson on May 10, 1861, Blandowski was taken to the U.S. Arsenal for treatment. He was moved to the Good Samaritan Hospital, where on May 23 he endured the amputation of the wounded leg. The surgery proved to be too great a shock. He weakened and died three days later on Sunday, May 26, 1861.[12]

Constantin Blandowski's funeral on the following day was attended with great military ceremony. It began at 7:30 A.M. at the Good Samaritan Hospital, located on 24th Street between Cass and O'Fallon Streets. Mounted orderlies led the procession away from the hospital to the cemetery. The funeral escort, a band, and Blandowski's coffin followed. Members of his unit, Company F, 3d Volunteers, came next, preceding his relatives riding in carriages. Officers of the U.S. Army, also riding in carriages, followed the family. Members of the Society of the Turners (a German organization) and representatives of the various volunteer and Home Guard regiments led twelve carriages loaded with citizens, the last of the spectacle.[13]

General Nathaniel Lyon and his staff attended the funeral, at which Lyon made a few private remarks to the wife and family. Captain Constantin Blandowski was laid to rest with full military honors at Picker German Protestant Cemetery, the cemetery of the Holy Ghost Evangelical and Reformed Church, often called Picker Cemetery after the minister who founded the congregation.[14]

A surprising number of mysteries surround the brief life of Captain Blandowski in St. Louis. The first concerns the date of his arrival in St. Louis. It would be interesting to know more about his sudden appearance on the Teutonic social scene and his romance with Miss Steinhauser.

Another mystery concerns the question of whether he ordered his men to fire on the crowd at Camp Jackson. Though it is reported in one newspaper account, neither of the city's two major English-language newspapers, the *Missouri Republican* and the *Missouri Democrat*, mention Blandowski's wounding or his subsequent purported order to fire. Only the *Daily Missouri State Journal* specifically reports Blandowski's involvement. In 1866 James Peckham repeated the story in his book, *General Nathaniel Lyon and Missouri in 1861*. Contemporary witnesses, however, testified to observing the firing but to hearing no orders given for the exchange. Whether Blandowski gave the order remains uncertain, but it would appear from events that he had a strong motivation to do so.

In the Camp Jackson affair, many small incidents occurred simultaneously. A number of witnesses reported that members of the crowd fired pistols at the troops. It has generally been asserted that Blandowski's wound came from one of these encounters. There is evidence, however, that Blandowski's mortal wound may have been the result of friendly fire.

After Blandowski's burial, the *Missouri Republican* reported that his death had been caused by a Minié rifle ball, the standard military issue of the time. The report was met with considerable skepticism. The *Missouri Republican* was, despite its name, the newspaper which most often sided with the Democratic Party. Further, the newspaper was controlled by the Knapp family, a prominent member of which was Lieutenant Colonel John Knapp, the commander of the 1st Regiment of Missouri Volunteer Militia. To counter the public's justifiable skepticism, the *Missouri Republican* printed certification from Dr. T. Griswold Comstock, physician at the Good Samaritan Hospital, where Blandowski was treated. Dr. Comstock swore that Captain Blandowski died from a wound "by a Minie rifle ball causing an injury to the head of the fibula and tibia."[15]

Given the divided sympathies of Missouri's citizens, one might be suspicious of Dr. Comstock's motives in this conclusion. At the time of the incident, Dr. Comstock was a well-respected member of the community. After brief military service in 1862 as surgeon of the 1st Regiment, Missouri Volunteer Infantry, U.S.A., Comstock returned to the Good Samaritan Hospital where he served for more than twenty years. Late in life he became president of the medical staff of St. Louis Children's Hospital.[16]

The last mystery concerns the final resting place of Captain Blandowski. The Picker Cemetery, where he was buried in 1861, was a twenty-acre tract bounded by Compton, Wyoming, Louisiana, and Arsenal Streets in south St. Louis. The last burial in this cemetery was performed in 1901, at which time it was closed. Not long afterward, disinterments began because of demands for the property. The last bodies were removed from the tract in 1916. The original Picker Cemetery is now the site of Roosevelt High School at the modern address of 3220 Hartford Street.

Local tradition has it that Blandowski's body was reburied at the Independent Evangelical Protestant Cemetery, also then known as the New Picker Cemetery. This cemetery, located at the modern address of 7133 Gravois Road, was first used in 1862. Because a third Picker Cemetery was later established, the New Picker Cemetery containing Blandowski's second grave inevitably became known as Old Picker Cemetery (since the original Picker Cemetery had been obliterated by urban development), just as the newest of the three cemeteries became New Picker Cemetery. The location of a stone alleged to mark the grave of Captain Blandowski in Old Picker Cemetery (7133 Gravois Road) is shown on the map at right. No physical evidence has been found to establish that the grave is in fact the grave of the first officer of the Union army to be mortally wounded in the Civil War.[17]

June 11: Governor Jackson and General Lyon Meet at the Planters' House

The Planters' House stood on the west side of Fourth Street, occupying the entire block between Pine and Chestnut Streets. Nothing remains of this elegant hotel.

The Planters' House was more than a hotel. Before the Civil War, it was a social center and an important meeting place. In June 1861 it was the scene of a stormy conference between the Federal and state authorities trying to determine the future of Missouri.

Ground was broken at Fourth and Pine Streets for the Planters' House in 1837. On April 3, 1841, the four-and-one-half story hotel was opened to the public. It was soon known

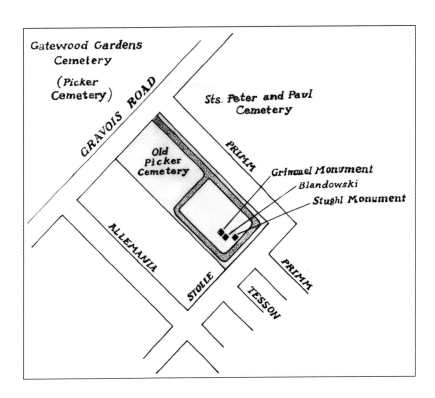

as "the epitome of elegance and grandeur, a place of romance and gayety, a center of lavish entertaining and extravagant spending." Four-horse busses met arriving steamboats or the ferry from Illinois Town, as East St. Louis was then known. Ladies gathered in the hotel's parlor while gentlemen gathered in the bar to drink Planters' Punch, one of several drinks invented there. Meals were fifty cents, and the dinner menu offered twenty-six entrées.[18]

Part of the attraction of the Planters' House were the people who stayed there. Before the Civil War, Phineas T. Barnum, Tom Thumb, the "Swedish Nightingale" Jenny Lind, and President Martin Van Buren all signed their names to the guest register. Charles Dickens created quite a stir during his brief visit in 1842. In his *American Notes*, Dickens recorded his endorsement of the Planters' House: "It is an excellent house and the proprietors have some bountiful notions of providing the creature comforts."[19]

Governor Claiborne Jackson and former governor Sterling Price, now commander of the Missouri State Guard, arrived at the Planters' House on the evening of June 10, 1861. They had ridden from Jefferson City in a private railroad car to meet with the Federal authorities in St. Louis in an attempt to prevent Federal domination of the state government. Jackson and Price came to the meeting with somewhat different motives.

Purported Burial Site of Captain Constantin Blandowski. *Map by Jennifer Ratcliffe-Tangney, 1994.*

The governor hoped to gain time to prepare the state for joining the Confederacy. Price, having earlier negotiated a truce of sorts with General Harney, was apparently sincere in his desire for reconciliation, though his knowledge of his adversaries, Frank Blair and General Nathaniel Lyon, should have told him of the extreme difficulty of his mission.[20]

After breakfast on June 11, Jackson, Price, and Jackson's aide, Thomas L. Snead, notified Lyon of their presence. Jackson and Snead wore civilian clothes, but Price donned the full regalia of his Mexican War uniform, including a plumed cocked hat and high cavalry boots. Lyon's reply arrived, noting that he would send a carriage to take them to the U.S. Arsenal. Governor Jackson, already in high dudgeon because he had to make the trip from his capital to St. Louis, refused this further indignity. He demanded that the meeting take place in his room at the Planters' House.[21]

Shortly after 11:00 A.M., Lyon, Blair, and Horace A. Conant, Lyon's aide, arrived at the Planters' House and were directed to Jackson's room. Seated around a large oval mahogany table, the six men debated Missouri's future for four hours. Snead remembered that the interview "was at last terminated by Lyon's saying that he would see every man, woman, and child in Missouri under the sod before he would consent that the State should dictate to 'his government' as to the movement of its troops within her limits, or as to any other matter however unimportant." Concluding the interview, Lyon announced: "This means war. One of my officers will conduct you out of my lines in an hour." Jackson, Price, and Snead boarded a train and left immediately for Jefferson City.[22]

The Civil War years were hard on the Planters' House. In 1865 the owners abandoned it briefly before leasing it to another hotelier who repaired, refurnished, and reopened it later that year. Soon the Planters' House returned to its status as "a first class hotel in every respect." In 1887 a fire forced the hotel to close, and the building was razed several years later. A new Planters' Hotel was built on the site and operated until 1922, when it was converted into an office building.[23]

Planters' House Hotel. *Photograph by Hoelke and Benecke, ca. 1875.*

Collision between the Federal Troops under Colonel M'Neil and the Citizens of St. Louis, Mo.—The Fire of the Troops Taking Effect upon the Recorder's Court, Which Was Then in Session. *The caption erroneously identifies the unit's commander as M'Neil; the commander was actually Colonel Kallmann. Wood engraving from* Frank Leslie's Illustrated Newspaper, *June 29, 1861, p. 97. Missouri Historical Society Photograph and Print Collection.*

June 17:
Home Guards Fire at
the Recorder's Court

Another clash between citizens and Home Guards occurred near the corner of Seventh and Olive Streets.

General Nathaniel Lyon and most of his Union forces left St. Louis in early June 1861 to pursue Governor Jackson and the Missouri State Guard. One of the regiments remaining in the St. Louis area was the 2d Regiment, United States Reserve Corps, also called the 2d Reserves. Colonel Herman Kallmann led this Home Guard regiment, which had been organized in St. Louis on May 7, 1861, and participated in the capture of Camp Jackson three days later.[24]

On the morning of June 17, 1861, five companies (B, C, E, F, and I) of the 2d Reserves were returning from the depot of the North Missouri Railroad at Collins and North Market Streets, where they had been guarding railroad bridges. Their march down Seventh Street was uneventful until the column reached St. Charles Street. At that point there was a mild altercation with a civilian who insisted on insulting the troops. Captain Edmund Wurpel, commander of Company B, had the offender released and "told him to go on about his business."[25]

The soldiers marched ahead through the intersection of Olive and Seventh Streets. The head of the column was at Locust Street when shots were fired, one from above and another from the pavement level. Captain Jacob Riseck, marching toward the rear of the column with Company I, was wounded in the shoulder. Another soldier fell to the pavement.[26]

Believing the shots to have come from the balcony of the drugstore and engine house on their flank, the soldiers in the last two companies of the column took it on their own initiative to turn east and fire. What the soldiers did not realize was that the Recorder's Court Room occupied the floor above the engine house and was holding session. The court was riddled by bullets. The presiding judge narrowly escaped. Mr. Nehemiah M. Pratt, a police officer, and three others in the courtroom were killed instantly. Deputy Marshal Frenzel was mortally wounded by four shots to his legs.[27]

The incident produced the predictable battle in the pages of the *Missouri Republican* and *Missouri Democrat*. The *Republican* produced witnesses claiming that no shots were fired at the soldiers. A soldier at the rear of the column, some witnesses swore, precipitated the incident by accidentally discharging his musket. The *Democrat* attempted to refute this claim, pointing out that the wounded Union officer had been hit by a ball in the left shoulder that lodged in his right hip, evidence that the shot which struck him had indeed been fired from above. The *Democrat* also produced civilian witnesses who saw or heard shots from the building on the east side of Olive Street. It appears likely that shots did originate from a second-story balcony but from the building adjacent to the Recorder's Court Room, not from the courtroom's balcony.[28]

After the incident, the 2d Reserves marched to the corner of Seventh and Chestnut and stopped to restore order in the ranks. From there they advanced to Seventh and Walnut where they halted again to "close off communication with Chestnut Street." As other troops from within the city arrived to relieve them, the companies of the 2d Reserves were dismissed one by one without further incident.[29]

July 3: Western Department Created

The United States Army created the Western Department on July 3, 1861, to consist of Illinois and all states and territories west of the Mississippi but east of the Rocky Mountains. It was succeeded by the

---

Commanders of the Department of the Missouri, 1861-1865

Major General Henry W. Halleck	November 19, 1861-March 11, 1862
Brigadier General John M. Schofield	June 5-September 24, 1862
Major General Samuel R. Curtis	September 24, 1862-May 24, 1863
Major General John M. Schofield	May 24, 1863-January 20, 1864
Major General William S. Rosecrans	January 30-December 9, 1864
Major General Grenville M. Dodge	December 9, 1864-July 1865

Source: Dyer, *Compendium of the War of the Rebellion,* 255.

Commanders of the District of St. Louis, 1861-1865

Brigadier General John M. Schofield	November 21, 1861-April 10, 1862
Colonel Lewis Merrill	April 10-August 6, 1862
Brigadier General J. W. Davidson	August 6-November 13, 1862
Brigadier General Eugene A. Carr	November 13, 1862-February 23, 1863
Brigadier General J. W. Davidson	February 23-June 6, 1863
Brigadier General William K. Strong	June 6-November 30, 1863
Brigadier General C. B. Fisk	November 30, 1863-March 25, 1864
Brigadier General Thomas Ewing, Jr.	March 25, 1864-November 21, 1864
Brigadier General Alfred Pleasonton	November 21, 1864-December 9, 1864
Brigadier General Thomas Ewing, Jr.	December 9, 1864-April 5, 1865
Bvt. Brigadier General J. L. Beveridge	April 5-April 8, 1865
Brigadier General George D. Wagner	April 8-June 20, 1865
Brigadier General J. A. Williamson	June, 20-July 21, 1865

Source: Dyer, *Compendium of the War of the Rebellion,* 547.

Department of the Missouri two months later, on November 9. The Western Department's two commanders were Major General John C. Frémont, from July 25-November 2, 1861, and Major General David Hunter, from November 2-November 9, 1861.[30]

The Department of the Missouri controlled Union military activity in Missouri, Iowa, Minnesota, Wisconsin, Arkansas, and the western part of Kentucky. In 1862 it was reorganized to include Missouri, Arkansas, Kansas, and the Indian Territory. Colorado and Nebraska were added later in the year. The headquarters for the department was in St. Louis. Within the Department of the Missouri was the District of St. Louis, which directed military activity within the St. Louis area.

July 25:
"The Pathfinder" and
"General Jessie"
Take Command

The Brant mansion was located on the south side of Chouteau Avenue and occupied the full block between Eighth and St. Paul Streets. For a few months in 1861, it was the headquarters for all military activity west of the Mississippi River.

Major General John Charles Frémont, "the Pathfinder of the West," arrived in St. Louis on July 25, 1861, to take command of the Union army's Western Department. Frémont's position was significant because of the large area the department controlled. Yet, in less than four months, Frémont would leave St. Louis under a cloud of presidential displeasure.

In 1841 Frémont had the good fortune—or good judgment—to marry Jessie Benton, daughter of Missouri's U.S. senator Thomas Hart Benton, a leader in the growing movement opposed to the spread of slavery. In the 1840s Frémont explored the West as an engineering officer in the U.S. Army. He resigned from the army in 1848 after a bitter quarrel with General Stephen Kearny in the aftermath of the Mexican War in California. In 1850 Frémont was elected to the U.S. Senate from the new state of California, and he became widely associated with antislavery sentiment. In 1856, much to the approval of abolitionists everywhere and to the particular approval of St. Louis' German population,

Frémont was the first presidential candidate of the Republican Party.

Frémont's arrival in St. Louis might have been greeted as the return of a long-lost native son, but Jessie found the city ominously quiet. "As we drove through the deserted streets we saw only closed shutters to warehouses and business places; the wheels and the horses' hoofs echoed loud and harsh as when one drives through the silent streets late at night," she remembered. Despite her familiarity with the city, Jessie Frémont believed St. Louis to be "the rebel city of a rebel state" and a "hostile city" that "showed itself as such."[31]

Controversy beset John and Jessie Frémont almost from the day of their arrival. One of their first acts was to rent the Brant mansion at 806 Chouteau Avenue as their home and headquarters. The Brant mansion was the dominant building in a sanctuary for the city's well-to-do. While occupied by Joshua B. Brant and his second wife, Sarah Benton, the home "was the scene of many lavish and brilliant social affairs." The "palatial" and "opulent" residence, a three-story villa surrounded by a walled garden, was rented for the shocking sum of six thousand dollars annually, at a time when a private in the Union army earned only thirteen dollars a month. Adding to the controversy was the fact that the Brant home was rented from the widow Sarah Benton Brant, Jessie Benton Frémont's aunt.[32]

Jessie Frémont argued that the mansion was "strongly built and fire-proof." In addition, with three streets bordering the walled grounds, the Brant mansion was "convenient for the review of the regiments which came pouring in from neighboring states." Part of the basement of the home was quickly converted into a small armory. The first floor housed various staff officers and administrators, including a printer and telegrapher. General and Mrs. Frémont and their inner circle occupied the second floor. Sentries stood guard in the halls and in the streets surrounding the mansion.[33]

Jessie Frémont played an active part in her husband's military administration, so much so that some began calling her "General Jessie." She seemed to enjoy being at the center of all the activity. "The offices and halls at headquarters were humming with life, and the clank and ring of sabre and spur were sounding-notes of coming battle all the day long, and far into the nights," she recalled. Though her direct involvement scandalized some, she was effective in her role as her husband's liaison with the Western Sanitary Commission. She was also instrumental in bringing Dorothea Dix to St. Louis to inspect the makeshift hospitals organized to care for the wounded from the battle of Wilson's Creek, Missouri, in August 1861.[34]

From the Brant mansion, Frémont brought order to St. Louis. He stopped open enlistment for the Confederate army and forced the removal of pro-Southern portraits and other displays from shopkeepers' windows. He ordered construction of a ring of fortifications around St. Louis as he directed military affairs throughout the state. Unfortunately, Frémont also snubbed the politically powerful Frank Blair, quarreled with Governor Gamble over the control of the Missouri militia, and gave little scrutiny to lucrative defense contracts awarded to his friends and supporters.

The event that led most directly to Frémont's removal from command occurred on August 30, 1861. On that date Frémont issued a proclamation that put Missouri under martial law, announced the death penalty for guerrillas caught behind Union lines, and freed the slaves of masters disloyal to the United States.[35]

Despite warnings of Frémont's radical tendencies from Postmaster General Montgomery Blair, Frank Blair's brother, President Lincoln was shocked by Frémont's action. At the time Lincoln was very concerned about the sympathies of the slaveholding population of the border states, particularly Kentucky. Frémont's radical stance on abolition threatened to nullify President Lincoln's efforts to keep the border states in the Union. Lincoln wrote privately to Frémont to explain the ramifications of Frémont's proclamation on national policy. The death penalty, applied indiscriminately, would certainly result in the execution of Union prisoners, Lincoln argued. He further asked Frémont to amend his proclamation to conform to the national policy of seizing slaves and other property only if they were supporting the Confederate war effort.[36]

Frémont refused to take Lincoln's informal advice, claiming that he would only modify his position if ordered to. Jessie Frémont left St. Louis on September 8, 1861, to argue her husband's case. She arrived in Washington, D.C., two days later. Tired and perhaps overwrought, Jessie was not prepared for the frosty reception she received from Lincoln. Her attitude toward the president only made matters worse. The day after her visit, Lincoln ordered Frémont to change his proclamation.[37]

On September 21, troops from the pro-Confederate Missouri State Guard surrounded Lexington, near Kansas City, and captured more than three thousand Union defenders. Frémont was widely blamed for the disaster, just as he had been after General Lyon's defeat at Wilson's Creek on August 10. On the evening of November 2, Frémont, now on campaign with his army near Springfield, was approached by a messenger who delivered a letter from President Lincoln. At 10:30 P.M., Frémont wrote to his wife: "I have just received the order relieving me of my command, directing me to turn it over to General Hunter. Get quietly ready for immediate departure from St. Louis. I shall leave this place forthwith."[38]

Frémont returned to St. Louis on Friday evening, November 8. There he was met by his wife and a large crowd of admirers whose "unceasing cheers and shouts," in Jessie's opinion, "sounded like the tide after a high wind." Frémont greeted his well-wishers with

Above:
The Brant Mansion, Residence and Headquarters of General Frémont. *Graphite on paper by Alexander Simplot, 1861. Missouri Historical Society Art Collection.*

Right:
Proclamation of Martial Law. *Broadside, 1861. Missouri Historical Society Archives.*

PROCLAMATION

Head Quarters Western Department,
ST. LOUIS, MO., August 14, 1861.
I hereby declare and establish

Martial Law

In the City and County of St. Louis.

Major J. McKINSTRY, U. S. Army, is appointed Provost Marshal. All orders and regulations issued by him will be respected and obeyed.

J. C. FREMONT,

Major General Commanding.

a short speech, in which he reportedly reviled Lincoln as "weak" and "imbecile." Later that month, "the Pathfinder" and "General Jessie" boarded a train for New York City.[39]

After the war the residential area around the Brant home began to decline. By the 1880s the area was covered by railroad yards, mills, and factories. In 1902 the one-time headquarters of Frémont's army was sold for use as a warehouse. Two years later the building was demolished and its site used for a factory.[40]

August 21: Union Soldiers Train at Benton Barracks

Benton Barracks was located on the northern side of St. Louis. Though nothing from the Civil War era remains, its importance to the war effort should be noted. Benton Barracks was a square of 150 acres with its southern edge along Natural Bridge Road. The St. Louis fairground occupied the land between Grand Avenue and the eastern edge of the Benton Barracks acreage.

As early as August 21, 1861, troops from Illinois, Indiana, Iowa, and Ohio began arriving at St. Louis for training. At first, these men made camp west of the St. Louis Fairgrounds in an encampment designated Camp Benton, named in honor of Missouri's late senator Thomas Hart Benton. General Frémont, the commanding general in St. Louis and Benton's son-in-law, decided that he needed a facility capable of training large numbers of soldiers. From Colonel John O'Fallon, Frémont rented the 150 acres, including Camp Benton, for a patriotically nominal amount.

Barracks were constructed in five east-west rows, each 740 feet long. Each row was approximately 40 feet wide. Warehouses, stables, and other structures soon followed. A two-story building to be used as the commanding general's headquarters was built on the eastern edge of Benton Barracks. Though General Frémont helped dedicate the building, it was occupied by Benton Barracks' commander, Colonel B. L. E. Bonneville.

On September 18, 1861, General Samuel R. Curtis succeeded Colonel Bonneville in command of Benton Barracks. In order to maintain control of the area, Curtis was given authority over Benton Barracks and all other

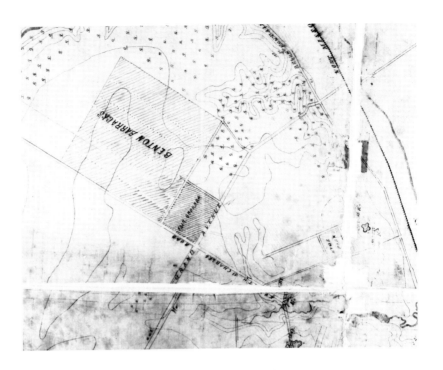

facilities, civilian or military, within a mile of it. Civilians within this radius were required to move out. All but one local character, James Horne Tooke, complied. In an encounter with Tooke, an avowed atheist, Curtis solved the problem by appointing Tooke chaplain of Benton Barracks. "Parson Tooke," as he became known, agreeably played his role.

The next commander of Benton Barracks was General William T. Sherman. Considered unfit for duty, Sherman had been sent to St. Louis under the command of General Henry W. Halleck, commander of the Department of the Missouri. Sherman assumed command of Benton Barracks on December 23, 1861, but was ordered back to a combat command less than two months later.

In June 1862 the War Department ended the practice of allowing paroled soldiers to go to their homes on furlough and required them to go to one of three parole camps based on the geography of their units. Soldiers from regiments raised in Illinois, Iowa, Minnesota, Missouri, and Wisconsin were to report to Jefferson Barracks. When the site proved to be unsuitable, Benton Barracks was chosen as the site for the camp of paroled prisoners. The paroled soldiers were generally dissatisfied and contentious, some even refusing to perform guard duty for their own security on the legalistic grounds that bearing arms violated the conditions of parole. From mid-1863, however, exchanges of Union and Confederate prisoners on parole virtually ceased, increasing the need for prisoner of war camps but decreasing the need for camps of parole.[41]

Detail of Military Map of St. Louis, ca. 1863, Showing Location of Benton Barracks, Hyde Park, and Fort No. 10. *Missouri Historical Society Map Collection.*

Major General Frémont, U.S.A., and Staff Inaugurating Camp Benton, at St. Louis, Missouri, before Starting for Lexington. *Wood engraving after a photograph from* Harper's Weekly, *October 12, 1861, p. 644. Missouri Historical Society Photograph and Print Collection.*

Benton Barracks at St. Louis. *Lithograph by Alexander McLean, ca. 1862. Postal envelope from the collection of William E. Winter.*

The 19th Iowa Infantry Regiment arrived at Benton Barracks on September 5, 1862. The camp must have been a welcome sight to the tired soldiers, for it was a dusty march from the steamboat landing. In his diary, one of the Iowans wrote: "Benton Barracks are situated five miles from the city. Everything is conveniently arranged for the accommodation of a very large number of troops. It contains one mile square of ground and has every variety of building for camp purposes. They are all whitewashed and kept in good repair. At present there are 19000 troops quartered here but so ample are the grounds that it seems as if there were scarce as many hundred."[42]

General William Kerley Strong commanded at Benton Barracks for only a brief period, from June 6, 1863, until his retirement in October.

Strong's one accomplishment during his brief tenure certainly did not sit well with the soldiers: he stopped the sale of liquor within a one-mile radius of the camp.[43]

The 2d Missouri Cavalry, "Merrill's Horse," was probably the first regiment to be organized at Benton Barracks. It was formed there in the last months of 1861. Birge's Regiment of Western Sharpshooters, later to become the 14th Missouri Infantry, was mustered in at Benton Barracks in September and October of the same year. By April 1862 it was estimated that as many as twenty-three thousand recruits and soldiers were stationed at Benton Barracks. The 29th Missouri Infantry Regiment was organized there from July to October 1862, and the 32d, 33d, and 35th Missouri Infantry Regiments followed later that year. The 40th and 41st Missouri Infantry Regiments were both organized there in August 1864 in response to the threatened invasion of St. Louis by Confederates under General Sterling Price.[44]

The first black soldiers were mustered in at Benton Barracks in December 1863. The 1st, 2d, and 3d Missouri Infantry (Colored) would, within a few months, become the 62d, 65th, and 67th Regiments, United States Colored Troops, in a general reorganization of the black troops. For these soldiers, Benton Barracks was much more than a military encampment. Schools were organized by the Christian Commission to teach reading and spelling, skills formerly denied by law to slaves.[45]

The black soldiers slowly gained the respect of at least some white St. Louisans. On January

17, 1864, eleven soldiers, one of them black, and an officer were riding in a streetcar with civilians. At Fourteenth and Morgan Streets, a conductor came on board and objected to the black soldier riding inside the car rather than on the platform. The conductor insisted that he move or leave the car. Rather than abandon their comrade to the conductor's demands, the soldiers all left the car in a group as the civilians applauded their collective action.[46]

During its existence, Benton Barracks was reportedly a major attraction for spectators from the city, as the drills and parades of the large numbers of troops provided considerable entertainment for the civilians. But in September 1865, Benton Barracks was returned to the use of its owner.

September: Frémont's Fortifications Surround St. Louis

In the summer of 1861, St. Louis was a collection point for troops from all over the midwestern United States. General Lyon and then-general Frémont both sought to protect the city by a series of fortifications along its western edge and through batteries along the river. Two heavy guns, Columbiads, were set up a short distance outside the city on the Gravois Road, probably near the intersection of Spring and Gravois. Another was placed at Rock Springs, a community extending from Arsenal to Delmar, west of Grand. It is most likely that the gun was emplaced along the main route into the city near Vandeventer and Market.[47]

The Iron Mountain Railroad ran south from St. Louis through the resort community of Sulphur Springs, built in 1860 by James Burgess two miles southeast of Barnhart, Missouri. Three Columbiads were placed at a position "of the first strategic importance" in September 1861, probably at the Iron Mountain Railroad Landing. (To reach this site, follow Interstate 55 south to Highway M-Barnhart. Turn left and continue to the stoplight. Go left two-tenths of a mile to Sulphur Springs Road and turn right to Sulphur Springs Landing. Though there are no signs of the redoubt that held the Columbiads, the Iron Mountain Railroad Landing is evident.)[48]

In September 1861 St. Louis was visited by Secretary of War Simon Cameron. Because of a lack of funds, he directed that the building of fortifications stop. Despite Cameron's directive, work somehow continued. By the end of 1861, St. Louis was enclosed within a ring of ten forts and several detached batteries. Fort Number One was located near the United States Marine Hospital; all the other forts were numbered consecutively as they continued northward around the city. The forts were not large, but it was hoped they would offer good rallying places in the event of a Confederate incursion. At the time it was rumored that General Frémont's intention in siting these forts was as much to overawe the citizens of St. Louis as it was to protect them from invaders.

General Frémont's Fortifications around the Western Edge of St. Louis, September 1861. *Missouri Historical Society Map Collection.*

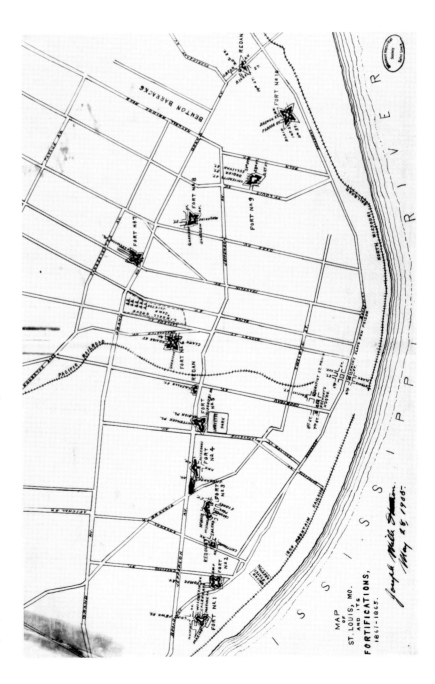

Fortifications at
St. Louis, Missouri.
Wood engraving from
Frank Leslie's
Illustrated
Newspaper, *August
16, 1862, after
M. Henry Lovie.
Missouri Historical
Society Photograph and
Print Collection.*

The first five forts were constructed under the supervision of Lieutenant Julius Pitzman of the United States Engineer Corps. The second five forts were the responsibility of Major Justus McKinstry of the Quartermaster Corps. McKinstry changed the contract basis and, as a result, Fort Number Six cost nearly as much as all the first five forts added together.

John Hogan's house was on Grand Avenue, facing east, not far from Fort Number Seven. Hogan, the city's postmaster from 1857 to 1861, was a former Methodist minister, a Democrat, and a slaveholder, but he took the initiative to visit the garrison of the fort. He offered the abundance of his garden and his fruit trees to the officer in charge, and soon soldiers were visiting twice weekly to join in the bounty. During the summer, Hogan also allowed the Union soldiers to use the water from his cisterns, although he was insistent that they not spill a drop. The soldiers, in turn,

served as complete protection for the neighborhood, keeping a strict watch at all times.

Hogan's friendship with the soldiers had another benefit. It became customary on the occasion of a Union victory to fire the cannon in salute, and the concussion often shattered window glass in the blocks surrounding the fort. Hogan never failed to receive advance warning and a reminder from the commanding officer of Fort Number Seven to open his doors and windows, thus keeping his glass intact.[49]

General Frémont's forts were never tested by the actions of Missouri's Confederates.

Characteristics of the Ten St. Louis Forts

Fort Number One	Each side about 400 feet long. Held three heavy guns.
Fort Number Two	Each side about 400 feet long. Mounted four guns.
Fort Number Three	Main line about 600 feet long. Small powder magazine attached.
Fort Number Four	About 500 feet long with powder magazine attached.
Fort Number Five	Each side about 400 feet long. Held four Columbiads.
Fort Number Six	Held four heavy guns.
Fort Number Seven	Each side about 400 feet. Held four heavy guns.
Fort Number Eight	Each of the five sides about 450 feet long. Five guns.
Fort Number Nine	Each of the five sides about 450 feet long. Five guns.
Fort Number Ten	Each side about 400 feet long. Mounted four heavy guns.

Source: Hyde and Conard, *Encyclopedia of the History of St. Louis, 814-16.* Lauenstein, "Notes on the Fortifications of St. Louis."

Eads Boatyards in Carondelet. *Photograph by E. Humphries, ca. 1880. Missouri Historical Society Photograph and Print Collection.*

October 12: First U.S. Ironclad Launched in Carondelet

The boatyard where James Eads built many of his ironclads was located between the 5600 and 6600 blocks of Broadway in south St. Louis on property now owned by the St. Louis Shipbuilding and Steel Company. The original ways were removed in 1933. There are no relics of the Civil War in the area.[50]

For a view of what the riverfront might have looked like during the Civil War, visit Bellerive Park at 5800 Broadway. The small park is on the east side of Broadway at Bates Street. A marker gives a brief history of Carondelet. The Carondelet Historic Center, 6303 Michigan, contains exhibits showing the city's history, including a scale model of one of Eads' gunboats, the USS Carondelet. *For information, call 314-481-6303.*

On October 12, 1861, the first ironclad warship built by the United States slipped down the marine railway of Captain James B. Eads' boatyard in Carondelet and floated free in the Mississippi River.

Seven months earlier, former St. Louisan and now attorney general Edward Bates had written to Eads asking him to come to Washington, D.C., to present his ideas concerning the use of gunboats to close the Mississippi River to the seceding states. Bates called on Eads because of his reputation as an innovative riverman. At age twenty-two, he

had invented a diving bell to recover cargoes from sunken river steamers. Soon he was designing boats with machinery that could recover not only cargoes but also entire hulls. Only forty-one at the war's outbreak, Eads was a prosperous and prominent engineer living in semiretirement.[51]

Eads received a warm reception for his ideas from Lincoln's cabinet, and he fully expected to be asked to proceed with his plans. Unfortunately, though Secretary of the Navy Gideon Welles liked Eads' ideas very much, jurisdiction for inland waterways belonged to the United States Army, and Secretary of War Simon Cameron had been the only one of Lincoln's cabinet members who was not impressed with the feasibility of Eads' ideas.

After several weeks' delay, Cameron changed his mind, and army authorities began to consider plans for gunboats seriously. By mid-June, General in Chief Winfield Scott had sought the aid of both Commander John Rodgers, an experienced naval officer, and naval constructor Samuel M. Pook in consulting with western steamboat builders on the proper design of gunboats. The overall responsibility for creating the fleet of river gunboats was assigned to the army's quartermaster general, Montgomery C. Meigs.[52]

Just as Meigs was preparing the announcement inviting bids on the gunboat designs that the army and navy had developed, he received a letter from Frank Blair and two other St. Louisans. Together they reminded Meigs of Missouri's capacity for building gunboats at either St. Louis or Cape

Girardeau. In a separate letter, Montgomery Blair reminded Meigs that St. Louis contractors should be carefully considered. If the gunboats were built on the Ohio River, he argued, the water might well be too low for them to reach Cairo, Illinois, in time to be of use in the war. In the summer of 1861, everyone expected a short war.[53]

The bids were opened on August 5, 1861. Eads' bid, $89,600 per boat, was the lowest of the seven bids received. In accepting the contract, Eads agreed to a penalty of $600 per boat per day for each day past the delivery date, October 10, 1861. Eads had three months in which to build seven ironclad gunboats and have them ready to receive their armament.[54]

Four gunboats were laid down at the Carondelet Marine Railway under Eads' direct supervision. Eads arranged for three others to be built under the supervision of Captain William L. Hambleton at Eads' Mound City Marine Railway and Ship Yard on the Ohio River near Cairo, Illinois. Not everything went smoothly. The Carondelet area contained a large number of Southern sympathizers who bragged of sabotage plans for the construction activity, creating worries about security. Workmen threatened to strike for higher wages, despite being paid two dollars for each ten-hour day and twenty-five cents an hour for overtime.[55]

The gunboat construction program was a boon to St. Louis, but no bonanza. Eads put five hundred men to work at Carondelet and another three hundred at Mound City. Unfortunately, this was only a fifth of the expectation proclaimed by the editors of the *Missouri Democrat* in an outburst of civic boosterism. Thirteen sawmills, including five in St. Louis, were soon cutting white oak into lumber for the gunboats. Before long, Eads' crews were working a seven-day week. Where

possible, the machine shops, blacksmiths, foundries, and rolling mills were working night shifts as well.[56]

While Eads built the hulls for the gunboats, Commander Rodgers and his assistant decided to test the armor plating under artillery fire. Borrowing two ten-pounder Parrott rifled guns from the arsenal, they set up a test on a sandy beach on the Illinois side of the Mississippi River. Beginning at eight hundred yards, the guns were fired from progressively closer ranges, moving to five hundred yards, then two hundred yards, and finally one hundred yards. At one hundred yards the test was stopped because the pieces of shattered ball were flying back and threatening the gun crews. The iron passed the test.[57]

On October 12, 1861, two days beyond the due date, Eads launched *Carondelet,* the first of his seven gunboats. Three days later, *St. Louis* followed. *Louisville* and *Pittsburgh* came next, followed by the three boats from the Mound City works, *Cincinnati, Mound City,* and *Cairo.* Although it was not the first launched, *St. Louis* was the first of the gunboats to be outfitted and commissioned. Therefore, to the *St. Louis* goes the honor of being the first ironclad gunboat in the service of the United States.[58]

When completely fitted out, the gunboats were a formidable sight. They were 175 feet long, 51 feet wide, and drew about 5 feet of water. These "Pook Turtles," nicknamed in honor of Samuel Pook, carried a rectangular casemate with sloped armored sides and a paddlewheel amidships near the stern. The casemate had openings for thirteen massive guns. Three were in the bow, four along each side, and two at the stern. A crew of 175 manned the gunboat, which, when fully loaded and ready for service, made 9 miles per hour.[59]

As they were commissioned, the Eads gunboats became part of the Western Gunboat Flotilla. The steamers were commanded by navy officers, though operated by the army. All of the seven "Cairo Class" gunboats compiled good combat records. Five survived the war. *Cairo* was sunk in the Yazoo River by a mine on December 12, 1862. After the transfer of the *St. Louis* to the U.S. Navy in September 1862, it was realized that there was already a ship of that name. The *St. Louis* was therefore renamed *Baron de Kalb.* On July 13, 1863, *Baron de Kalb* was lost on the Yazoo River in the same fashion as the *Cairo.*[60]

USS *Louisville* under Way. *Salted paper photograph, ca. 1862. Missouri Historical Society Photograph and Print Collection.*

December 24: McDowell Medical College Welcomes Prisoners

The McDowell Medical College stood at the northeast corner of Eighth and Gratiot Streets, on property now owned by Ralston-Purina. During the Civil War years, the college was known by a much more ominous name: the Gratiot Street Prison.

The McDowell Medical College was founded by of one of St. Louis' most colorful characters, Dr. Joseph Nash McDowell. McDowell came to St. Louis in the late 1830s, and in 1840 he organized a medical department for Kemper College. In 1845 this effort failed, but McDowell reached an agreement with the University of the State of Missouri to continue his curriculum, an arrangement which held until 1857. At that point, he organized his school as an independent institution, the McDowell Medical College.[61]

In medical circles, McDowell was held in high regard. Unfortunately, he also gave evidence of "an erratic temperament that at times approached insanity" and was an outspoken Southern sympathizer. To make his position clear, McDowell had once placed a loaded revolver on the table in front of him before discussing a political question with his audience. As one pro-Union St. Louis minister described the influential physician, "Any stranger would have noted him in a crowd as an unusual character."[62]

On May 30, 1861, Union soldiers arrived at McDowell Medical College to search it for the arms and ammunition rumored to be kept there by McDowell, purportedly for self-defense. McDowell's small arsenal included two cannon used in celebratory salutes, especially on Independence Day, and as a warning to protesters who objected to the dissection of human corpses at the college. Threatened by the action of the Unionists, Dr. McDowell and one son, Drake, left St. Louis to join the Confederate army. In early August the McDowells arrived in the camp of Missouri State Guard general M. Jeff Thompson in southeast Missouri—somehow they had managed to bring the two cannon with them. McDowell's other son, Max, stayed behind in St. Louis to recruit for the Missouri State Guard but was captured and held in the Myrtle Street Prison, known until shortly before as Lynch's Slave Pen.[63]

Gratiot Military Prison. *Photograph of sketch by M. M. Patterson, 1864. Missouri Historical Society Photograph and Print Collection.*

The first Union use of McDowell Medical College was as a barracks. The expected arrival of Confederate prisoners of war, however, caused a flurry of activity directed at converting the college into the Gratiot Street Prison. In mid-December 1861, fifty men, including at least fifteen former slaves, were put to work cleaning and renovating the college. To the blacks fell the distasteful task of removing the human bones—three wagonloads of them—found in the basement, relics of the earlier study of anatomy. Cooking ranges and sleeping bunks were constructed, and the room formerly used for dissecting purposes was converted into a dining room.[64]

The McDowell Medical College welcomed its first prisoners on Tuesday, December 24, 1861. Led by a United States band playing "Hail, Columbia!" and guarded by the 25th Indiana and 2d Iowa Infantry Regiments, some twelve hundred Confederate soldiers were marched from the Pacific Railroad Depot to the college in a procession that the *Missouri Democrat* described as "a la Camp Jackson." Included in the prisoners were Colonel Magoffin, reportedly the brother of Governor Beriah Magoffin of Kentucky, and S. T. Chapman, the son of the next-door neighbor of Frank Blair.[65]

Reflecting the nature of the conflict in Missouri, St. Louis prisons differed from other military prisons. Here political prisoners, or so-called "prisoners of state," were housed with Confederate soldiers and Union criminals, including deserters. After a hearing, the political prisoners would be released on bond, exiled to the Confederate States, or transferred to Alton Prison for completion of their sentences.[66]

Opinions vary about the severity of the conditions in the prison. One modern author claims that Gratiot Street Prison was "fairly clean, as jails of the day went." Another says that conditions were very bad, with sickness widespread and mortality high. Reverend Galusha Anderson, a frequent visitor to Gratiot Street Prison and an ardent Unionist, argued that all of the military prisons in St. Louis were sanitary and well kept. There was enough wholesome food, and "so far as it was possible" the prisoners were clothed and warm in winter.[67]

The diary of Griffin Frost, a Confederate officer and inmate of the prison in 1863, tells a different story:

Jan. 2—Discover this morning that Gratiot is a very hard place, much worse than Springfield; fare so rough, it seems an excellent place to starve....

Jan. 5—There are now about eight hundred prisoners in Gratiot, and more coming in every day from all parts of the country. We are allowed only two meals a day, and it keeps the cooks busy to get through with them by dark. Some two or three hundred eat at a time, and the tin plates and cups are never washed from the first to the last table ... all [is] dished up and portioned out with the hands; knives, forks and spoons not being allowed....

Jan. 20—All through the night may be heard coughing, swearing, singing and praying, sometimes drowned by almost unearthly noises, issuing from uproarous gangs, laughing, shouting, stamping and howling, making night hideous with their unnatural clang. It is surely a hell on earth.[68]

A more famous prisoner of the Gratiot Street Prison, Confederate mail runner Absalom Grimes, remembered his time in the prison as a sort of badge of Southern honor. "In those stirring war days," he wrote, "no man was of importance or standing until he had been locked up in Gratiot Street prison at least a few days."[69]

Major Absalom Grimes, Confederate Mail Runner. *Photograph, ca. 1863. Missouri Historical Society Photograph and Print Collection.*

1862

January 8: Commercial Interests Battle in the Chamber of Commerce

By 1857 the Chamber of Commerce had outgrown its quarters. A group of wealthy investors joined together to build new quarters for the commercial hub of the city. The Chamber of Commerce moved into its new home on June 8, 1857. The limestone building, designed in an Italian style, was located on the east side of Main Street between Market and Walnut Streets. In its era, the building was one of the most imposing in the city.

On January 8, 1862, the members of the Chamber of Commerce, the collective voice of the city's business interests, met for the annual election of officers. One slate of candidates was described by the *Missouri Democrat* as "true and faithful Union men"; their opposition, though it included "some good men," was characterized as "framed in the interest of disloyalty and secessionism." Since its organization in 1836, the Chamber of Commerce had been politically conservative. In the 1860 election, few members supported the Republican Party, instead preferring the more centrist Douglas Democrats or John Bell and the Constitutional Union ticket.[70]

As the proceedings continued, Albert G. Edwards moved to admit eighty new members, but there was protest that Edwards, a Unionist, was trying to gain support for the "loyal" candidates. It was rapidly becoming apparent that the distinction between "loyal opposition" and "disloyalty" would be difficult to discern in Missouri. Derrick A. January, the outgoing president of the Chamber of Commerce, was a good example; his name had been included in a list of disloyal citizens drawn up and published by the provost marshal the previous month. The members of the Chamber voted on the new-member candidates, but five black balls were found in the ballot box, enough to block their admittance. Rather than continue with a vote for officers, the Unionists withdrew and quickly decided to form their own organization.[71]

Two days later, the Union Merchants Exchange opened just a short distance away in a building on Third Street. The remaining members of the Chamber of Commerce were shocked by the rapidity of this development. The newly elected Chamber officers resigned in an attempt to bring about a reconciliation. However, the members of the new exchange refused to compromise because they

Merchant's Exchange Building. *Lithograph by Alexander McLean. From Jacob N. Taylor and M. O. Crooks,* Sketchbook of St. Louis, *St. Louis, 1858. Missouri Historical Society Library.*

considered some of the Chamber members to be disloyal. Later in the week the Union Merchants Exchange defiantly voted to exclude anyone from its membership who also held membership in the Chamber of Commerce. After its first week of existence, the Union Merchants Exchange numbered 216 members, nearly five times the size of the now diminished Chamber of Commerce.[72]

On January 26 General Henry W. Halleck moved openly against pro-Southern sympathizers in the St. Louis area by ordering, among other things, that all officers of the Mercantile Library and the Chamber of Commerce take the state oath of loyalty within ten days or risk arrest if they continued their duties. The *Missouri Democrat* advised the members of the Union Merchants Exchange to stay away from the Chamber of Commerce until "it is purged of every vestige of treason and the last stain of disloyalty is scoured out." Soon the Chamber found itself excluded from public life, to the point of being excluded from President George Washington's birthday parade while the Union Merchants Exchange marched in full force.[73]

The Chamber of Commerce continued a moribund existence until September 1862, when Provost Marshal Bernard G. Farrar ordered it disbanded while forbidding its members to reconvene anywhere else in the state. On November 26 the Union Merchants Exchange moved into the building formerly occupied by the Chamber of Commerce and remained there until December 21, 1875. The membership kept the word *Union* in their name for the ten years after the end of the war. The battle for commercial supremacy was over; the Union Merchants Exchange had won.

February 26: Wounded Arrive from Fort Donelson

The casualties of the war in Tennessee, first from Fort Donelson and later from Shiloh, flowed up the Mississippi River to St. Louis and into one of the city's sixteen hospitals. One of the earliest military hospital facilities was located at the corner of Fifth Street (modern Broadway) and Chestnut Streets opposite the Old Courthouse.

On Sunday, February 16, 1862, after an eleven-day campaign that had begun with the capture of Fort Henry on February 6, General U. S. Grant earned his nickname "Unconditional Surrender" by demanding the capitulation of the Confederate forces under General Simon B. Buckner at Fort Donelson, Tennessee. Grant and Flag Officer Andrew Foote had capably demonstrated what soldiers and gunboats, several of them from James Eads' boatyards in St. Louis, could accomplish working together.

When St. Louis received the news the next day, the city celebrated "the jubilee of victory." At Benton Barracks, an impromptu parade of the 2d Michigan Cavalry, 2d Iowa Infantry, 3d Missouri Infantry, 5th Michigan Cavalry, and other troops filed past the headquarters of General William K. Strong, the camp's commander. Strong proclaimed that with the fall of Forts Henry and Donelson, "the decisive blow was given to this accursed rebellion." Many civilians were also excited, especially those involved in steamboating; the same day, Federal authorities announced the seizure of numerous steamboats for the movement of troops and supplies for the army.[74]

Grant took twelve thousand prisoners at Fort Donelson, more than a thousand of them wounded. By February 20 the first of the Confederates began arriving in St. Louis, many to be rerouted to prison camps in Alton, Chicago, and other points. The steamer *War Eagle* arrived on February 26 with one hundred and fifty Union and Confederate wounded aboard. Most went to a hospital on Fourth Street between Morgan and Franklin Avenues. Thirty-five went to the military hospital at Fifth and Chestnut Streets, adding to the more than two hundred soldiers already quartered there. The five-story building, known in 1862 as "City General Hospital," had been rented by the Sanitary Commission the previous September and prepared for use as a hospital.[75]

While assuring its readers that the captured Confederates would be cared for with all civility, the *Missouri Democrat* could not refrain from commenting on the "barbarism and coarse brutality which pervades them." Admitting to "our own possible prejudices," the newspaper thought the Confederates appeared "ignorant and ferocious" and, although "gleams of animal cunning" could be seen, there was no evidence of "manly self-respect or intelligence" among them.[76]

A young St. Louis woman of Southern sympathies wrote to her brother, a Confederate artilleryman serving east of the Mississippi, to tell him she had seen the Fort Donelson prisoners arriving. The "secesh women (as the *Democrat* calls us) went wild over them," she assured her brother. "Most of the officers were paroled and I can tell you they had a gay time."

She attended a reception for them, estimating the throng to include five hundred Confederates, but St. Louis' southern hospitality backfired; to her brother she was sad to report that "Old Halleck thought they were treated too well so he sent them to Columbus, Ohio, where they have not a friend."[77]

In March, Baptist minister Galusha Anderson was asked to supervise the religious work in City General Hospital. Soon, regimental chaplains or pastors of the city's churches were leading services that were simple and brief, "presenting some truth that comforted and helped those that were in trouble." The sick and wounded listened eagerly, Anderson thought, reminded of "their churches at home, of loved ones with whom they had often met." As he made his rounds, Anderson was careful to avoid references to the war and political difference. In his opinion, this helped wounded Confederates realize that, in the hospital at least, they were equals with Union soldiers. "Suffering," he concluded, "had made them kin."[78]

April 20:
Doc Jennison Jailed in the Myrtle Street Prison

The Myrtle Street Prison, formerly Lynch's Slave Pen, was located at the corner of Myrtle and Fifth Streets. Myrtle Street, now Clark Avenue, was the third street south of Market Street. Broadway is the modern name for Fifth Street.

Charles Rainsford "Doc" Jennison—the hero of the free-soilers in Kansas and Missouri and a scourge to anyone whose misfortune put them in the path of "Jennison's jayhawkers"—was on his way to St. Louis. Jennison's escort was not his beloved 7th Kansas Volunteer Cavalry, and his destination was not a place of honor. "Doc" Jennison was under guard, and he was headed for the Myrtle Street Prison.

Born in New York in 1834, Jennison grew up near Madison, Wisconsin, where, at the age of nineteen, he took up the study of medicine. In 1854 he married, and in 1857 the Jennisons moved to Kansas. Jennison soon became active in the border conflict with Missouri. His principal contribution to this conflict was the concept of a "self-sustaining" war: when Jennison led a raid into Missouri, his men were encouraged to take what they could carry and to burn what they had to leave behind. Jennison himself boasted that mothers in

Missouri's western counties hushed their unruly children with a warning of "Jennison's jayhawkers."[79]

Typical of his approach to the problems of guerrilla warfare was his capture of Independence, Missouri, in September 1861. Blocking the exits from town, Jennison's men rounded up all the adult male citizens, both loyal and disloyal, and herded them to the town square. There they were guarded by part of Jennison's command while another part searched Independence for horses, mules, firearms, and other valuables, stealing from good Union men and Southern sympathizers alike. Known Union men were then released from custody, while the remaining prisoners were harangued and promised that ten prominent secessionists of Jackson County would be executed for every Union man killed in the vicinity. Jennison and his men then returned to Kansas City with their booty.[80]

On September 4, 1861, Jennison was commissioned colonel of the 7th Kansas Volunteer Cavalry, in his opinion official sanction for his method of warfare against Missouri bushwhackers. By mid-December, however, Jennison had made enemies of both the guerrillas and the Union military authorities. General Halleck, in command in St. Louis, wrote plaintively to headquarters in Washington: "The conduct of the forces under Lane and Jennison has done more for the enemy in this State than could have been accomplished by 20,000 of his own army. I receive almost daily complaints of outrages committed by these men in the name of the United States, and the evidence is so conclusive as to leave no doubt of their correctness." Several days later, he wrote again expressing the opinion that Jennison and his men "disgrace the name and uniform of American soldiers and are driving good Union men into the ranks of the secession army." Jennison's view was almost certainly different. After the border wars of the 1850s, Kansans saw Missourians, especially those living in the border counties, as Southern sympathizers. In reality, at least a third and perhaps more than half of the residents of Missouri's western counties were neutral or loyal to the Union.[81]

It was not only Jennison's means that caused official trouble, it was also his end: freedom for slaves, regardless of the politics of their masters. Jennison and the 7th Kansas were fanatical abolitionists. One of the regiment's companies was commanded by John Brown, Jr., the son of the man who led the abortive slave revolt at Harper's Ferry, Virginia, in 1860 and who was hanged for his abolitionist zeal.

Whenever Jennison's men returned to camp from an expedition, liberated slaves followed in their column's wake. Although the Federal government was not yet ready to address the issue of slavery, Jennison's policy of "practical abolitionism" could not be ignored.[82]

The U.S. Army dealt with the problem in the time-honored fashion; they moved it. Jennison and his 7th Kansas soon found themselves ordered to Humboldt, Kansas, too far away to tempt the regiment from prosecuting the war against Missourians. The unit was soon joined by the 8th Iowa Infantry and a batallion of the 7th Missouri Infantry, and since the aggregation constituted a small brigade, Jennison was appointed acting brigadier general. Soon it was known that the 7th Kansas was to be marched to New Mexico, reinforcements for Union general E. R. S. Canby in resisting the advance of Confederate general Henry H. Sibley.[83]

Jennison was furious. Recognizing that the War Department had creatively developed a solution for keeping him and his men from their mission in Missouri, Jennison impulsively resigned his commission on April 10, 1862, to become effective on May 1. Five days after it was tendered, his resignation was accepted. In the meantime, Jennison paraded the 7th Kansas and explained his reasons for leaving the service. Chief among them was his accusation that the Union high command, in particular General Samuel D. Sturgis, Jennison's commander in Kansas, was "secesh at heart" and interested in prosecuting the war in Missouri only if it did not interfere with slavery.[84]

Jennison's men, however, were enlistees rather than officers. They could not suddenly be seized by indignation or moral principle and resign as Colonel Jennison could. Jennison's men had a practical response; in the next few days perhaps as many as one hundred troopers just rode off. Others took the time to get furlough papers from Jennison. He was denying no one who asked. By April 15, perhaps as many as one in five members of the regiment was unaccounted for.[85]

Sturgis, although he was already unpopular with the Kansas radicals, issued orders to arrest Colonel Jennison and Captain George Hoyt, Jennison's most ardent supporter within the 7th Kansas Cavalry. On April 17, Jennison and Hoyt were arrested in Leavenworth, Kansas, and Jennison was soon sent under guard by train to St. Louis. To the provost marshal in St. Louis, Sturgis expressed the wish that Jennison should "be placed in such close custody as will place his escape beyond the pale of possibility—and I hope you will send him at once to Alton [prison]." On his arrival in St. Louis, Jennison was secured instead in the Myrtle Street Prison.[86]

The Myrtle Street Prison, or "Hotel de Lynch" as the *Missouri Democrat* styled it, was a two-and-a-half-story brick structure used until a year before by Bernard M. Lynch as a slave pen. In 1859, his business growing briskly, Lynch purchased the building and converted it for use in the slave trade by barring the windows and adding bolts and locks. He abandoned his business in early 1861, and his facilities were soon appropriated by Union military authorities. The Myrtle Street Prison had a capacity of one hundred men, but it was often overcrowded. Jennison's stay in the prison was not the typical one. He was lodged not in a cell but in the overseer's quarters, and his wife and daughter visited with him freely. He was soon receiving a steady stream of visitors including newspapermen, prominent citizens, the British consul, and even General Franz Sigel.[87]

On April 22 the *Missouri Democrat* took up Jennison's cause, arguing for his release on parole until charges were brought against him. The newspaper reported that numerous Union army officers expressed regret over Jennison's confinement, particularly because "his imprisonment is too gratifying to the secessionists." The *Missouri Democrat* editorialized that he was "surely the victim of the dirty malice of the pro-slavery generals Sturgis, Denver, and Mitchell—who now command Kansas."[88]

The *Missouri Republican* fired back at its competitor. "What has Jennison done that the people should be called upon to praise and honor him?" the *Republican* asked. The newspaper's editors were shocked that this "jayhawker and outlaw" who "made a business of running off the negroes and stealing the property of the citizens of this State living on the western border" should be thought of sympathetically. As a reminder, the *Republican* quoted an article appearing in the *Democrat* during the border troubles with Kansas in November 1860 that explained how the Kansans had started as a band of "merely Free State men" and "had soon degenerated into a mere banditti." Jennison and others like him, the *Democrat* had claimed then, "avenged their wrongs by indiscriminate robbery" as they "sacrificed revenge for greed." To the public, the *Republican*'s recommendation regarding Jennison was that he should be "arrested, tried, and hanged, with all possible dispatch."[89]

Despite the arguments and the recommendations of the *Missouri Republican*, the sympathies expressed by the *Missouri Democrat* won out. The *Democrat* was not alone in its crusade. Abolitionist newspapers across the North took up Jennison's cause, and one modern historian has suggested that "blackmail threats" by influential abolitionists may also have played a role in preventing the court-martial. Jennison was released on April 25, although not until he had fulfilled the unusual requirement of posting a bond of twenty thousand dollars. Had Jennison wished, he could have gone to the St. Louis Theater to see "the talented tragedian" John Wilkes Booth perform in *Richard III*. Instead, he joined his family at Barnum's Hotel.[90]

On Saturday evening, April 26, more than two thousand St. Louisans, predominantly Germans, assembled in front of Jennison's hotel for a "large and splendid" demonstration. After a serenade by the crowd and an accompanying band, Jennison addressed the assemblage to present his version of the facts. He had resigned, he said, "because as a Free State Kansas man he could not serve under the men who had lead the oppressive Border Ruffian raids in that State." Cheers followed his assertion that the proceedings against him had been caused by the fact he was an abolitionist. After a brief justification of his operations in western Missouri, Jennison concluded by paying tribute to the Germans of Missouri "whose valor, patriotism and devotion to liberty had undoubtedly saved the State" and with the wish that "all men might recognize in Jennison the Jayhawker, while a faithful soldier of the Union, an undoubted, undisguised fighting Abolitionist."[91]

Jennison left St. Louis for Washington, D.C., to pursue his interest in returning to the command of the 7th Kansas Cavalry. Kansas senator James Lane's influence was sufficiently strong with President Lincoln that orders were to be prepared and sent to St. Louis returning Jennison to command. As soon as this became known, Missouri's Congressional delegation visited Lincoln en masse to protest. The Missourians left the White House with the assurance that Jennison would not be given a command. Jennison meanwhile had traveled to St. Louis. There he presented himself to the inspector general to be mustered in as colonel of the 7th Kansas. Unfortunately for Charles R. Jennison, the orders received specified that "Charles R. Jennings" was to take command and, absent other orders from Washington, D.C., the inspector general was unwilling to act contrary to his orders.[92]

Recognizing that the Regular Army, like City Hall, was difficult to fight, Jennison the Jayhawker returned to Leavenworth, Kansas, and opened a livestock business. It was soon claimed that the lineage of most Kansas horses was "out of Missouri, by Jennison."[93]

1863

May 13: Prominent Southern Sympathizers Banished from St. Louis

The riverfront at the foot of Pine Street was the scene of one of the more moving incidents of the Civil War in St. Louis.

On May 11, 1863, St. Louis came to a halt. The occasion was the commemoration of the capture of Camp Jackson just two years earlier. A column of six thousand Union soldiers marched from downtown St. Louis through throngs of spectators to Lindell Grove, where a crowd of thirty thousand citizens waited. There all were treated to an oration by the lawyer-politician Charles D. Drake, former "States' Rights" Democrat turned Radical Republican. Drake promised "to put on record . . . the true character of that ill-starred camp." His intention, he proclaimed, was to overcome the "diligent efforts" that had been made "to cover up the truth" and "to transmit [the camp's] history to the future in a cloud." Forgotten were the ambivalent emotions and mixed political leanings of many in the Missouri Volunteer Militia. Forgotten were the innocent bystanders who died at the hands of Union troops at Camp Jackson. This was an occasion for the vilification of all Southern sympathizers.[94]

Just two days later, a pathetic display at the riverfront showed just how far the fortunes of the city's Southern sympathizers had fallen.

At 5:00 P.M. on May 13, twenty-one St. Louisans were put aboard the steamer *Belle Memphis* to be banished to Confederate-held territory south of Memphis, Tennessee. Most of the exiles were guilty of holding the wrong political convictions, although some of the women were guilty of aiding their Confederate husbands, brothers, or friends too openly.[95]

One of the women was Mrs. Margaret Parkinson McLure. The fifty-year-old widow of William Raines McLure had come into a sizeable inheritance from her parents that, combined with income from the real estate investments of her late husband, made her a woman of substantial wealth. The McLure family's country home on Natural Bridge Road, called Pine Lawn, was noted for its spacious lawns and pine tree landscaping. The estate gave its name to the community that later developed there.[96]

Mrs. McLure and her sons held strong Southern sympathies. William Parkinson McLure returned to St. Louis from Denver to see his mother before he entered the Confederate service. After he left for the South, Mrs. McLure began visiting the city's prisons and caring for Confederate soldiers. She also carried mail and cooperated in the movement of contraband goods. After her son was killed in combat in 1862, Mrs. McLure's actions became ever bolder.[97]

On the evening of March 20, 1863, as Mrs. McLure returned to her downtown home on Chestnut Street between Sixth and Seventh Streets, she was put under house arrest by Union authorities. A few days later, most of the contents of her home were removed and replaced with cots so her home could be used temporarily as a prison for women.[98]

In addition to Mrs. McLure, four other women were accused of being "secret rebel mail agents": Mrs. Charles Clark, Mrs. Addie M. Haynes, Mrs. R. Lowden, and Miss Harriet Snodgrass.[99]

Another of the exiles placed on the boat that evening was Eliza "Lily" Brown Graham Frost. Described in the newspapers as "Mrs. General D. M. Frost," she should have evoked sympathy from her fellow citizens, but she did not. Her husband, Daniel Marsh Frost, was, by Unionist accounts, the villain of Camp Jackson. After that incident, Frost joined the Missouri State Guard and then became a brigadier general in the Confederate army. Conditions became ever more difficult for Lily and the children, who had remained behind in St. Louis. Accused of spying as a result of exchanging letters with her husband, the pregnant Lily was separated from her children and included in those to be banished from the city. Four other women who were wives of Confederate officers were sent out of the city with Mrs. Frost: Mrs. Joseph Chaytor, Mrs. Montrose Pallen, Mrs. David Sappington, and Mrs. William Smizer.[100]

Miss Lucie Nicholson, the eleventh woman in the group, apparently wore with pride the charge that "she was a volunteer in the rebel army." There is no doubt that she was an ardent Confederate sympathizer. The *Missouri Democrat* published a letter she wrote to a friend just a month before her banishment in which she lamented: "Oh how I wish Price would come. I would rather see every house in Missouri burned to the ground than to see it remain in the hands of the Federal Government."[101]

An hour before the women were placed on the boat, an officer of the provost marshal, two guards, and an omnibus called for the women at their "prison," the McLure home, and drove them to the wharf at the foot of Pine Street. There they saw the thirteen men brought under guard from the Gratiot Street Prison who would be exiled with them. The prisoners passed between ranks of soldiers from Company K, 23d Missouri Infantry, who had been assigned to keep spectators back from the scene. The exiles were escorted to a cabin aboard the *Belle Memphis* and guarded by a company of the 1st Nebraska Infantry. As the steamer pulled away and disappeared downriver, there were no demonstrations at the riverfront, although a few women friends of those on board were seen waving their handkerchiefs in a parting salute.[102]

The *Belle Memphis* landed in Memphis on Friday evening, May 15. The next morning the prisoners were transferred to ambulances and wagons and, under the watchful eyes of the 1st Nebraska, escorted fifty miles east to LaGrange, Tennessee. Mrs. Frost, Mrs. McLure, Mrs. Smizer, and Miss Nicholson rode together in an ambulance "which had been used the day before to move the dead and still had bloodstains on the floor." Food was scarce for the exiles, and they were forced to depend on the generosity of the people along their route. At LaGrange, the group was turned over to a detachment from Colonel Edward Hatch's Illinois cavalry, who escorted them south to Holly Springs, Mississippi, the edge of Confederate territory. There the exiles were left to their fates.[103]

Ironically, while the St. Louis exiles were traveling south, many of the "Camp Jackson boys" were moving north. After Camp Jackson, many of the Missouri militiamen with secessionist sympathies enlisted in the 1st Missouri Infantry, C.S.A. That regiment was now part of the 1st Missouri Brigade under the overall command of former St. Louisan and now Confederate general John S. Bowen. The Missourians had been among the first units to resist the Union army as it crossed the Mississippi River in the campaign that two months later led to the fall of Vicksburg. Now prisoners of war, the Missourians were aboard the steamer *Daniel G. Taylor* as it arrived opposite St. Louis on May 17, 1863. The steamer anchored in mid-river for several hours but then moved off to Alton, where its passengers were taken to the Alton Prison.[104]

July 4:
Union Soldiers Riot in
Hyde Park

Hyde Park is a short distance north of downtown St. Louis, just east of Interstate 70. From westbound Interstate 70, the Salisbury Street exit will take the visitor to the southern edge of the park. Nothing remains from the Civil War era.

On Independence Day 1863, Hyde Park was the scene of a riot by Union soldiers that resulted in the deaths of at least five people and the wounding of a dozen more.

Nearby Benton Barracks was home to a large number of soldiers, including many former prisoners awaiting their paroles to return them to active duty. Hyde Park was a recreational site for the soldiers. There they could relax and, if desired, purchase beer from an establishment run by a certain Mr. Kuhlage, but on previous visits the soldiers had, according to the *Missouri Democrat,* built up "a feeling inimical to Mr. Kuhlage." Apparently, the "inimical feeling" stemmed from suspicions that Mr. Kuhlage was a secessionist. In Mr. Kuhlage's defense, another reported cause of the soldiers' animosity was his unwillingness to continue to serve beer to the troops after they failed to pay for it.

One of the Independence Day attractions was to be a "balloon and horse" ascension. Hundreds paid fifty cents for the opportunity to see the event. Others paid only twenty-five cents but ended up with nearly the same access to the balloon ascension as those with the higher priced tickets.

Everything went well until mid-afternoon, when a large crowd collected at the entrance to Hyde Park. Disturbed by the slow process of ticketing, some of the young men began removing boards from the fence in order to gain entrance. The police were called to stop this incursion, but the provost marshal and soldiers of the 2d Missouri Artillery arrived first to stop the interlopers.

Not long after, another disturbance broke out in Kuhlage's barroom. Though Kuhlage had tried to prevent a riot by stopping the sale of beer, a general brawl broke out when a bartender made the mistake of flourishing a pistol and cutting a soldier with a knife. Kuhlage's barroom was nearly demolished.

The soldiers' brawl caused a panic among the men, women, and children who were enjoying the day at Hyde Park. A rush started for the park gates, but tragedy was averted by the timely arrival of the police. One of the rioters was arrested by a policeman for stealing a coat, but not before two army officers came to the police officer's assistance to prevent an attack by others.

Things quieted down until around 5:00 P.M., when patience with the balloonist's failed attempts at ascension wore thin. The ticket price differential also was a cause for friction with those who had paid more for what was presumably a choice view of the event. The unruly crowd stormed the balloon, upset it, and used its fire to ignite the evening's fireworks, which had been stored nearby. In under five minutes, the show was over.

The rioters then returned to Kuhlage's house to see if there was any more mischief to be done. Unfortunately for the crowd, twenty men of the 2d Missouri Artillery were already on the scene. As the crowd surged toward Kuhlage's, the lieutenant commanding the soldiers tried to stop it by having his men fire blanks from their rifles. Unfortunately, not all the soldiers responded to the command as desired: when the lieutenant ordered his men to fire, bullets were heard whizzing through Hyde Park. Four paroled soldiers, members of the mob, were killed. Two civilians, Louis Francis Demette and J. M. Smith, were killed, and several others were wounded.[105]

In the following days, the city coroner's jury held its inquest and came to a verdict. They concluded that the men of the 2d Missouri Artillery were responsible for the deaths by firing "without sufficient provocation." The jury recommended that the guilty parties be identified and tried for murder.

The available soldiers of the 2d Missouri Artillery were assembled for review and potential identification by witnesses, but only thirty of the battery's fifty-seven men could be collected. No positive identifications were made. A second review was made of the remaining soldiers, but the outcome was the same. In the words of the *Missouri Democrat:* "Thus ends the Coroner's long, laborious, and faithfully prosecuted effort to answer the demands of Justice and the public in this important matter."[106]

September 13: Incendiaries Terrorize the Riverfront

The St. Louis riverfront at the foot of Carr Street was the scene of several attacks on river steamers. Carr Street is the first east-west street north of the Martin Luther King bridge, just a few blocks north of the grounds of the Jefferson National Expansion Memorial and the Gateway Arch.

Young Frank Martin pushed his skiff out into the Mississippi River just before 6:00 P.M, hoping for a quiet evening of fishing. As he moved into the river, he worked his way around the "magnificent steamer" *Imperial*—considered to be one of the finest, largest, and fastest boats on the Mississippi—as it lay tied up at the wharf for repair. Martin watched in disbelief as a shadowy figure used a torch to set fires just under *Imperial*'s cabin deck. He cried out at the top of his voice, catching the attention of a black man named Pulliam on a nearby steamer. Pulliam joined Martin in spreading the alarm.

Fireboats rushed alongside *Imperial* but to no effect. *Hiawatha*, lying just north of *Imperial*, soon burst into flame. A quick-thinking ferry captain saved *J. C. Swon*, berthed just south of *Imperial*, by towing her out into the river. *Post Boy*, a small sidewheeler, caught fire from *Hiawatha* and, in turn, the sternwheeler *Jesse K. Polk* was consumed by flames.[107]

Two weeks later, in the early hours of September 28, a fire broke out under mysterious circumstances on the steamer *Platte Valley*. A watchman raised the alarm, and

a dozen volunteers arrived to put out the fire, which had started inside a locked room. Three days later, fire was discovered aboard *Chancellor* as she was tied up for repair at the docks in Carondelet on the city's south side. After the incident, *Chancellor* was moved north to the foot of Carr Street. *Platte Valley* or *Chancellor* may have been the victim of an "infernal machine," one of the more sophisticated tools of arsonists during the Civil War. From the outside, an infernal machine might appear to be an innocent valise or small suitcase. Inside, however, was a series of mechanisms intended to start a fire. An alarm clock with the bell removed was used to time the event, the "ringing" of the alarm springing the lock of a gun. The gun's hammer would strike and explode a percussion cap, igniting a tube of powder, which in turn exploded a bottle of "Greek fire," most likely a solution of phosphorus in bisulfide of carbon. This explosion would cause the turpentine-soaked pieces of cloth with which the suitcase was filled to burst into flame.[108]

On Sunday, October 4, *Chancellor*, only slightly damaged in the earlier attack, was again a target, and this time the firefighters were too late. *Forest Queen*, lying just north of *Chancellor*, soon burst into flames. A ferry towed *Forest Queen* into midstream and cast her loose to drift. Meanwhile, *Catahoula* had also drifted downstream. Thinking to improve her safety, the ferry moved *Catahoula* to the opposite shore, but she was soon struck by the burning *Forest Queen*. *Catahoula*, too, was lost.[109]

As loudly as the St. Louis headlines decried the "awful conflagration," the din of alarm would have been even louder had local authorities known that the fires were most likely the result of an organized plot by

St. Louis from the Illinois Side Showing the Steamer Sultana *(right) and the Courthouse (left). Detail of panoramic photograph, ca. 1864. From the Collections of the St. Louis Mercantile Library.*

members of the Confederate "secret service." Had a second attempt a year later succeeded, the city would have been thrown into panic.

In September 1864 John Breckenridge Castleman returned to his room at the Union Street Hotel after his midday meal. A knock on the door alerted him to a visitor, followed in rapid succession by several others. With the group assembled, Castleman reviewed each man's assignment and distributed bottles of Greek fire to be used in another attack on the steamboats. Armed and with their targets fresh in their minds, the incendiaries (as fire-starting terrorists were then known) left Castleman's room one by one to make their way to their positions by 2:00 P.M., the time chosen for their work to begin. This time, however, the assault was entirely unsuccessful. Castleman was very disappointed with the efficacy of the Greek fire, and he later claimed that had his men used "old fashioned matches" they would have destroyed all the boats then at St. Louis.[110]

In November 1864 Judge Advocate General Joseph Holt, chief of the U.S. War Department's Bureau of Military Justice, reported to Secretary of War Stanton that information about the plot had been received from supposed St. Louisan Francis Jones, a prisoner who informed on fellow Confederate terrorists to mitigate his own punishment. Jones seemed to take pride in the extent of the organization, freely identifying supposed Confederate agents in Boston, New York, Philadelphia, Chicago, Springfield, St. Louis, and ten other cities.[111]

Using this information, Colonel J. H. Baker, provost marshal general in St. Louis, arrested ten men in February 1865, two of whom also turned against their comrades. Edward Frazor, the reputed leader of the group, told Baker of a meeting he had attended with Confederate secretary of war Judah Benjamin in the summer of 1864. Benjamin paid Frazor and a companion $35,000 in gold to meet their claims for the destruction of U.S. property, apparently including their results in St. Louis. Frazor, like fellow agent Jones, readily disclosed the names of his accomplices. He identified eighteen men involved in this "infamous pursuit," five of them in the St. Louis area and several of whom Colonel Baker could link to the steamboat fires in 1863.[112]

In concluding his report, Colonel Baker estimated that more than seventy steamboats owned in St. Louis had been destroyed during the four years of war, though only nine had been destroyed by combat. Of the remainder, Baker expressed no doubt that most were destroyed by the men who were now his prisoners or "by similar emissaries of the rebel government."[113]

October 26: U.S. Corral Supplies Horses for the Cavalry

From U.S. Highway 40, take Grand Avenue north to its intersection with Cass Avenue. The cavalry depot's western edge ran along Grand; Cass Avenue ran nearly through the center of the U.S. Corral. As a result of urban development, nothing remains of the depot.

In 1860 the United States Army included only 5 regiments of horse soldiers. Two-and-a-half years later, 174 cavalry regiments were in service with the Union army, and an additional 28 regiments and 6 battalions were in the process of organization. The unprecedented stresses that this growth placed on the army's system for purchasing and training horses soon became apparent. On July 28, 1863, General Orders No. 236 created a separate Cavalry Bureau to take charge of the organization and equipment of the United States Cavalry. Perhaps more importantly, it would be responsible for providing mounts and remounts for the troopers.[114]

The Cavalry Bureau was to establish depots to collect, care for, and train cavalry horses, thus assuring that cavalry already in the field and new regiments were provided with serviceable horses. In order to meet the army's needs, the bureau was organized into Eastern and Western Divisions. The Eastern Division had its main depot at Giesboro Point near Washington, D.C. The Western Division chose the existing facilities in St. Louis as its depot, and it began operations on October 26, 1863.[115]

A period map in the collections of the Missouri Historical Society locates the United States Corral on the east side of Grand Avenue with its southern edge along the St. Charles Road (now called Dr. Martin Luther King Drive). Cass Avenue ran almost directly through the center of the depot. The high ground along the St. Charles Road near the southwestern corner of the U.S. Corral was the site of a small earthwork known as Battery D. Just off the northeast corner of the depot stood Fort Number 5. The battery and the fort were part of the series of strongpoints that guarded the landward approaches to St. Louis.[116]

The irregular seven-sided shape of the U.S. Corral was enclosed on all sides. Long stables, grain and forage warehouses, a saddle repair shop, a blacksmith shop, a carpenter shop, an armory, business offices, quarters for employees, and even a fire brigade gave the depot the appearance of a thriving village. Horses were brought to the depot by their owners for sale. After an examination, including exercises in running and jumping, the horses were purchased for artillery or cavalry duty. The depot also received horses deemed no longer fit for active service with the army. These animals were either recuperated and reissued, or they were condemned and sold for nonmilitary use. Stabling was available for 9,000 horses, but the depot typically held only 5,000. In the one year of its existence, the U.S. Corral purchased and received 47,524 horses.[117]

Although the U.S. Corral and other depots of the Cavalry Bureau generally solved the problems of supplying horses for the cavalry, they did not solve the problem of supplying mounts trained for active service. One veteran cavalry division commander, writing of his experience in 1864, asserted that he had to use his veteran regiments to "drive" the horses and men of new cavalry regiments into action. A modern historian of the United States cavalry claims that "the bolting of untrained horses ridden by unskilled riders, the first time they were exposed to gunfire, remained a serious hazard to the Union cavalry to the very end of the war."[118]

The Cavalry Bureau held an independent existence for little more than a year. Its authority cut across too many vested interests, including the Quartermaster's Department, the Ordnance Bureau, the commanders of armies, and, at times, the wishes of state governors. To complicate matters, the Cavalry Bureau never had strong leadership. Of its four bureau chiefs, the first, Major General George Stoneman, was in charge for five months and showed remarkably little interest in his assignment. Its fourth and last bureau chief, August Kautz, was in charge for only ten days before the life of the independent Cavalry Bureau came to an end on April 17, 1864.[119]

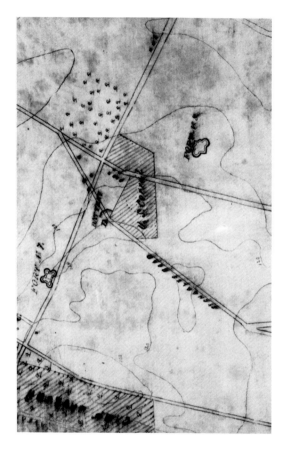

Right: Detail from Military Map of St. Louis, ca. 1863, Showing Location of the U.S. Corral. *Missouri Historical Society Map Collection.*

Below: Hospital and Yard for Condemned Government Horses and Mules. *Graphite on paper by Alexander Simplot, 1863. Missouri Historical Society Art Collection.*

1864

May 17:
Citizens Organize the Grand Mississippi Valley Sanitary Fair

The greatest civic event of the Civil War years was held along Tucker Boulevard (then called Twelfth Street) between Washington and Olive Streets.

Mayor James S. Thomas declared May 17, 1864, to be a public holiday so everyone could attend the procession and opening ceremonies of the Grand Mississippi Valley Sanitary Fair. The fair was the highpoint in the fund-raising work of the Western Sanitary Commission and the St. Louis Ladies' Union Aid Society, whose mission was to alleviate the suffering of wounded soldiers, their families, and refugees from the war.

When the first wounded soldiers arrived in St. Louis after the battle of Wilson's Creek in August 1861, members of the St. Louis Ladies' Union Aid Society were on hand to meet the train with bandages and clothing. From this

modest beginning, the society grew to become the main auxiliary of the Western Sanitary Commission in the St. Louis area.[120]

On June 13, 1861, President Abraham Lincoln had signed into being the United States Sanitary Commission, whose purpose was to advise and assist the Army Medical Bureau. In St. Louis, community leaders believed that an independent sanitary commission west of the Mississippi River was needed to adequately serve the needs of soldiers in the area. After wounded soldiers and refugees brought the realities of civil war to St. Louis in the summer of 1861, Jessie Benton Frémont prevailed upon her husband, General John C. Frémont, to sanction the plan to establish the Western Sanitary Commission. It was approved on September 5, 1861.

The first members of the commission were James E. Yeatman, Carlos S. Greeley, Dr. J. B. Johnson, George Partridge, and Reverend Dr. William Eliot. The scope of the Western Sanitary Commission was much broader geographically and socially than the Ladies' Union Aid Society, but in St. Louis the two organizations worked cooperatively to serve the needs of all "who suffer at the cause of the Union, and also sick and wounded prisoners of war."[121]

On February 1, 1864, representatives of the Western Sanitary Commission and the St. Louis Ladies' Union Aid Society, along with other interested citizens, met in the lecture

Mississippi Valley Sanitary Fair Building. *Lithograph by Alexander McLean, 1864. Missouri Historical Society Photograph and Print Collection.*

Above:
Booth Auctioning
Items Honoring
General Grant,
Mississippi Valley
Sanitary Fair.
*Photograph by Robert
Benecke, 1864.
Missouri Historical
Society Photograph and
Print Collection.*

Right:
Booth Auctioning
General Lyon's Last
Letter, Mississippi
Valley Sanitary Fair.
*Photograph by Robert
Benecke, 1864.
Missouri Historical
Society Photograph and
Print Collection.*

hall of the St. Louis Mercantile Library. There they began planning for their most extravagant fund-raising effort yet, the Grand Mississippi Valley Sanitary Fair. Major General William S. Rosecrans, then commander of the Department of the Missouri, was named president of the fair. Yeatman headed up the Fair's executive committee, which had charge of the event's operations.[122]

The site selected for the fair was the area on then Twelfth Street between Washington and Olive Streets. In 1864 this area was the western edge of the city's business district. The main building, 114 by 525 feet, was on Twelfth Street from Olive to St. Charles Streets. In the building's center was an octagon 75 feet across and 50 feet high, decorated with mottoes, flags, battle trophies, and arbors of evergreens and flowers.[123]

The Grand Mississippi Valley Sanitary Fair opened on May 18, 1864, after the previous day's inaugural festivities. Once the citizens had paid their fees to be admitted to the fair, they were presented with a wide variety of ways to show their support for the Union cause by spending more money. Sales at the various booths, eating and drinking establishments, and places of recreation, such as the skating pond, were apparently brisk, but raffles drew the most attention. The biggest raffle was of Smizer Farm, a five-hundred-acre tract complete with buildings that was donated by the county court. The farm was valued at nearly forty thousand dollars. Other prizes in this raffle included a rosewood piano, a pedigreed stallion, and a picture titled *Adoration of the Holy Trinity by All the Saints.*[124]

Another raffle held on the closing night, June 18, 1864, featured three bars of Nevada silver, each valued at four thousand dollars. Being the closing night of the fair, this raffle was also an attempt to move as much of the unsold merchandise as possible. Before the evening was over, more than seven thousand prizes had been awarded.[125]

A novel feature of the fair that attracted much favorable attention was the fact that guard duty was performed by black soldiers from the regiments then at Benton Barracks. While black soldiers and black patrons of the fair caused little stir, another activity was more controversial: liquor sales. Though stronger spirits were prohibited, the executive committee finally gave way to the demands of the German community for sales of wine and beer. As Reverend Galusha Anderson, a Baptist minister, observed, "The Germans, being so large a part of our population, and so ardently devoted to the maintenance of the Union, were given a large space in the building, where they patriotically sold lager beer, and a host of people patriotically drank it."[126]

Another activity drawing much participation was the opportunity to buy votes for one dollar each and cast them for "favorite general." The general receiving the most votes was to be presented with a sword valued at fifteen hundred dollars. More than half of the 4,517 votes cast went to General Winfield Scott Hancock. In order of their finish, votes also went to Generals McClellan, Sherman, Butler, and Grant.[127]

The Grand Mississippi Valley Sanitary Fair was organized to raise money. It succeeded admirably. Total receipts were $618,782.28, which, after expenses, provided a profit of $554,000. From the profits, the Western Sanitary Commission immediately donated $50,000 to the St. Louis Ladies' Union Aid Society for its work in hospitals. The largest use of the profits, $345,000, was for medical supplies. Another $64,000 was used for the aid of soldiers, their families, refugees, and freedmen. The Western Sanitary Commission also provided an annuity of $1,000 monthly for the Ladies' Freedmen's Relief Association for activities specifically aiding the families of freedmen and black soldiers.[128]

Financial success, however, may not be the best measure by which to judge the impact of the Grand Mississippi Valley Sanitary Fair. In the words of Reverend Anderson, "The Fair was a blessing not only to refugees and freedmen, to the sick and wounded in hospitals, to the widows and orphans of our slain heroes, but it was also a measureless boon to St. Louis. It was one more mighty agency for curing us of our selfishness. For a time at least it broke in upon our commercialism, and led us to think of others and to do something for their welfare."[129]

August 23: Homeward Bound, Northern Style

The 10th Missouri Infantry Regiment, U.S.A., was unusual in that seven of its companies were recruited from Illinois, two companies were from Iowa, and only one, Company K, was from Missouri. Despite its uncharacteristic beginnings, the return of the 10th Missouri to St. Louis to muster out at the expiration of its three-year term of service must have been a typical experience.

The 10th Missouri Infantry Regiment, U.S.A., was organized in St. Louis in August 1861. Its initial service was to guard the Pacific Railroad at various points within Missouri, but in April 1862 the regiment moved across the Mississippi. After participating in the battles of Farmington, Iuka, and Corinth, Mississippi, the 10th Missouri was assigned to railroad guard duty around Memphis. By March 1863 the regiment was again part of Grant's active field force. In the campaign for Vicksburg, the regiment was present at Port Gibson, Raymond, Jackson, Champion Hill, Big Black River Bridge, and the Vicksburg siege. After Vicksburg, the 10th Missouri went with Grant to Chattanooga where, on November 23-24, 1863, it participated in the assault on Tunnel Hill. Under Sherman's overall command, the regiment moved forward to Kingston and then Resaca, Georgia, until its three-year enlistments began expiring in August 1864.

In its three years of service, the 10th Missouri established a good combat record. Three officers and 98 enlisted men were killed or mortally wounded in its campaigns. An additional 2 officers and 228 enlisted men died of disease, bringing the unit's total losses to 5 officers and 326 men.[130]

On August 19, 1864, the regiment started for home. It traveled by rail from Resaca to Chattanooga, Nashville, and Louisville before arriving in East St. Louis, Illinois, on the afternoon of August 23. At the station, the veterans were met by the St. Louis City Post Band and the Veterans Reception Committee and escorted back across the Mississippi River to Missouri.[131]

After landing, the regiment formed in column and marched up Carr Street to Fifth Street (now Broadway). The column turned south on Fifth Street and marched one block to Washington Avenue, where it turned back toward the river in order to pass the headquarters of General William Rosecrans, commander of the Department of the Missouri. Pausing briefly at headquarters, the men gave three cheers before continuing the march. At Fourth Street, the regiment again turned south and continued to Chestnut Street. At Chestnut, the column turned right and halted when reaching the corner of Chestnut and Fifth Streets, the northwest corner of the courthouse. The soldiers were ordered to stack arms, and they were then treated with refreshments.[132]

After a brief rest, the regiment moved forward to a reception in its honor. From a speaker's platform, the 10th Missouri was greeted by its one-time commander, Colonel

Samuel A. Holmes, Mayor James S. Thomas, and members of the Veterans Reception Committee. After the mayor's greetings, Colonel Holmes addressed his comrades. Praising the living and eulogizing the dead, he reminded the veterans that "men who have made such sacrifices in such a cause as you have made deserve and will forever have the gratitude of your country."[133]

After three cheers for Colonel Holmes, three for the Veterans Reception Committee, and three for the 10th Missouri, the regiment's current commander, Colonel Francis C. Deimling, delivered a brief response in gratitude to Colonel Holmes and the committee. More cheers for Colonel Holmes and the organizers followed.[134]

The men spent the night at Schofield Barracks. The next day they moved to Benton Barracks, where they made out their individual discharge papers. A month later the men were mustered out and paid before each made his own way home.[135]

September 29: Confederates Raid Cheltenham Post Office

Augustus Muegge and His Family at Their Home. *Photograph, ca. 1870. Missouri Historical Society Photograph and Print Collection.*

At the time of the Civil War, Cheltenham was a village four miles outside the southwestern city limits. Today it is well within the city. The two-story brick building that was Cheltenham Post Office still stands at 6437 Manchester. The building is in private hands and is not open to visitors.

Postmaster Augustus Muegge of Cheltenham arrived at the militia camp on Olive Street Road around 8:00 P.M. on September 29, 1864. He frantically told his story: he and his wife had been attacked by Confederate raiders. Union troops were sent in pursuit out Laclede Station Road but gave up when they reached Old Watson Road and had seen no signs of the marauders. If Muegge was right, this was the only appearance of armed secessionists in St. Louis since the days of Camp Jackson in 1861.

The village of Cheltenham was large enough to boast a railroad station and a United States Post Office. The Post Office was half a mile from the station and located inside the Muegge's general store on the corner of Manchester and Valley (now Dale) Avenues. In September 1864 the village was no doubt in a state of alarm, just as St. Louis was, because of the threat from General Sterling Price's advancing Confederate columns.[136]

According to Muegge, four men rode up to his store in the early evening, perhaps as early as 5:00 P.M. Two men remained mounted as the other two dismounted and walked into the store. After looking around, they inquired about the distance to the nearest military post. Mrs. Muegge, suspicious of the visitors' intent, called out a warning to her husband in German to be careful.

Next, the intruders asked about Muegge's politics. He replied that he was a Union man. Then they asked whether he had ever held office. Muegge said he was the United States Postmaster for Cheltenham. In response, one of the men drew his pistol and announced, "It's just such men as you that we want to kill."[137]

The ever alert Mrs. Muegge threw herself between her husband and the intruder, causing the would-be killer to pull up his arm. Heeding his wife's call to run for his life, Mr. Muegge sprang down the hall, went out the back door, and made his escape. As soon as he could find a horse, he made his way to the Union militia camp.[138]

How seriously the Union troops took Muegge's report is difficult to determine. The *Missouri Republican* reported just after the event that a scout was sent out "immediately." The *Missouri Democrat* claimed that, despite considerable effort on Muegge's part to get the Union troops interested, he could find no one "who had authority to act." Because every bridge and ford crossing the Meramec River was well guarded in apprehension of Sterling Price's advancing army, it was assumed that it was not possible for the raiders to have escaped in that direction.

The descriptions of the "Rebel guerillas" varied widely. The *Missouri Republican* reported that they were "splendidly mounted and finely dressed, with 'dusters' over their fine clothes." Displaying the regular Confederate uniform, they were "evidently old soldiers." The *Missouri Democrat* described the Confederates as also wearing long dusters "under which the collar of the rebel uniform" was visible. The riders wore moccasins with long Mexican spurs and "might have some Indian blood from their complexion and features," the newspaper added. Whatever their source or their intention, the Confederate riders have disappeared into history.

The *Missouri Republican* offered this rationale for the excitement at Cheltenham Post Office: "The most plausible explanation is that the fright of the Postmaster induced him in imagining a great deal more than he saw, and in his statement drew largely upon his fancy."

It is unfortunate that apparently no one took the time to interview the postmaster's wife.

September 30: Union Troops Rush to Kirkwood

From downtown St. Louis, follow U.S. 40 west to Lindbergh Boulevard south. When Lindbergh Boulevard crosses Manchester Road, its name changes to Kirkwood Road. From the intersection of Manchester and Lindbergh/Kirkwood Road, go south 1.3 miles to Argonne Drive. Turn right (west) on Argonne and drive for two blocks, stopping at the Kirkwood Historical Society at 302 West Argonne Drive. The society's collection includes Civil War diaries, letters, and uniform items. For hours, call 314-965-5151.

The development of Kirkwood as the first permanent planned suburban community west of the Mississippi River was initiated in 1851. During most of the Civil War, Kirkwood was an unincorporated village with no local government of its own. Located strategically on the Pacific Railroad and high above the Meramec River, it was far from the protection offered by St. Louis. On September 30, 1864, the village found itself in a flurry of military activity when two brigades arrived to resist what was believed to be the vanguard of General Sterling Price's Confederate forces.[139]

On September 19 Price and twelve thousand cavalrymen crossed into Missouri from Arkansas, converging on Fredericktown. Price's corps, three divisions under James F. Fagan, John S. Marmaduke, and Joseph O. Shelby, was a great concern to Union general William S. Rosecrans at his headquarters in St. Louis.

Unknown to Rosecrans, seven regiments and one battalion of Price's column were mounted infantry with no training in cavalry tactics. Nearly four thousand of Price's men were unarmed. Despite these weaknesses, Price's force was the "most powerful body of cavalry" assembled west of the Mississippi River during the Civil War.[140]

As Price's column moved northward, officials in St. Louis were jolted into action. On September 26 Rosecrans issued orders that, on recommendation of the mayor and "many leading business men of the city," required all business to be suspended at noon of the next day to allow the formation of citizen guard units. Enough St. Louisans responded to the call to form five regiments and three battalions, one of them of black citizens. On September 30, fearing a Confederate advance across the Meramec River, Rosecrans ordered Union militia units moved from St. Louis to Kirkwood as a defensive measure.[141]

Major General Andrew Jackson Smith, a proven combat officer, was on hand to lead the Federal troops. Fortunately for Rosecrans, Smith was the harbinger of the arrival of his complete veteran corps. Smith's troops had been diverted to St. Louis from Tennessee by way of the Mississippi River when Price's movements became known. Until his veterans arrived, however, Smith would lead two brigades of militia units. One brigade, consisting of twelve hundred men of the 3d, 6th, and 10th Enrolled Missouri Militia, was commanded by C. D. Wolff. George F. Meyers commanded Smith's other brigade, fifteen hundred soldiers of the 11th and 13th Enrolled Missouri Militia and a company called the "National Guard of St. Louis." The 7th Kansas Cavalry and three companies of militia cavalry accompanied the footsoldiers.[142]

On September 27, eighty miles southwest of St. Louis at Pilot Knob, Price's column was badly hurt by General Thomas Ewing's Union forces defending Fort Davidson. To add insult to the injury of this bloody rebuff, the Union garrison withdrew, eluding capture by the Confederates. Learning that Rosecrans was being heavily reinforced by Smith's combat-tested soldiers, Price concluded that St. Louis was not vulnerable to attack. He turned his army west, marching across the state to defeat at the battle of Westport, near Kansas City.[143]

As a result of the timely movement of Union forces, the "Battle of Kirkwood" was never fought.

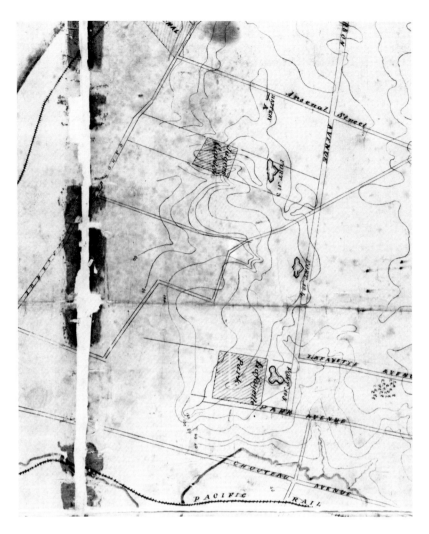

Detail from Military Map of St. Louis, ca. 1863, Showing Location of Forts No. 4, 5, and Lafayette Park. *Missouri Historical Society Map Collection.*

October 29: Confederates Executed at Fort No. 4

Fort No. 4 stood just a short distance south of Lafayette Square in an area now bounded by Jefferson, Shenandoah, Missouri, and Ann Streets. On the afternoon of October 29, 1864, the fort was the scene of a public execution.

James Wilson enlisted in the Union army in May 1861 and rose rapidly in rank. By December he was first sergeant of Company G, 10th Cavalry, Missouri State Militia. Not long after the regiment's redesignation as the 3d Cavalry, Missouri State Militia, Wilson was commissioned captain, and he was promoted to major on June 20, 1863. Wilson's promotions came because he proved himself to be an exceptional combat leader. His regiment fought many actions against Confederate regular and guerrilla forces, and in the bloody struggles in

southeast Missouri, quarter was seldom asked or given by either side.[144]

On September 26, 1864, the first day of the battle of Pilot Knob, Missouri, Major Wilson led the force that temporarily drove the Confederates out of the Arcadia Valley. The following day, during the Confederate assault on Fort Davidson, he and others were cut off and captured. The next day the Union prisoners, both military and civilian, began an eighty-mile march to a point about ten miles west of Union, Missouri, arriving there on October 2. The following day Major Wilson and six enlisted men were singled out and turned over to the Confederate guerrilla leader Timothy Reeves.[145]

Reeves and Wilson were old enemies whose men had often traded roles as the hunter and the hunted. A week before the battle at Pilot Knob, Union cavalry burned Doniphan, Missouri, Reeves' hometown. There is also evidence that on Christmas Day of 1863, Wilson and the 3d Missouri Cavalry surprised Reeves' guerrillas in their camp where, unknown to Wilson, the guerrillas' families had come for the holiday celebration. The attack may have resulted in as many as thirty civilian casualties, including at least three of the guerrillas' wives.[146]

Whatever his motivation, Reeves now had the upper hand. Two witnesses later reported that Reeves said to Wilson, "Major, you are a brave man—but you never showed my men quarter, neither will I give you quarter." Wilson and the six enlisted men were then executed. The remainder of the prisoners were paroled and allowed to go home.[147]

News of the deaths reached General William Rosecrans in St. Louis on October 5. The next day, he issued Special Orders No. 277 calling for a Confederate major and six enlisted men to be held in solitary confinement until Wilson's fate was made certain. The bodies were found on October 23, by which time the badly decomposed corpses had been uncovered and partially eaten by hogs that roamed the woods where the bodies had been hastily buried.[148]

On October 25, 1864, Rosecrans' provost marshal general in St. Louis directed that the first Confederate major captured from General Sterling Price's raiding force be forwarded to him without delay for execution. On October 28, Special Orders No. 279 extended the retaliation to six Confederate enlisted prisoners. No Confederate majors from General Price's army were in custody. Six enlisted men were selected at random from among the prisoners in St. Louis at the time. Only one of the six selected had been in the same battle as the murdered Union soldiers. After the selections, it was learned that one of the prisoners, John N. Ferguson, was a teamster and had never carried arms; George Bunch was chosen to take his place.

Harvey Blackburn, the oldest of the six, was from the St. Louis area. The Blackburns had migrated from Kentucky to Missouri in the early 1800s. Before the Civil War, Harvey Blackburn lived in a community known as Possum Hollow near Florissant. In 1861 Blackburn left St. Louis for Arkansas, where he joined the Confederate cavalry.[149]

Around 2:00 P.M. on Saturday, October 29, 1864, the six soldiers were led from their confinement at the Gratiot Street Prison on Eighth and Gratiot Streets to a waiting covered wagon. They were escorted without music to Fort No. 4, just a short distance south of Lafayette Park. There six posts with seats attached had been erected in a north-south line along the west side of the fort. In the presence of some three thousand people, mostly soldiers, the prisoners were seated and each man's hands were tied behind his post.[150]

After the sentence was read, Charles Minnekin, one of the youngest of the prisoners, asked for permission to speak:

Soldiers, and all of you who hear me, take warning from me. I have been a Confederate soldier four years and have served my country faithfully. I am now to be shot for what other men have done, that I had no hand in, and know nothing about. I never was a guerilla, and I am sorry to be shot for what I had nothing to do with, and what I am not guilty of. When I took a prisoner I always treated him kindly and never harmed a man after he surrendered. I hope God will take me to His bosom when I am dead. Oh Lord, be with me.[151]

The firing party of fifty-four soldiers included men from the 10th Kansas and 41st Missouri Infantry Regiments, thirty-six of whom stood about ten paces distant from the condemned men. The remaining eighteen stood in reserve in case a second volley from the executioners was needed. Some of the Kansas men appeared uneasy at the prospect of firing on the prisoners. An officer harshly reminded them of their duty and that they should have no qualms because the Confederates had taken the lives of many Union men who were as innocent as these were. Blindfolds were then tied on the prisoners. Shortly after 3:00 P.M., on command, the thirty-six soldiers fired simultaneously. After the volley two of the victims groaned and one cried out, but all were dead in a few minutes. The six Confederates were buried in adjacent graves in Jefferson Barracks National Cemetery.[152]

Major Wilson's body was brought to St. Louis and lay in state in the rotunda of the courthouse for several days. On November 1 his remains were escorted to the depot of the North Missouri Railroad and shipped to Troy, Missouri, where he was buried in the city cemetery.[153]

On November 7 two Confederate majors captured during Price's defeat in western Missouri arrived at the Gratiot Street Prison. The provost marshal now had the material with which to complete his grisly requisition. The man chosen to die in revenge for Major Wilson was Major Enoch O. Wolf, an Ohio-born Texan veteran of General John Marmaduke's cavalry division. His death sentence was read to him the next morning. When it was learned that Wolf was a Mason, a local minister and the minister's Masonic lodge interceded to repeatedly delay Wolf's execution. In February 1865 Wolf was transferred to Johnson's Island Prison in Ohio and was exchanged, thus escaping his random death sentence.[154]

Confederate Soldiers Condemned by Special Orders No. 279

Harvey H. Blackburn, private	47 years old	Co. A, Coleman's Cavalry (Arkansas Rifles)
George T. Bunch	22 years old	3d Missouri Cavalry
James W. Gates	21 years old	3d Missouri Cavalry
Asa V. Ladd, private	34 years old	Co. A, Burbridge's Missouri Cavalry
Charles W. Minnekin	21 years old	Co. A, Crabtree's Arkansas Cavalry
John A. Nichols, private	21 years old	Co. G, 2d Missouri Cavalry

Source: *Missouri Democrat*, October 29, 1864. Scharf, *History of St. Louis City and County*, 444.

Utz Residence, 615 Utz Lane. *Photograph by Robert Elgin, 1965. Missouri Historical Society Photograph and Print Collection.*

December 26: Major James Utz Hanged as Spy

The pre–Civil War home of the Utz family still stands in Hazelwood. Major Utz is buried in Fee Fee Cemetery, a few miles from his home.

To view the Utz house, from Interstate 70 take the Lindbergh Boulevard exit and go north approximately 3.0 miles, crossing both Natural Bridge Road (Missouri 115) and McDonnell Boulevard (Missouri TT). Utz Lane is on the left (north) side of Lindbergh just before the interchange with Interstate 270. Follow the signs to Utz Lane. The Utz home is on the right at 615 Utz Lane. It is in private hands and not open to the public.

Fee Fee Cemetery is located at 11210 Old St. Charles Road. To visit Fee Fee Cemetery, return to Lindbergh Boulevard and turn south (right). Cross Interstate 70 and St. Charles Rock Road. Two intersections south of St. Charles Rock Road, turn right at Old St. Charles Road. Move immediately into the left lane. Turn left at the first intersection and immediately right into Fee Fee Cemetery. Follow the cemetery lane a short distance ahead to a small parking lot by the cemetery office and park. At the time of the Civil War, the current office building was the meetinghouse of Fee Fee Baptist Church. A plaque on the building tells its history.

To find the Utz grave, go to the front of the meetinghouse and go seventy steps into the graveyard on a line parallel to Old St. Charles Road.

The Utz family was among the earliest settlers in St. Louis County. In 1827 Julius Utz built this farmhouse in St. Ferdinand township about midway between the villages of Bridgeton and Florissant. After his death in 1837, the house became home to his nephew, Franklin T. Utz, and his wife, Amelia. On March 9, 1841, a son, James Morgan Utz, was born to the highly respected couple.[155]

In the spring of 1861, twenty-year-old James Utz left St. Louis to join the Missouri State Guard. In September 1862, after service in the Guard's 8th Infantry Battalion and the 9th Infantry Regiment, Utz was captured, but he was later exchanged. During the summer of 1864, Utz was promoted to major and assigned to duty as a "special agent" for the Confederate army. Utz' knowledge of Southern sympathizers in the St. Louis area was a key factor in this assignment. The Utz home was reputed to be the headquarters of the "night riders," secessionist sympathizers who raided Union outposts and property in the area, and the scene of many Confederate conclaves.[156]

In late July 1864, five men making their way south to join General Price's army were confronted by Union soldiers in Jefferson County. Three of the men were killed, one escaped, and one was wounded and captured. On the wounded man was found a letter written in cypher. The letter was taken to the district provost marshal in St. Louis, who put his staff to work decoding the message. The results of their work indicted Major James Morgan Utz.

The cyphered letter, signed "J. M. Utz," advised his correspondent to tell General Price that Utz' St. Louis contact was confined in Gratiot Street Prison and that he had difficulty reaching the man's replacement. He also reported that three militia regiments, two of them veteran, were on duty in St. Louis.[157]

On September 24 Utz and five conspirators, including eighteen-year-old Paul Fusz, an ancestor of the St. Louis auto-dealer family, made their way out of St. Louis driving a wagon loaded with medical supplies. Dressed in Union uniforms, they hoped to make their way west to meet General Joseph Shelby's Confederate cavalry command. Just beyond Manchester, between the town and the Meramec River, the group was stopped by a patrol of the 6th Missouri Cavalry, U.S. Their lack of papers aroused suspicion, and a search of the wagon revealed its contraband cargo, including a cypher book and letters from Confederate officers. The group was arrested and confined in Gratiot Street Prison.[158]

Major Utz was tried by military commission in St. Louis and found guilty on all three charges on which he was arraigned: being a rebel spy, recruiting for the rebel army within the lines of United States forces, and carrying correspondence and information to enemies of the United States. Franklin Utz, the major's father, no doubt helped console his son; he, too, was now an inmate in Gratiot Street Prison, having been confined on a charge of disloyalty. Despite their circumstances, they had hope. The younger Utz' uncle, St. Louis County Judge Frederick Hyatt, had frantically appealed to the president in an attempt to reduce the anticipated punishment.[159]

Without public notice, Major Utz was transferred from Gratiot Street Prison to the county jail at the southeast corner of Sixth and Chestnut Streets on Sunday evening, December 25, 1864. Shortly before noon the next day, he was led from his cell to the scaffold, accompanied by Father Ward of the Catholic Church who, years earlier, had baptized him in the Catholic faith. Utz' last request was that his body be turned over to his friends.[160]

At twenty minutes after noon, James Morgan Utz was hanged. After thirteen minutes, he was pronounced dead by the attending surgeon, and his body was taken for burial at Fee Fee Cemetery not far from the Utz family home. His pardon from President Lincoln arrived a short time later.[161]

On his gravestone are these words:

Friends weep for him who sleeps beneath this sod,
His cruel fate in sympathy deplore
But while you mourn, remember that his God
Has called him hence, where sorrows are no more.

1865

June 20:
Homeward Bound,
Southern Style

The riverfront was the scene of the last appearance of Confederate troops in St. Louis.

Homecoming for Missouri's Confederates was a much different experience than it had been for Missouri's Union soldiers.

On June 20, 1865, the veterans of the 9th Missouri Infantry Regiment, C.S.A., arrived at the St. Louis riverfront aboard the steamer *Maria Denning*. The 9th Missouri had been organized in late 1862 by consolidation of the 8th Missouri Infantry Battalion and the Missouri companies of Clarkson's Missouri Cavalry Battalion. Serving in brigades commanded by Generals D. M. Frost, J. B. Clark, and C. S. Mitchell, the regiment compiled a good combat record in the Trans-Mississippi Department while fighting at Prairie Grove, Pleasant Hill, and Jenkins' Ferry. At the time of its return to its native state, the 9th Missouri was commanded by Major Harry H. Hughes.[162]

The 9th Missouri was the first Confederate unit to arrive in St. Louis during the week. It was followed by the 8th, 10th, 11th, and 16th Missouri Infantry Regiments and the 3d and 4th Cavalry Battalions. In each case, before the men were allowed to leave their steamers, they were required to take the oath of allegiance to the United States.[163]

On June 23, 1865, the Confederate veterans learned that their transition to civilian life was not going to be as easy as they had perhaps hoped. That day, Major General Grenville M. Dodge, commander of the Department of the Missouri, issued the following order:

Paroled officers and men of the late rebel armies are forbidden to wear within this department the uniform, or any part thereof, or other insignia of said rebel service. Exception, however, will be made in the case of private soldiers who are destitute of means, and such persons will be permitted for a short time to wear such clothing as is in their possession after stripping from the same all Confederate or State buttons and other insignia of the rebel service. In the case of officers of every rank no exception will be made, but such persons will be held to a prompt and strict compliance with this order, and any violation of its terms by either officers or soldiers will be considered as an act of hostility to the government of the United States, and will be punished accordingly.[164]

Though the war was over and the veterans of both sides were coming home, it would still take time for peace to come to Missouri.

Furl that Banner, for 'tis weary;
Round its staff 'tis drooping dreary;
Furl it, fold it, it is best;
For there's not a man to wave it,
And there's not a sword to save it,
And there's not one left to lave it
In the blood which heroes gave it,
And its foes now scorn and brave it:
Furl it, hide it, let it rest.

Father Abram Joseph Ryan
Confederate Chaplain

Decoration Day. *Wood engraving after Otto Walter Beck from* Harper's Weekly, *May 30, 1891, p. 400. Missouri Historical Society Library.*

Chapter 5 In

Forest Park

From U.S. Highway 40, take the Kingshighway Boulevard exit north. Follow Kingshighway approximately 0.7 miles north to West Pine. Turn left on West Pine, staying in the center lane. West Pine dead-ends at Lindell. Turn left (west) on Lindell. Continue west on Lindell for 1.1 miles to DeBaliviere (St. Louisans pronounce it "de-BOL-liver"). Turn left at DeBaliviere, following the signs to the Jefferson Memorial.

The Jefferson Memorial was built in 1913 with proceeds from the World's Fair of 1904 and named in honor of President Thomas Jefferson. It houses the offices of the Missouri Historical Society (founded in 1866), although the Library and Archives were recently moved further west to 225 South Skinker. Forest Park, once well outside the city's limits, is reportedly the third largest city park in the United States. Among the many treasures in its thirteen hundred acres are four monuments of Civil War interest.

From these honored dead we take increased devotion to that cause for which they gave the last full measure of devotion; that we here highly resolve that these dead shall not have died in vain; that this nation, under God, shall have a new birth of freedom; and that government of the people, by the people, and for the people, shall not perish from the earth.

President Abraham Lincoln
Gettysburg
November 1863

Memoriam

1. Edward Bates Statue

From the south side of the Jefferson Memorial, follow Washington Drive west 0.8 miles to a small island in the roadway near the base of Art Hill, north of the St. Louis Art Museum. Use caution when visiting the Bates statue because traffic moves around the triangular island in all directions.

The first statue in the city of St. Louis to honor a hero of the Civil War was not dedicated to a soldier but to a civilian: Edward Bates.

Bates began his public career in 1818 when he was appointed attorney for the Northern District of Missouri. Though only twenty-five years old, Bates had practiced law in St. Louis for two years and had already developed powerful political alliances. In 1823 he became United States district attorney and in 1826, with the support of Senator Thomas Hart Benton, won election to the United States House of Representatives. Having lost Benton's support in the intervening years, Bates failed in his bid for reelection in 1828. He then moved into state politics, where he united opposition to Benton's programs while creating a nucleus that would become the Whig Party in Missouri.

After 1836 Bates left politics to return to his law practice. In 1842 he joined in partnership with Hamilton R. Gamble, future governor of Missouri and husband of Caroline Coalter, the sister of Bates' wife. Though Bates owned slaves until 1844, he increasingly came to favor limiting the expansion of slavery. He also championed the creation of colonies in Africa and Central America for freed slaves.

Bates came to national prominence in 1847 when he was chosen as presiding officer for the River and Harbor Convention in Chicago. The delegates, including Congressman Abraham Lincoln, were impressed with his closing speech. Three years later Bates was honored with the request to serve as secretary of war for President Millard Fillmore, an opportunity he declined for personal reasons. As a Whig, Bates continued to work to end the expansion of slavery, a goal which ironically moved him closer to the position of his adversary Thomas Hart Benton. Bates again came to public attention at the Republican Convention of 1860, where he was considered a potential compromise candidate between Lincoln and William Seward. Bates received strong support on the first ballot, but Lincoln won the nomination two ballots later.

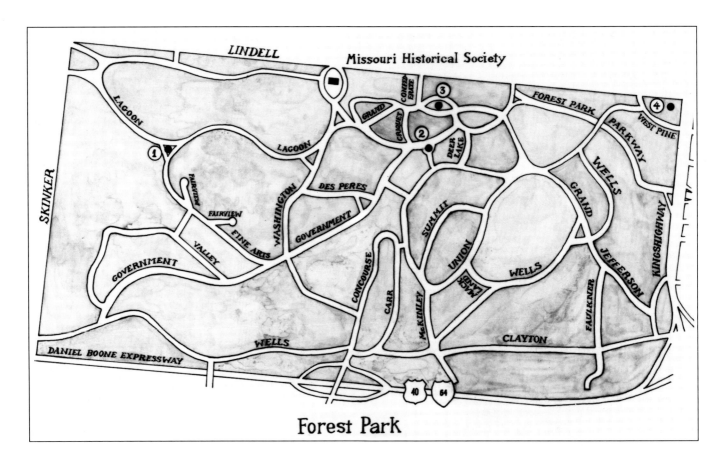

Forest Park. *Map by Jennifer Ratcliffe-Tangney, 1994.*

After Lincoln's election, Bates accepted the president's offer to become attorney general of the United States. Despite the fact that he had a son serving on each side during the Civil War, Bates was an unswerving supporter of the Lincoln administration. Lincoln came to rely on him as a "conservative counterweight" to the more radical Republicans in the cabinet. Bates privately hoped to be made chief justice of the Supreme Court when the position opened in October 1864, but Lincoln responded to increasing pressure from radical Republicans by nominating Salmon P. Chase to the post. Bates resigned and returned to St. Louis. He died in the city on March 25, 1869, and was buried in Bellefontaine Cemetery.[1]

The monument to Edward Bates was unveiled on June 24, 1876, the opening day of Forest Park. The statue, completed several years earlier, was originally intended for placement in Lafayette Park, but no action had been taken because the sculptor had not been paid. Forest Park's commissioners paid the outstanding balance to buy the statue for their park. The Bates monument originally stood at a prominent location near the southeast entrance of Forest Park but was moved to its present, less prominent location as a result of a highway expansion in 1934-1935.[2]

The bronze statue is ten feet high and stands on a red granite pedestal of the same height. Bates wears a full-skirted Prince Albert coat as he stands as if addressing a court. His hand holds a book resting on a stand in the shape of an eagle, above which is the seal of the State of Missouri.

Four medallions, one on each face of the pedestal, were added by the sculptor later. From the front face of the statue and moving around to the right, the individuals represented are James B. Eads, the builder of the first ironclads to serve the Union army on the Mississippi River; Hamilton R. Gamble, Bates' brother-in-law and law partner, as well as the governor of Missouri for much of the Civil War era; Charles Gibson, a protégé of Bates in the practice of law who served under him during the Civil War as solicitor of the court of claims (today's solicitor general) when Bates was Lincoln's attorney general; and Henry Sheffie Geyer, who assisted as legal counsel in the Dred Scott case and went on to serve as successor to Missouri's Thomas Hart Benton in the United States Senate from 1851 to 1857. A close associate of Bates, Geyer was president of the Bates Association, which helped raise money for the monument.[3]

James Wilson Alexander MacDonald (1824-1908), the sculptor of the Bates statue, ran away from home in Ohio and from an apprenticeship as a blacksmith to find work in St. Louis. In the city he studied art and anatomy while working in the printing business. In 1852 MacDonald and two partners began the newspaper *Morning Signal,* which would later be sold and become the antislavery *Missouri Democrat.* MacDonald used his profits from the sale of the newspaper to continue his art studies, this time in New York. By 1857 he was back in St. Louis in the sewing machine business. After the Civil War he returned to New York and began his career in earnest as a portrait artist and sculptor. The statue of General George Armstrong Custer at the United States Military Academy was done by MacDonald two years after the Bates sculpture.[4]

2. General Franz Sigel Statue

From the Bates statue, continue to the left on Washington, passing directly in front of the St. Louis Art Museum. Follow Fine Arts down the hill to Government and turn left. Follow Government for about 0.7 miles to the Sigel statue, located in a circular island.

Perhaps the most impressive statue of a Civil War figure in St. Louis belongs to the least impressive soldier: Major General Franz Sigel.

Sigel was born on November 18, 1834, in the Grand Duchy of Baden. At seventeen, he entered the military academy at Karlsruhe and graduated in 1843 near the top of his class. His aptitude gained him an immediate appointment as an officer in the 4th Infantry Regiment. The young Sigel was strongly influenced by the liberal views gaining popularity across Europe, causing him to resign from the army in 1847 because of the military's "oppression of the lower classes." He entered the University of Heidelberg in 1848 to study law, but he resigned almost immediately to join Baden's revolutionary army, organizing an independent battalion at Mannheim. In July 1849, after the revolution was put down by Prussian troops, Sigel fled to Switzerland. According to Sigel's modern biographer, "his failures on the battlefield were overshadowed by his devotion to the revolutionary movement and by his unflinching courage and willingness to fight to the death."[5]

Dogged by Prussian spies, Sigel moved from Switzerland to Italy, but he was forced to continue to flee, emigrating from England to

the United States. He arrived in New York City on May 15, 1852, and there became active in the militia as an instructor in tactics while teaching at a German academy. In January 1854 Sigel married Miss Elsie Dulon in New York City.[6]

Offered a position as a professor at the then prestigious Deutsches Institut in St. Louis, Sigel moved to the city in August 1857 with his wife and two sons. By 1861 he was director of schools in St. Louis, whose population included a large German minority. In a move directed to please his constituents, Sigel attempted unsuccessfully to introduce the German language into the schools. His strongly pro-Union political stance, typical of most of the German residents of St. Louis, was evident from his occasional articles for the St. Louis German newspapers.[7]

Sigel was a popular figure among the city's Germans. He commanded the 3d Regiment, U.S. Volunteers, in the capture of Camp Jackson in May 1861 and was shortly thereafter promoted to brigadier general of volunteers. General Sigel's initial months as an American general were successful ones, but at Wilson's Creek in August 1861 his flanking column was heavily repulsed and fled the field. He recovered his military reputation with significant contributions to the Union success at the battle of Pea Ridge in northwest Arkansas early in 1862, resulting in his promotion to major general on March 22, 1862.

Transferred east to Virginia, Sigel's luck changed rapidly. In 1864 he was beaten at the battle of New Market by a small force of Confederates that included the boy soldiers

General Franz Sigel Statue, Forest Park. *Photograph by Emil Boehl, ca. 1900. Missouri Historical Society Photograph and Print Collection.*

from the Virginia Military Institute. He was removed from active field operations and on May 4, 1865, resigned his commission. Sigel lived nearly four decades after the war, dying at age seventy-seven in New York City.[8]

The Sigel statue was created by Robert Cauer (1863-1947), a German sculptor who performed a number of commissions in St. Louis. Cast at the Lauchhammer foundry in Saxony, the monument was donated by the Sigel Monument Association, Judge Leo Rassieur, president. The statue was dedicated on June 23, 1906, as a memorial to all German-Americans who fought for the Union. It was the first addition to Forest Park after the World's Fair of 1904. The inscription on the front side of the monument's base reads, "To remind future generations of the heroism of the German-American patriots of St. Louis and vicinity in the Civil War of 1861-65."[9]

Despite his military shortcomings, Sigel held enormous political influence with the immigrant German population, a group of significant political importance to Lincoln's war aims. It was the memory of the German-American role that produced the Sigel statue early in the twentieth century. Sigel is also honored in the naming of a St. Louis elementary school and towns in Illinois and Pennsylvania.[10]

Confederate Memorial. *Photograph by David Schultz, Missouri Historical Society, 1994.*

3. The Confederate Memorial

From Government in front of the Sigel statue, continue just a short distance to McKinley on the left (north) side of the street. Follow McKinley into a grove. The monument is closely guarded by trees.

George Julian Zolnay, a Hungarian who began his tenure as professor of sculpture at Washington University in 1903, won a design competition for the Confederate Memorial in 1912. The commission was sponsored by the Ladies' Confederate Monument Association, which had stipulated that the monument could show "no figure of a Confederate soldier, or object of modern warfare." Despite this concession, the idea of commemorating Confederate soldiers was unsettling for some of the city's politicians. After a stormy session of the city council, an ordinance was approved accepting the monument, provided that the Confederate Monument Association of St. Louis maintain it.[11]

The cornerstone of the monument was laid on September 23, 1914, and the monument itself was unveiled with much ceremony on December 5, 1914. "General" Bennett H. Young, commander in chief of the United Confederate Veterans, made the dedicatory address. Young was quite a celebrity, having just published a memorial volume to the Confederate cavalry entitled *Confederate Wizards of the Saddle*, in which Missourians figured prominently. As a youth, he was a trooper in John Hunt Morgan's 8th Kentucky Cavalry. First Lieutenant Young also led the Confederate raid from Canada to attack St. Albans, Vermont, the northernmost land action of the Civil War. After the war, he became a prominent attorney and was active in the affairs of Confederate veterans. Following Young's speech was a short address by Mrs. H. N. Spencer, chairwoman of the committee, and another by Seymour Stewart, commander in chief of the Sons of Confederate Veterans.[12]

The granite shaft of the Confederate Memorial is thirty-two feet tall. On the western face is a bronze relief of two women and a small boy sending a young man off to the war. Above this scene, in low relief, is the figure of an angel representing the "Spirit of the Confederacy." Below the figures is an inscription which reads, "Erected in memory of the soldiers and sailors of the Confederate States by the United Daughters of the Confederacy of St. Louis."

On the opposite side of the shaft are two inscriptions. The first was written by Dr. R. C. Cave, a St. Louis writer and lecturer. It reads as follows:

> To the memory of the soldiers and sailors of the Southern Confederacy, who fought to uphold the right declared by the pen of Jefferson and achieved by the sword of Washington. With sublime self sacrifice, they battled to preserve the independence of the states which was won from Great Britain, and to perpetuate the constitutional government which was established by the fathers. Actuated by the purest patriotism they performed deeds of prowess such as thrilled the heart of mankind with admiration. "Full in the front of war they stood," and displayed a courage so superb that it gave a new and brighter luster to the annals of valor. History contains no chronicle more illustrious than the story of their achievements; and although, worn out by ceaseless conflict and overwhelmed by numbers, they were finally forced to yield. Their glory, "on brightest pages penned by poets and by sages, shall go sounding down the ages."[13]

Following this statement is a brief quotation attributed to Robert E. Lee: "We had sacred principles to maintain and rights to defend for which we were in duty bound to do our best, even if we perished in the endeavor."

The monument was built by Charles Axtall Rosebrough at a cost of approximately twenty thousand dollars. Wilbur Tyson Trueblood and Frederick Charles Bonsack were the architects. Since its erection, the monument has been damaged by vandals, and today it is maintained with the cooperation of the Sterling Price Camp (St. Louis), Sons of Confederate Veterans.[14]

4. Francis Blair Statue

Leave the Confederate Memorial and head west. Turn right (north) immediately at Confederate, which leads back to Lindell. Turn right (east) on Lindell, heading back toward Kingshighway Boulevard. The Blair statue is in a large island on the right. Unfortunately, access to the Blair statue is limited by the lack of parking at this corner of Forest Park.

Francis P. Blair, Jr., Statue at Kingshighway and Lindell Boulevard. *Photograph by Emil Boehl, 1902. Missouri Historical Society Photograph and Print Collection.*

Francis Preston Blair, Jr., was honored with this statue for his life of service as a member of the United States House of Representatives, a major general and corps commander in the Union army, and a United States senator.

Blair arrived in St. Louis in 1842 at the age of twenty-one to practice law with his brother, Montgomery. Their father, Francis Preston Blair, Sr., was the editor of a powerful Democratic newspaper, Washington D.C.'s *Congressional Globe*, from 1830-1854 and was a close friend of Andrew Jackson. Though a slaveowner himself, the elder Blair believed the Union took precedence over sectional interests. Convinced that the Democratic Party had betrayed the principles of "Jacksonian Democracy," Blair and his sons wholeheartedly endorsed the emerging Republican Party in the late 1850s.[15]

Francis "Frank" Blair, Jr., was elected to the U.S. Congress from Missouri's First District (St. Louis) in 1856 and in 1860. Concerned about the intentions of Missouri's state leaders, Blair took an active role in recruiting the Home Guards to counter the secessionist Minute Men of St. Louis. A colonel at the time of the capture of Camp Jackson in May 1861, Blair led the 1st Regiment of U.S. Volunteers. In August 1862 he was rewarded with a promotion to brigadier general of volunteers for his efforts in successfully organizing seven regiments for the Union and, later that year, was promoted to major general. His brother, Montgomery, had earlier been rewarded for the family's support of Lincoln by appointment as postmaster general in Lincoln's cabinet.[16]

Blair's active military service began as a brigade commander in the early stages of Grant's campaign for Vicksburg. In his memoirs, Grant recalled his concern about the politician-general:

General F. P. Blair joined me at Milliken's Bend a full-fledged general, without ever having served in a lower grade. He commanded a division in the campaign. I had known Blair in Missouri, where I had voted against him in 1858 when he ran for Congress. I knew him as a frank, positive and generous man, true to his friends even to a fault, but always a leader. I dreaded his coming; I knew from experience that it was more difficult to command two generals desiring to be leaders than it was to command one army officered intelligently and with subordination. It affords me the greatest pleasure to record now my agreeable disappointment in respect to his character. There was no man braver than he, nor was there any who obeyed all orders of his superior in rank with more unquestioning alacrity. He was one man as a soldier, another as a politician.[17]

After Vicksburg, Blair served briefly as the commander of the Union XV Corps before leading the XVII Corps under Sherman in the march through Georgia. He resigned from the military in November 1865 and, after a brief experiment as a Mississippi cotton planter, returned to Missouri to enter politics. He was nominated twice for appointments by President Andrew Johnson, but he was too moderate for the Radical Republicans controlling the U.S. Senate. In 1868 he was a candidate for vice president but was unsuccessful largely because of his lenient position on restoring the former Confederate states to the Union. Missouri Democrats and liberal Republicans united in 1871 to elect Blair to fill an unexpired term in the United States Senate. Senator Blair worked to eliminate voting restrictions on former Confederate officers and officials. In failing health, he retired just two years before his death in 1875. He is buried in Bellefontaine Cemetery.[18]

The Blair monument was begun by Wellington W. Gardner in 1880. Gardner worked on the statue in the studio of Howard Kretschmar, then a teacher at Washington University. In 1881 Gardner won first prize at the Agricultural and Mechanical Exposition for his bust of President Garfield. The next year he won the competition for the Blair monument. The statue, made of bronze and standing nine feet tall, was donated by the Blair Monument Association, and the granite

pedestal, eleven feet tall, was paid for by the city. The arm gesture captured by the sculptor was praised by Blair's acquaintances as characteristic.[19]

An inscription on the front (east) side of the pedestal gives Blair's dates of birth (February 19, 1821) and death (July 8, 1875). On the west side is the following inscription:

This monument is raised to commemorate the indomitable free-soil leader of the west; the herald and standard bearer of freedom in Missouri; the creator of the first volunteer Union army in the South; the saviour of the state from secession; the patriotic citizen-soldier, who fought from the beginning to the end of the war; the magnanimous statesman, who, as soon as the war was over, breasted the torrent of proscription, to restore to citizenship the disfranchised Southern people, and finally, the incorruptible public servant.

Late in the afternoon of May 21, 1888, some fifteen thousand people assembled at the Lindell Avenue entrance of Forest Park to watch Mrs. Christine Graham, Blair's daughter, unveil the statue. A violent rainstorm caused the elaborate ceremonies to be shortened, including the cancellation of the principal oration, but at least one of the dignitaries was undaunted by the uncooperative weather, as General William T. Sherman stepped to the podium to give praise to Francis P. Blair, Jr. "I have been with Frank Blair when the thunder of artillery would make the storm which has swept over us seem as the rumbling of distant wagons," he told the crowd. "I assure you," he continued, "that he was worthy of the honor you do his memory in the heroic statue which stands before us at this moment." Sherman, who as a civilian had been a personal witness to Blair's work in St. Louis in the earliest days of the war, defined Blair's place in history when he concluded that Frank Blair "did more than any single man to hold this great central city of our Union to her faithful allegiance to the General Government, so necessary to the perpetuity of the Union."[20]

Benton Park and the Friedrich Hecker Monument

From Interstate 44, take Jefferson Avenue south one mile to its intersection with Arsenal Street. Turn left (east) on Arsenal, and Benton Park will be on the right (south). No parking is allowed on the Benton Park side of Arsenal. For the easiest access to the Hecker monument, continue on Arsenal to Lemp Street. Turn right on Lemp and then right again at the intersection with Wyoming. Follow Wyoming west to the south side of Benton Park. The Hecker monument is visible from the street.

Friedrich Hecker. *Photograph by Robert Benecke, ca. 1880. Missouri Historical Society Photograph and Print Collection.*

Many political refugees arrived in America in the late 1840s after the failed republican revolutions in central Europe, but few were as prominent as Friedrich Franz Karl Hecker.

Hecker arrived in New York City on October 4, 1848, to a welcome that he described as the greatest reception for a European since the arrival of Lafayette. As a prominent lawyer in Germany, Hecker had been a fiery and outspoken champion of the people, and he came to America determined to continue the fight for republican reforms in his native land. He moved west and settled on a farm near Belleville, Illinois, becoming a leader in the St. Louis area German community. He was an active supporter of the first presidential candidate of the Republican Party, John C. Frémont, and enthusiastically rallied German support for Abraham Lincoln's candidacy four years later.[21]

When war broke out, the fifty-year-old Hecker enlisted as a private in a Union three-month regiment in St. Louis. He was soon summoned by friends to Chicago to command the 24th Illinois Infantry, a German regiment named "the Hecker Regiment" in his honor. His tenure with the 24th Illinois was stormy. Hecker's orders dismissing undesirable officers—and potential political rivals—were appealed all the way to Secretary of War Simon Cameron before an unsatisfactory compromise was worked out in November 1861. Hecker took sick leave in protest.[22]

Another German regiment, the 82d Illinois Infantry, was mustered into service in October 1862, and Colonel Hecker was appointed to command it. After moving to the Eastern Theater of the war, the regiment was made part of Major General Carl Schurz' division, XI Corps, Army of the Potomac. On the afternoon of May 2, 1863, at Chancellorsville, Virginia, the 82d Illinois had the misfortune to be directly in the path of General Thomas J. Jackson's flank attack. Hecker grabbed the regimental colors and ordered his men forward, but Confederate fire brought him down almost immediately. After his recovery, he led a brigade in Schurz' division in the Chattanooga campaign, but he retired from military service in early 1864.[23]

Hecker returned to active participation in politics, his patriotism heightened by his combat experience. In a Fourth of July oration in Trenton, Illinois, in 1871, Hecker boldly proclaimed his view of his new fatherland: "I am the destiny of the old world—I am America, and I will plant the banner of the deliverance of humanity in every land." On a similar occasion in Stuttgart, Germany, Hecker praised the "three miracles of America" that he had seen in his lifetime: the abolition of slavery, the return of huge armies to civilian pursuits, and the decision of the victorious not to bestow medals on their generals. Hecker died on March 24, 1881, and was buried near Summerfield, Illinois.[24]

Benton Park was created by city ordinance on June 25, 1866, converting a graveyard of seventeen acres to a city park. The land had been used for burials from 1840 until 1865, at which time the bodies were removed to Arsenal Island. The park's original acreage has been slowly reduced by the encroachment of the surrounding streets. On Sunday, October 1, 1882, a crowd of fifteen thousand gathered to witness the unveiling of the Hecker monument. Dr. Emil Preetorius, editor of the *Westliche Post*, opened the ceremonies, which included orations in German and English, songs, and instrumental music. Miss Stella Hecker, a granddaughter, then unveiled the monument.

The tall obelisk of gray granite sits on the highest point in Benton Park and overlooks a small lagoon. The shaft bears a photographic image of Hecker on its north face, replacing a bronze relief done by German-American sculptor Karl Stubenrauch. A bronze oak wreath once graced the south side of the monument; an oak wreath has been engraved in its place. St. Louisan Ernst C. Jannsen was the monument's architect.[25]

On the east and west sides of the monument are the years "1848" and "1861," the dates of the two revolutions that gave meaning to the life of Friedrich Franz Karl Hecker.

Reservoir Park and the German-American Memorial

From Interstate 44, take the Grand Boulevard exit south. Reservoir Park and the German-American memorial are immediately south of the highway on the east (left) side of Grand Boulevard. The monument originally faced north but was moved in 1969 to facilitate highway redesign.

In 1913 the German-American Alliance and St. Louis citizens of German descent undertook to create a memorial to "the German spirit of enlightenment in America." To do so, they chose to honor three German-Americans associated with *Anzeiger des Westens* and *Westliche Post*, St. Louis' most influential German-language newspapers during the Civil War: Carl Daenzer, Emil Preetorius, and Carl Schurz.[26]

The Naked Truth. *Sculpture by Wilhelm Wandschneider. Photograph by Franz Linkhorst, Berlin, Germany, 1914. Missouri Historical Society Photograph and Print Collection.*

Carl Daenzer was born in the Grand Duchy of Baden in 1820 and came to America after the failed revolution of 1848-1849. After his arrival in St. Louis in the 1850s, he took a job as an associate editor of Henry Boernstein's *Anzeiger des Westens.* He left the newspaper on August 5, 1857, after a dispute with Boernstein and organized the *Westliche Post.* In the years before the Civil War, Daenzer's *Westliche Post* took an editorial stance that was strongly Republican and antislavery. Poor health forced him to give up his position in 1860, but a visit to Germany revived him, and he returned to St. Louis in 1862. The *Anzeiger des Westens* having failed during his absence, Daenzer started the *Neue Anzeiger des Westens* but soon dropped the word *Neue* (new). He remained active with the newspaper until 1898, when it was consolidated with its erstwhile competitor, the *Westliche Post.* Daenzer then returned to Germany.[27]

Emil Preetorius was born in Germany on March 15, 1827. He graduated with a doctoral degree in law from the University of Heidelberg in 1848 before becoming an active revolutionary, a decision that resulted in his emigration when the revolution failed. Dr. Preetorius settled in St. Louis in 1853, actively supported Lincoln in the 1860 election, and was elected to the Missouri legislature in 1862 as an ardent abolitionist. On November 30, 1864, he left the legislature to become part-owner and editor-in-chief of the *Westliche Post,* a position he held until his death in 1905. Over the years, Preetorius became highly esteemed in St. Louis. Among his many contributions to the city was service as president of the Missouri Historical Society in 1892-1893.[28]

Carl Schurz was already a national celebrity when he moved from Detroit to St. Louis in 1867 to become editor and part-owner of the *Westliche Post.* Born in Prussia on March 2, 1829, Schurz, like Daenzer and Preetorius, fled his homeland because of his involvement in the 1848-1849 revolution. He arrived in New York in 1852 and first came to St. Louis in 1854, visiting fellow revolutionary Friedrich Hecker on his farm near Belleville, Illinois. Liking the Midwest, the Schurz family settled in Watertown, Wisconsin, where Schurz began a newspaper. He was a strong supporter of Frémont's Republican candidacy in 1856, and his vocal support gained him a position as chairman of the state delegation to the Republican National Convention. Schurz was then recruited to the party's national committee with the expectation that he would turn out the "foreign" vote.[29]

After Lincoln's election, Schurz was appointed "minister plenipotentiary and envoy extraordinary" to Spain. The president rewarded Schurz' relentless requests for military service once war broke out by granting him the rank of brigadier general in March 1862. Despite his very limited prior military experience and his lackluster performance in the Union army, Schurz was promoted to major general on March 17, 1863. In the battles at Chancellorsville and Gettysburg, his division was "thrown into headlong rout," and the German-American units it contained became the objects of scorn of the Army of the Potomac. However, Schurz actively campaigned for Lincoln in the election of 1864, and the success of his political efforts overcame the shortcomings of his military ones. After his arrival in St. Louis in 1867, Schurz was elected to the United States Senate (1869-1875), served as secretary of the interior (1876-1880), and exercised influence in every presidential election until 1904. Daenzer, Preetorius, and Schurz all died within a year of each other; Schurz died last on May 14, 1906.[30]

In 1913 a panel awarded the commission for the German-American memorial to German sculptor Wilhelm Wandschneider. Wandschneider's design, titled *The Naked Truth,* created a furor: its single bronze female figure was nude. Adolphus Busch, a major contributor, threatened to withdraw his support from the controversial memorial but was dissuaded by the charm of Wandschneider and his wife. Every German-American group in the city participated in the monument's dedication in 1914, just weeks before the Kaiser's army went to war in Europe. *The Naked Truth* safely survived the Great War, despite urging by the Women's Christian Temperance Union that it be melted down and "utilized for munition purposes."[31]

Bellefontaine Cemetery

From Interstate 70 in north St. Louis, take the West Florissant exit north approximately 0.7 miles to Bellefontaine Cemetery at 4947 West Florissant. Visiting hours are from 8:00 A.M. to 5:00 P.M. daily, including Sundays and holidays. The cemetery office is open Monday through Friday from 8:00 A.M. until 4:30 P.M. For information, call 314-381-0750.

Opposite the cemetery office is a small building housing waiting rooms and restrooms. It is open when the cemetery office is open, and it is sometimes used by the friends of the deceased during funerals. Please enter the building quietly.

It would almost be possible to retell the history of the Civil War in Missouri simply by moving from gravesite to gravesite within Bellefontaine Cemetery. Included among the many citizens of Civil War importance buried there are three governors of Missouri, four mayors of St. Louis, the highest ranking Confederate general buried in St. Louis, one member of President Lincoln's cabinet, three Confederate congressmen, and more Civil War Medal of Honor winners than are buried at any other location in St. Louis.

Bellefontaine Cemetery was established in 1849 after a cholera epidemic made clear the need for additional cemetery capacity. The cemetery's trustees recruited Almerin Hotchkiss, then superintendent of Greenwood Cemetery in Brooklyn, to design the cemetery. Hotchkiss arrived in St. Louis in September 1849. By the next May, the cemetery was ready. Hotchkiss served as superintendent for the next forty-six years.

Bellefontaine Cemetery, once a rural cemetery, today lies surrounded by urban development. When inside the cemetery, however, the visitor will notice how effectively Hotchkiss' landscaping removes the influence of the surrounding city.

The burial places of seventy-one individuals are included in the tour of Bellefontaine Cemetery that follows; the names are listed in alphabetical order in the accompanying table to ease identification of individual graves.

1. Robert Julius Rombauer
Lieutenant Colonel, U.S.A.
Block 24, Lot 2524

Rombauer was born in Munkacs, Hungary, in 1830. In 1848 he suspended his studies in Vienna to join the Hungarian revolution as an artillery officer. He was taken prisoner, and on his release he fled to America with his mother and brothers. On May 2, 1857, by then established in St. Louis, Rombauer married Countess Dembinsky, the Hungarian widow of a Polish nobleman who had died in St. Louis several years earlier. The Rombauers were married for sixty-six years.

When the Civil War broke out, Rombauer became lieutenant colonel of the 1st Regiment, United States Reserve Corps, and commanded its first battalion at Camp Jackson on May 10, 1861. His brother Roderick led Company B of the same regiment.

After the war, Rombauer was involved in railroading, but he was also active in civic affairs, serving as president of the St. Louis Public Library, president of the board of assessors, and as a member of the board of education. In 1909 he authored *The Union Cause in St. Louis in 1861*, an important account of the early days of the Civil War in Missouri. Rombauer died on September 25, 1925, in his ninety-sixth year.[32]

2. Minor Meriwether
Lieutenant Colonel, C.S.A.
Block 32, Lot 3897

Born in Christian County, Kentucky, on January 15, 1827, Meriwether was educated as an engineer at the University of Tennessee. In the years before the Civil War, he served as chief engineer of river levees in western Tennessee.

Meriwether entered Confederate service in October 1861. His first assignment was to aid in the construction of the fortifications at Columbus, Kentucky, Island Number 10, and Fort Pillow, Tennessee. Subsequently he served on the staff of General Sterling Price in northern Mississippi.

When Price returned to the west side of the Mississippi River, Meriwether joined the staff of General John Pemberton as chief engineer and supervised the construction of several of the forts in the defenses of Vicksburg. After Vicksburg's fall, he was assigned to the task of maintaining the railroads in the Deep South. In 1864 Meriwether moved to the staff of General Joseph E. Johnston in Georgia and then to the staff of General Richard Taylor. After the war, Meriwether returned to Memphis and became a business associate of former cavalryman Nathan Bedford Forrest. Meriwether was at Forrest's bedside on October 29, 1877, and recorded the famous general's last command: "Call my wife." In 1883, he moved to St. Louis where he practiced law until his death on June 6, 1910.[33]

Stops in Tour of Bellefontaine Cemetery
(In alphabetical order)

Name	Tour No.	Name	Tour No.
Almstedt, Colonel Henry	66	MacDonald, Colonel Emmett	22
Anderson, John Richard	18	McDowell, Dr. Joseph Nash	50
Bates, Edward	13	McGunnegle, Lieutenant Wilson	63
Blair, Major General Francis P., Jr.	71	McNeil, Brevet Major General John	3
Blodgett, Colonel Wells Howard	55	McPheeters, Major William M., M.D.	67
Bonneville, Brevet Brigadier General Benjamin L. E.	33	Meriwether, Lieutenant Colonel Minor	2
		Miller, Brevet Brigadier General Madison	70
Brown, Brevet Brigadier General Philip Perry, Jr.	69	Noble, Brevet Brigadier General John Willock	43
Brownell, First Lieutenant Francis E.	58	O'Brien, Lieutenant Henry D.	45
Buell, Major General Don Carlos	20	Parsons, Brevet Major General Lewis Baldwin	68
Cabell, Major Edward Carrington	14		
Campbell, Captain Given	25	Peckham, Colonel James	17
Carter, Major Frank	53	Pesch, Private Joseph	42
Cavender, Brevet Brigadier General John Smith	26	Pitzman, Major Julius	41
		Polk, Colonel Trusten	51
Childs, Sergeant William Ward	40	Pope, Major General John	32
Clark, Colonel Meriwether Lewis	10	Price, Brigadier General Edwin E.	29
Conn, Captain Luther	12	Price, Major General Sterling	30
Cunningham, Major Edward, Jr.	48	Rainwater, Major Charles Cicero	6
Eads, James Buchanan	61	Rombauer, Lieutenant Colonel Robert Julius	1
Edwards, Brigadier General Albert Gallatin	60	Scott, John Guier	15
Farrar, Brevet Brigadier General Bernard Gains	24	Sessinghaus, Private Gustavus	19
		Simpson, Brigadier General Samuel Parsons	34
Field, Roswell Martin	37		
Filley, Chauncey I.	44	Smith, Major General Andrew Jackson	27
Filley, Oliver Dwight	21		
Fletcher, Brevet Brigadier General Thomas Clement	49	Snead, Colonel Thomas Lowndes	52
		Stevenson, Brevet Major General John Dunlap	16
Fout, First Lieutenant Frederick W.	7		
Freeman, Thomas W.	59	Stewart, Lieutenant Alphonso Chase	56
Gamble, Hamilton Rowan	28	Stewart, Lieutenant General Alexander Peter	57
Garland, Colonel Hugh A.	54		
Gibson, Sir Charles	11	Stifel, Colonel Charles G.	39
Guerin, Private Fitz W.	47	Thomas, James S.	38
Hammel, Sergeant Henry A.	5	Vest, Senator George Graham	46
Hart, Brevet Brigadier General Orson Henry	31	Wade, Colonel William	35
		Wherry, Brevet Brigadier William Mackey	64
Hitchcock, Major Henry	65		
Holman, Brevet Brigadier General John Henry	8	Wimer, Colonel John M.	36
		Wood, Brevet Brigadier General William D.	23
Hutchinson, Colonel Robert Randolph	9		
McCulloch, Captain Robert	4	Yeatman, James E.	62

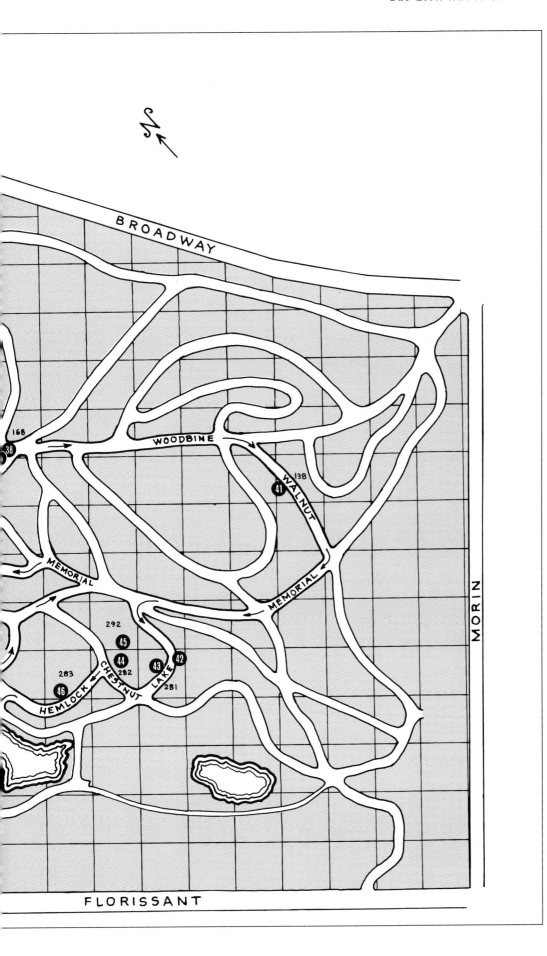

Bellefontaine
Cemetery. *Map by Pat
Baer, 1994.*

3. John McNeil
Brevet Major General, U.S.A.
Block 35, Lot 1103

McNeil's Civil War service was performed entirely within Missouri. A native of Nova Scotia (born February 14, 1813), he moved to St. Louis in 1840 to engage in the fur trade. He served in the Missouri legislature in 1844-1845. From 1855 to the outbreak of war, he was president of the Pacific Insurance Company in St. Louis.

McNeil became colonel of the 3d Regiment, United States Reserve Corps, in St. Louis in May 1861 and was involved in the capture of Camp Jackson. He also gained a small victory with his regiment at Fulton, Missouri, on July 17, 1861, shortly before the troops' ninety-day enlistments expired. In June 1862 he became colonel of the 2d Missouri State Militia Cavalry and was promoted to brigadier general of U.S. Volunteers in November. His service took him to all parts of the state, where he operated against pro-Southern guerrillas. McNeil's alleged brutality to civilians of Southern sympathies and his lack of mercy for captured opponents earned him hatred as a "butcher." On October 18, 1862, McNeil ordered ten prisoners held at Palmyra, Missouri, shot in retaliation for the disappearance, and presumed murder, of a Union man. The political repercussions of the "Palmyra Massacre" dogged McNeil for the next two decades.

At the battle of Westport, Missouri, in 1864, McNeil was relieved of command by General Alfred Pleasonton for failure to attack when ordered. Despite this setback, McNeil commanded the District of Central Missouri until April 12, 1865, at which time he resigned and was promoted to the rank of brevet major general.

After the war McNeil was twice clerk of the criminal court of St. Louis County and county sheriff. He held a series of Federal positions including superintendent of the St. Louis branch post office. He died in St. Louis on June 8, 1891.[34]

4. Robert McCulloch
Captain, C.S.A.
Block 36, Lot 3278

Soon after his birth in Osceola, Missouri, on September 15, 1841, both McCulloch's parents died, and he was sent to Rockbridge County, Virginia, to be raised by relatives. McCulloch was a cadet at Virginia Military Institute until April 9, 1861, when he left to join the Confederate army. With time he rose in rank to become captain of Company B, 18th Virginia Infantry.

McCulloch saw combat at First Manassas, the Seven Days' battles, Second Manassas, and Gettysburg, where he was wounded twice and participated in Pickett's Charge on July 3, 1863. Captured after the battle, he was later exchanged and returned to active duty until the end of the war.

In 1868 McCulloch married Miss Emma Paxton of Rockbridge County. The next year the couple moved to St. Louis, where McCulloch had found employment with the Bellefontaine Railway Company, a career he pursued until 1904. McCulloch attended the fiftieth anniversary reunion at Gettysburg in 1913 but died the next year on September 26, 1914.[35]

5. Henry A. Hammel
Sergeant, U.S.A.
Medal of Honor
Block 191, Lot 3766 (no marker)

With Privates Guerin and Pesch (both also buried in Bellefontaine Cemetery), Sergeant Hammel of Company A, 1st Missouri Light Artillery, was awarded the Medal of Honor for bravery demonstrated on April 28-29, 1863, while serving the guns of the steamer USS *Cheeseman*. Hammel's Medal of Honor was awarded on March 10, 1896.[36]

6. Charles Cicero Rainwater
Major, C.S.A.
Block 191, Lot 4517

Rainwater was born in Ray County, Missouri, on April 6, 1838. He graduated from Central College in Fayetteville in 1858 and married Miss Sarah H. Fowler of Benton County, Missouri.

Rainwater joined the Missouri State Guard as a private in April 1861, and he was promoted through the ranks from sergeant to captain. In June 1862 he was serving as captain, Company E, 6th Missouri Infantry. He was wounded in the head in July 1863 at Vicksburg and more severely wounded in the hip at Atlanta in July 1864, forcing him from active service. After the war Rainwater came to St. Louis to engage in the mercantile business, a career he pursued until his death on November 10, 1902. In 1891 Rainwater had the honor of leading the Confederate veterans who took part in the funeral procession of General William T. Sherman.[37]

7. Frederick W. Fout
1st Lieutenant, U.S.A.
Medal of Honor
Block 186, Lot X, Grave 72

A native of Germany, Fout performed his Civil War service with the 15th Battery,

Indiana Light Artillery, entering the service at Indianapolis. Near Harpers Ferry, (West) Virginia, on September 15, 1862, Fout voluntarily gathered the men of the battery together, remanned the guns (which had been ordered abandoned by an officer), opened fire on the enemy, and kept it up until after the surrender of his command. For this action Fout was awarded the Medal of Honor on November 2, 1896.[38]

8. John Henry Holman
Brevet Brigadier General, U.S.A.
Block 199, Lot Z, Grave 65

Born October 27, 1824, in North Livermore, Maine, John Henry Holman began his Civil War service as a second lieutenant in the 4th Regiment, U.S. Reserve Corps, one of the several regiments called into service in St. Louis in May 1861 by Blair and Lyon. He later became lieutenant colonel, 26th Missouri Infantry, and colonel, 1st Infantry Regiment, United States Colored Troops. The 1st Regiment was organized in Washington, D.C., in May and June 1863. It served in combat with the Army of the James in 1864 and in the Department of North Carolina in 1865.

On March 13, 1865, Holman was promoted to brevet brigadier general for "gallant and meritorious service." After the war he pursued his occupation as architect and master builder until his death on June 26, 1883, in St. Louis.[39]

9. Robert Randolph Hutchinson
Colonel, C.S.A.
Blocks 219/220, Lot 3163

Hutchinson was born in Petersburg, Virginia, on August 28, 1837, and was brought to St. Louis by his family when he was four. After receiving his early education in St. Louis, he graduated from the University of Virginia and the University of Berlin, Germany. Hutchinson was admitted to the Missouri bar in 1861.

At Camp Jackson in May 1861, Hutchinson was serving as first lieutenant in Company G of the 2d Regiment, Missouri Volunteer Militia. In June 1861 he joined the 1st Missouri Infantry, C.S.A., then organizing at Memphis, Tennessee, as Colonel John Bowen's assistant adjutant general. Hutchinson held this position until Bowen's death in July 1863. He then transferred to the Army of Northern Virginia where he took a similar position under General Robert Rodes. Hutchinson fought in all the army's battles until his capture at the battle of Cedar Creek. He remained a prisoner until June 1865.

Hutchinson married Miss Mary Mitchell, a St. Louisan, soon after his release. Prohibited

Meriwether Lewis Clark. *Photograph, ca. 1870. Missouri Historical Society Photograph and Print Collection.*

from serving as a lawyer in Missouri by the postwar administration, Hutchinson started a new career as a banker, working his way from cashier to president of the Mechanics Bank of St. Louis. He died in St. Louis on November 21, 1910.[40]

10. Meriwether Lewis Clark
Colonel, C.S.A.
Block 224, Lot 780

Meriwether Lewis Clark was the son of William Clark of the Lewis and Clark expedition. He was born in St. Louis on January 10, 1809. Graduating from the United States Military Academy in 1830, he served in the Blackhawk War and against the Sac Indians in 1832. Clark then left the service to pursue a career as an architect and engineer in St. Louis. He returned to military service as a Missouri volunteer during the Mexican War and as a major commanded a battery of Missouri artillery at the battle of Sacramento. After the war he was appointed surveyor-general for Missouri. In 1854 Clark commanded a military force that quelled riots in St. Louis.

In 1861 Clark was appointed brigadier general for the Ninth Division of the pro-Confederate Missouri State Guard, which included the counties of Washington, Franklin, Jefferson, and Crawford. In 1862 he served as the Guard's chief of artillery, and after transfer to the Confederate service he continued in this role for Generals Sterling Price and Earl Van Dorn. In the summer of 1864, Clark was transferred to the Ordnance Department at Richmond. In November he was given a command in the Army of Northern Virginia, a post he held until his capture at Amelia Court House on April 5, 1865.

After the war Clark was a faculty member of the Kentucky Military Institute until being appointed surveyor-general for the state of Missouri. He died in Frankfort, Kentucky, on October 28, 1881.[41]

11. Sir Charles Gibson
Solicitor of the Court of Claims, U.S.A.
Block 228, Lot 2299

Charles Gibson, born in Virginia in 1825, moved to St. Louis with his parents in 1836. Ten years later, he was admitted to the bar. While studying law, he also learned French, German, and Latin, a course of action that paid him invaluable dividends during his career. His career also benefited by his stature as a law partner and protégé of Edward Bates and as the husband of the niece of Hamilton Gamble, future governor of Missouri.

When Edward Bates became attorney general in President Lincoln's cabinet in 1861, he obtained an appointment for Gibson as solicitor of the court of claims. Gibson's family, despite its poverty, had at one time owned slaves, so he was sensitive to the interests of pro-Union slaveholders. In Washington, he was often a spokesman for conciliatory policies toward Missouri. When the Lincoln administration adopted what Gibson considered to be radical antislavery positions, he resigned and returned to St. Louis in 1864.

In later life, Gibson was an active, public-spirited citizen. His many interests included the creation of the Laclede Gas Company and the establishment of Forest Park. In the 1880s Gibson was knighted by the emperors of both Germany and Austria-Hungary for his success in representing their interests in St. Louis lawsuits. Sir Charles Gibson died in St. Louis on October 28, 1899.[42]

12. Luther Conn
Captain, C.S.A.
Block 228, Lot 2299

Born in Burlington, Kentucky, on March 14, 1842, Conn was educated at Carrolton, Kentucky, under future Confederate general John Magruder. When war came, Conn enlisted in the 3d Kentucky Cavalry, C.S.A., and was soon commissioned captain. While serving with General John Morgan on his raid through Ohio and Indiana, Conn was captured and imprisoned at Johnson's Island, Allegheny City, Point Lookout, Fort McHenry, and Fort Delaware until he was exchanged in the fall of 1864. Conn's last military assignment was as escort for President Jefferson Davis and other Confederate officials as they fled from Richmond to Georgia.

After the war Conn returned to Kentucky to resume farming, but he later moved to Arkansas to take up cotton planting. He moved to St. Louis in 1867 and entered the real estate business. One of the properties that he acquired over the years was Grant's White Haven farm, where he would spend his retirement raising horses. Conn married Miss Louise Gibson in 1871 while leading an active business life in the city. He was also involved in the development of Forest Park. Conn died in St. Louis on October 11, 1922.[43]

13. Edward Bates
Attorney General, U.S.A.
Block 223, Lot 1315

Edward Bates was born September 4, 1793, in Goochland County, Virginia, along the James River. In 1814 he moved to St. Louis to study law at the invitation of his brother Frederick, who was serving as secretary of the Territory of Missouri. Bates studied law in the office of Rufus Easton and in the winter of 1816-1817 was admitted to the bar. When the state government was organized in 1820, he was appointed Missouri's first attorney general.

In 1823 Bates married Julia D. Coalter. One of Julia's sisters married Hamilton R. Gamble. In the next fifteen years, Bates served in the Missouri House of Representatives, the U.S. House of Representatives, and the Missouri Senate. In 1856 he returned to private practice.

Though Bates had owned slaves until 1844, he gradually became prominent as an antislavery man. By 1859 he was considered by some to be the best candidate of the Republican Party for the presidential election of 1860. After Lincoln's election, Bates accepted the president's offer to become attorney general of the United States and thus became the first cabinet officer from west of the Mississippi River and, at age sixty-eight, the oldest member of Lincoln's cabinet.

As the war progressed, President Lincoln relied more and more on Bates to offset the Radical Republican views in his cabinet. Failing to receive Lincoln's nomination for the position of chief justice of the Supreme Court when the position opened in October 1864,

Bates resigned and returned to St. Louis, where he died on March 25, 1869. A monument to his memory was erected in Forest Park in 1876.[44]

14. Edward Carrington Cabell
Major, C.S.A.
Block 223, Lot 2148

Cabell was born in Richmond on February 5, 1816, into a family whose Virginia roots dated from 1723. He received his education at Washington College (now Washington and Lee University) and at the University of Virginia, completing courses in both civil engineering and law. In 1837 he moved from Virginia to Florida and in 1846 was elected to represent that state in the United States Congress, serving in this capacity until 1853. In 1850 he married Anna Maria Wilcox of Columbia, Missouri, and in 1860 became a member of the St. Louis bar.

During the Civil War, Cabell supported the cause of the Confederacy, and from 1862 to 1865 he served on the staffs of Generals Sterling Price and E. Kirby Smith. After the war he continued the practice of law in St. Louis, a career interrupted by one term in the Missouri Senate beginning in 1878. Cabell died in St. Louis on February 28, 1896.[45]

15. John Guier Scott
Congressman, U.S.A.
Block 219/223, Lot 1636

Born in Philadelphia on December 26, 1819, Scott studied engineering at Bethlehem Academy, Pennsylvania, before moving to Missouri in 1842 to work in the mining and iron business.

In 1862 Scott was elected to the United States Congress to fill a vacancy and served from December 7, 1863, to March 3, 1865. After the war he returned to St. Louis and engaged in the pharmaceutical business before resuming his career in mining in Crawford County, Missouri. In 1870 he returned to St. Louis, and ten years later he moved to east Tennessee. He died at Oliver Springs, Roane County, Tennessee, on May 16, 1892, and was buried in St. Louis.[46]

16. John Dunlap Stevenson
Brevet Major General, U.S.A.
Block 90, Lot 2115

John Stevenson was born in Staunton, Virginia, on June 8, 1821. After attending South Carolina College he studied law and was admitted to the Virginia bar. Shortly thereafter he moved to Missouri. In 1846 he organized a battalion of the 1st Missouri Mounted Volunteers for service in the Mexican War, serving with Stephen Kearny's command in the invasion of New Mexico. He returned to St. Louis after the Mexican War and served several terms in the state legislature and one term as president of the state senate before the Civil War.

On June 1, 1861, Stevenson became colonel of the 7th Missouri Infantry, U.S.A. At the battle of Corinth, Mississippi, he commanded a brigade under General James B. McPherson. Promoted to brigadier general on March 13, 1863, to rank from November 29, 1862, Stevenson commanded a brigade in Logan's division, XVII Corps, during the Vicksburg campaign.

At the beginning of the campaign for Atlanta, Stevenson and his command were assigned to guard Decatur, Alabama, and the rail lines. Dissatisfied with this post, he resigned in April 1864. In August he was recalled to duty to command the District of Harpers Ferry, West Virginia, where he remained until the war's end, receiving a promotion to brevet major general of volunteers. Stevenson remained in the military service until he requested release on December 31, 1870, at which time he returned to St. Louis to resume his law practice. He died in the city on January 22, 1897.[47]

17. James Peckham
Colonel, U.S.A.
Block 107, Lot 1540

Born in New York in 1830, Peckham came to St. Louis in 1859. He rapidly became a follower of Unionist Frank Blair. At the outbreak of the Civil War, Peckham joined the Union army and served as lieutenant colonel in the 11th Missouri Infantry and as colonel of the 29th Missouri Infantry.

Peckham's most important contribution was his publication of one of the first book-length accounts of the war in Missouri, *General Nathaniel Lyon and Missouri in 1861*, published in New York in 1866. Peckham died at Hot Springs, Arkansas, in 1869.[48]

18. John Richard Anderson
Baptist minister
Block 116, Lot 410 (The Baptist Lot)

Anderson was born in Shawneetown, Illinois, in 1818. He lived as an indentured servant until he gained his freedom in 1830. In St. Louis he worked as a newspaper carrier, learning to read while he did his work. By 1837 he was working for Elijah Lovejoy as a typesetter on the antislavery *Alton Observer* and was an unwilling witness to Lovejoy's murder by a proslavery mob. After Lovejoy's death he returned to St. Louis to become the pastor of the Second African Baptist Church. Under his leadership for the next twenty-five years, the church grew to include one thousand members.

Harriett Scott, wife of Dred Scott, was a member of Reverend Anderson's church. Historians speculate that it was Anderson who brought the case of Dred and Harriett Scott to the attention of Francis Butler Murdoch, formerly the Alton prosecutor of Lovejoy's murderers. It was Murdoch who filed the first papers on behalf of Dred Scott on April 6, 1846.

When Reverend Anderson died on May 20, 1863, his prominence in St. Louis was so great that the *Missouri Democrat* carried notice of his death, unusual recognition for a black minister. His funeral, reportedly the largest in the city since the death of Senator Thomas Hart Benton, was conducted by Reverend Galusha Anderson of the Second Baptist Church. Anderson lauded his black counterpart for his "modest, yet industrious and zealous course, marked by intelligence and prudence."[49]

19. Gustavus Sessinghaus
Private, Congressman, U.S.A.
Block 116, Lot 1886

Gustavus "Gustave" Sessinghaus was born near Cologne, Germany, on November 8, 1838. With his father and two of his four brothers, Carl and William, Sessinghaus emigrated to the United States and St. Louis in 1854. Here his father continued in his trade as a miller, establishing the 4 S (for "four Sessinghauses") flour mills that won gold medals at the Chicago World's Fair of 1893 and the St. Louis World's Fair of 1903-1904.

Like most of the German immigrants in St. Louis, the Sessinghaus family was strongly pro-Union. In May 1861, Gustave and his two older brothers, William and Theodore (who arrived in St. Louis in 1856), took their places in the 5th Regiment, U.S. Reserve Corps. After the expiration of his ninety-day enlistment, Gustave was exempted from military service because his work at the flour mills was determined to be essential to the war effort.

In later life, Sessinghaus was active in local political affairs and was elected vice president of the St. Louis school board. In 1883 he was elected to the U.S. House of Representatives as a Republican from the Third Congressional District. He died in St. Louis on November 16, 1887.[50]

20. Don Carlos Buell
Major General, U.S.A.
Block 114, Lot 77

Born on March 23, 1818, in Lowell, Ohio, Buell was educated at the United States Military Academy, graduating in the class of 1841, a class that contributed twenty general officers to the Civil War. Infantry service in garrison, on the frontier, and in the Mexican War followed. Shortly after the outbreak of the Civil War, Buell was commissioned a brigadier general of United States Volunteers. After assisting General George McClellan in the initial organization of the Army of the Potomac, Buell was sent west to command the Army of the Ohio, and his troops participated in the advance that led to the capture of Nashville, Tennessee, in February 1862. On April 6-7, 1862, his arrival at the battle of Shiloh helped turn back the Confederate assault, preventing an almost certain defeat of the Federal forces.

Promoted to major general, Buell moved into Kentucky late in 1862 to oppose the invasion of Confederates Braxton Bragg and Edmund Kirby Smith. On October 8 he commanded the Federal troops at the indecisive battle of Perryville. Bragg retreated but Buell was slow to follow and was relieved of command on October 24. After more than a year of waiting for orders, Buell was mustered out of volunteer service in May 1864. He resigned his commission in the Regular Army the next month.

Although recommended by U. S. Grant for restoration to duty, Buell was not recommissioned and retired to a civilian career. His Southern-born wife and his friendship with General McClellan added to the perception that he was unfriendly to the Republican administration. Buell died at his home near Paradise, Kentucky, on November 19, 1898.

Buell was the second husband of Mrs. Margaret Hunter Mason. Mrs. Mason's first husband, Brevet Brigadier General Richard B. Mason, had been the first military and civil governor of San Francisco. That city's Fort Mason is named for him. He died at Jefferson Barracks, St. Louis, in the cholera epidemic of 1849 and was buried in Bellefontaine Cemetery. When Mrs. Buell died in 1881, she was buried adjacent to her first husband, General Mason. When General Buell died, he was buried next to his wife.[51]

21. Oliver Dwight Filley
Mayor, St. Louis, 1858-1861
Block 120, Lot 3

Oliver Filley was born in Bloomfield, Connecticut, on May 23, 1806. In 1833 he moved to St. Louis and soon went into partnership with his brother, Chauncey, in the stove manufacturing business. In 1835 Filley married Chloe Velina Brown of Bloomfield. They had three sons and four daughters.

A close friend of Thomas Hart Benton, Filley became a leader in the embryonic Republican Party in 1856. He was elected mayor of St. Louis in 1858 for the usual one-year term and was reelected for a two-year term under the new city charter of 1859.

Filley was the first of four St. Louis mayors during the Civil War years. In 1861 he headed a movement for arousing and consolidating Union sentiment and acted as chairman of the Committee of Public Safety. After his public service, Filley was a successful merchant until his death on August 21, 1881, in Hampton, New Hampshire.[52]

22. Emmett MacDonald
Colonel, C.S.A.
Block 91, Lot 925

Born in Steubenville, Ohio, in 1837, MacDonald had arrived in St. Louis with his parents by the 1850s. In 1861, serving with the Missouri militia, he was captured at Camp Jackson. He later joined the pro-Confederate Missouri State Guard and fought against General Lyon's Union forces at Wilson's Creek. After the battle, he defended Lyon's corpse from Southern soldiers intent on mutilating it; he safely delivered the body to Federal authorities in Springfield.

MacDonald commanded a Missouri artillery battery at the battles of Lexington and Pea Ridge. In mid-1862, MacDonald raised a regiment of cavalry in Arkansas and was appointed colonel. The unit later served as part of General John Marmaduke's command and was involved in his raid into southwest Missouri in early 1863. On January 11, in a confusing "hit and run" battle near Springfield, MacDonald was killed by Federal artillery fire. He was first buried at Wesleyan Cemetery in St. Louis but was reinterred at Bellefontaine Cemetery on February 8, 1865.[53]

23. William D. Wood
Brevet Brigadier General, U.S.A.
Block 83, Lot 52

Born December 24, 1822, Wood served first as colonel and aide to Missouri's governor Hamilton Gamble and then as colonel, 11th Missouri Cavalry. In 1862-1863, Wood served as acting adjutant general for Missouri. Breveted to brigadier general on March 13, 1865, he died in St. Louis on February 2, 1867.[54]

24. Bernard Gains Farrar
Brevet Brigadier General, U.S.A.
Block 102, Lot 580

Born August 5, 1831, in St. Louis, Farrar was educated at Norwich University (Vermont) and the University of Virginia. His initial Civil War experience included service as major and aide to General Nathaniel Lyon and as lieutenant colonel and aide to General Henry Halleck. Farrar was then promoted to colonel to command the 30th Missouri Infantry, but he served with the regiment only a few weeks before being assigned to duty in St. Louis dealing with issues relating to escaped slaves. He rejoined the field army in time to lead a brigade in the Vicksburg campaign. He then helped organize a black regiment, which ultimately became the 6th U.S. Colored Heavy Artillery. He was breveted brigadier general on March 9, 1865, but resigned from the service two months later. Farrar died in St. Louis on June 6, 1916.[55]

25. Given Campbell
Captain, C.S.A.
Block 112, Lot 56

The son of James and Mary Given Campbell, Given Campbell was born on December 1, 1835. After his education at Salem, Kentucky, and at the University of Virginia law school, Campbell moved to St. Louis to study law under Charles Drake.

In February 1861 Campbell joined the Missouri Volunteer Militia and as captain led Company G of the 2d Regiment (Bowen's regiment) in General Frost's command. He was among those captured on May 10, 1861, when General Lyon seized the militia at Camp Jackson. After his release, Campbell joined the 2d Kentucky Cavalry (Morgan's) and then the 9th Kentucky Cavalry.

As the Confederacy collapsed after the surrender of Lee's army at Appomattox, Captain Campbell commanded a ten-man escort for President Davis as he fled south. Davis and his escort were captured at Irwinsville, Georgia, on May 10, 1865, four years to the day after Campbell's capture at Camp Jackson.

After the war Campbell returned to St. Louis but then moved to New Orleans to avoid the radicals in Missouri. He returned to St. Louis in 1873 to practice law and in 1878 served on the city council. Campbell died in St. Louis on November 20, 1906.[56]

Hamilton Gamble.
*Carte de visite
photograph by J. A.
Scholten, 1863.
Missouri Historical
Society Photograph and
Print Collection.*

26. John Smith Cavender
Brevet Brigadier General, U.S.A.
Block 112, Lot 7

Cavender was born on March 11, 1824, in Franklin, New Hampshire. He served first as captain, 1st Missouri Infantry, then major, 1st Missouri Light Artillery, and finally as colonel, 29th Missouri Infantry. On March 13, 1865, he was promoted to brevet brigadier general for "gallant and meritorious service at Donelson and Shiloh." Cavender died in St. Louis on February 23, 1886.[57]

27. Andrew Jackson Smith
Major General, U.S.A.
Block 104, Lot 11

A modern historian has called A. J. Smith "one of the most competent division and corps commanders" of the Civil War.

Born in Pennsylvania in 1815, Smith graduated from the United States Military Academy in 1838 and was commissioned in the 1st Dragoons. For the next twenty-three years, he served with the 1st Dragoons throughout the west.

On November 3, 1861, Smith resigned his colonelcy of the 2d California Cavalry to become chief of cavalry under General Halleck. On March 30, 1862, he was made a brigadier general of volunteers and was promoted to major general in May 1864.

He commanded one of Sherman's divisions at Chickasaw Bayou in December 1862 and a division of the XIII Corps at the battle of Arkansas Post the following month. He served in the Red River campaign, in Tennessee and Mississippi against General Nathan Bedford Forrest, in Missouri, and returned to Tennessee to take part in the battle of Nashville in December 1864. He then commanded the XVI Corps against Mobile. In 1866, with the postwar reductions in the army, he resumed his Regular Army rank of colonel and commanded the 7th United States Cavalry.

In 1869 Smith resigned from the army and moved to St. Louis, his wife's home, to take an appointment from President Grant as postmaster. He served as the city's auditor from 1877 to 1889 and commanded a brigade of Missouri militia during the strikes of 1877. He died in St. Louis on January 30, 1897.[58]

28. Hamilton Rowan Gamble
Governor, Missouri
Block 96, Lot 874

Born in 1798 in Winchester, Virginia, Gamble was educated at Hampden-Sidney College in Virginia. In 1818 he moved to St. Louis to join his older brother, Archibald, to practice law and in 1824 was appointed secretary of state of Missouri. Two years later he returned to private practice, this time in partnership with Edward Bates, his brother-in-law. Gamble's reputation in his profession grew steadily and in 1851 resulted in his election to the Missouri Supreme Court. His two fellow judges promptly elected him president, as the chief justice was then called. Gamble's most famous opinion while on Missouri's highest court was his dissent in the Dred Scott case. He was the only judge to favor granting Scott his freedom from slavery.

Ill health caused Gamble's retirement from the court in late 1854. He returned to private practice but kept a much reduced schedule for the next three years. In 1858 he and his family moved to Norristown, Pennsylvania, where he began his well-deserved retirement.

Gamble continued to follow events in Missouri. He returned to St. Louis in early 1861 to participate in the state convention considering secession, determined to encourage Missouri to remain in the Union. At the convention, Gamble urged that a committee be formed to prepare a report on the relationship of Missouri and the Union. The committee found no cause for the state to secede, and Gamble, who drafted the report, successfully guided it through the ten days of intense debate that followed. In July 1861, after Missouri's Southern-sympathizing governor, lieutenant governor, and secretary of state "abdicated" their positions, the Missouri legislature elected Gamble governor. Despite reservations about his health, Gamble accepted the position.

Gamble's administration was a turbulent one. The machinery of state government, from the treasury to the militia, had all but disappeared. Generals sent from Washington, D.C., had their own ideas about how affairs in the state should be run. The border with Kansas was often a battleground, and guerrillas roamed large areas of the state. The most difficult question Gamble faced was slavery. Not until June 1863 did he succeed in gaining approval for the gradual emancipation of Missouri's slaves.

On December 17, 1863, Gamble slipped and fell on the steps of the State Capitol and reinjured an arm severely fractured in a railroad accident a few months earlier. He died of pneumonia in St. Louis on January 31, 1864.[59]

29. Edwin W. Price
Brigadier General
Missouri State Guard, C.S.A.
Block 96, Lot 1734

Edwin Price, born June 10, 1834, was the eldest child of Sterling and Martha Head Price. He attended school in Chariton County and at the University of Missouri in Columbia. In 1855, Price married Miss Kittie Bradford and took up farming in Chariton County.

Price and his father, Sterling, were at the Planters' House in downtown St. Louis when Lyon surrounded Camp Jackson on May 10, 1861, and thus evaded capture. Edwin returned to Chariton County and as colonel of the 3d Regiment, Third Division, Missouri State Guard, took part in the battles at Carthage, Drywood, and Lexington. When the division's commander, John B. Clark, was elected to the Confederate Congress, Price was promoted to brigadier general to replace him.

Price was captured by Union forces near Stockton, Missouri, in February 1862. In October, with the active involvement of President Jefferson Davis, Price was exchanged for a Union general. He rejoined his father, then in Mississippi, but promptly resigned his Confederate commission and returned to Missouri, later obtaining a pardon from President Lincoln. Price publicly renounced the Confederacy with such conviction that the *Missouri Republican* predicted his father would soon follow his example. General Price later privately explained his son's behavior as part of a plan to return him safely to Missouri as a "recruiting agent" for the Confederacy, but the episode did the Prices no good in their standing with Missouri's Governor Reynolds

Major General Sterling Price, C.S.A. *Carte de visite photograph by Saunders' City Art Gallery, Lexington, Missouri, 1863. Missouri Historical Society Photograph and Print Collection.*

or President Davis.

Father and son reconciled at war's end, the elder Price passing his land holdings to Edwin to avoid confiscation by the Federal authorities. Edwin Price died in St. Louis on January 4, 1908.[60]

30. Sterling Price
Congressman, U.S.A.
Governor, Missouri
Major General, C.S.A.
Block 96, Lot 1734

Born in Virginia on September 20, 1809, Sterling Price was educated at Hampden-Sydney College and later studied law. Moving with his family to Missouri in 1831, he purchased a farm in Chariton County. After six years in the general assembly of Missouri, including four as speaker, Price was elected to Congress in 1844. He resigned his seat in 1846 to lead the 2d Missouri Infantry in the war against Mexico.

Price was elected governor of Missouri in late 1852 for the 1853-1857 term. In March 1861 he presided over the state convention considering secession. In May he accepted command of Missouri's militia forces from pro-Southern governor Claiborne Jackson.

Price and his Missouri Confederates fought Union general Nathaniel Lyon at Wilson's Creek and went on to capture Lexington,

Missouri, before being forced to retreat to northwest Arkansas in the winter of 1861-1862. Price again fought the Federals in March 1862 at Pea Ridge, Arkansas. He was commissioned major general, C.S.A., to rank from March 6, 1862. He led troops in the unsuccessful battles of Iuka and Corinth, Mississippi, in October 1862, and at Helena, Arkansas, in 1863. In September and October 1864, Price launched a raid from Arkansas that took his troops across Missouri from Pilot Knob (near Ironton) to Westport (near Kansas City), where the campaign dissolved under increasing Federal resistance.

After the war, Price went to Mexico, but after the collapse of the Archduke Maximilian's Mexican Empire, he returned to St. Louis on January 11, 1867. He died in St. Louis on September 29, 1867, at a residence on 11 South Sixteenth Street (between Market and Walnut). His funeral was conducted on October 3 at the First Methodist Episcopal Church on the corner of Eighth and Washington.[61]

31. Orson Henry Hart
Brevet Brigadier General, U.S.A.
Block 87/88, Lot 1282 (no marker)

Born in Hartford, Connecticut, in May 1832, Hart enlisted as a private in the 7th New York State Militia. He later served as adjutant of the 70th New York Infantry and as a staff officer with Generals Daniel Sickles, William French, and Joseph Hooker. He was made a brevet brigadier general on March 13, 1865, for "faithful and meritorious service" during the war. Hart died in St. Louis on August 17, 1872.[62]

32. John Pope
Major General, U.S.A.
Block 86, Lot 197

Pope was born in Louisville, Kentucky, on March 16, 1822. After graduating from West Point in 1842, Pope did four years of survey duty before fighting in the Mexican War, where he received brevet promotions to the rank of first lieutenant and captain. After the Mexican War, he performed assignments in the Topographical Engineers, receiving his regular army commission to captain in 1856.

Promoted to brigadier general of volunteers on June 14, 1861, Pope served capably in the capture of New Madrid and Island No. 10 in March and April 1862. In May, under General Halleck, Pope and his troops participated in the advance on Corinth, Mississippi. He had been promoted to major general in March 1862.

At the height of his military career, Pope was brought east to command the Union army of Virginia, which included all the eastern Federal troops except those on the Peninsula with General McClellan. Unable to comprehend his enemy's movements, Pope allowed General Robert E. Lee to unite his two wings under Generals Thomas J. Jackson and James Longstreet and drive the Union army from the plains of Manassas back toward Washington, D.C.

Pope was then sent to the Department of the Northwest where he helped quell a Sioux uprising in Minnesota. From then until his retirement in 1886, Pope held various departmental commands until his seniority gave him promotion to major general in the regular service on October 26, 1882. He died in Sandusky, Ohio, on September 23, 1892.[63]

33. Benjamin L. E. Bonneville
Brevet Brigadier General, U.S.A.
Block 85, Lot 1111

Born April 14, 1796, near Paris, France, Benjamin Louis Eulalie Bonneville graduated from the United States Military Academy in 1815. His long service in the army was distinguished by his exploration of the Rocky Mountains (1831-1835) and service in the Mexican War. The Bonneville Salt Flats of Utah are named for him.

In 1861 Bonneville served as colonel, 3d U.S. Infantry, and as commander of Benton Barracks, St. Louis. Later that year he retired from the Regular Army in his rank as colonel. On March 13, 1865, Bonneville was honored with a brevet promotion to brigadier general for "long and faithful services in the army." He died in Fort Smith, Arkansas, on June 12, 1878, and was buried in St. Louis.[64]

34. Samuel Parsons Simpson
Brevet Brigadier General, U.S.A.
Block 76, Lot 193

Born in St. Louis on December 7, 1830, Simpson began his service in 1861 as first lieutenant and adjutant of the 3d Regiment, U.S. Reserve Corps. He later served as lieutenant colonel in both the 12th Missouri State Militia Cavalry and the 31st Missouri Infantry. Simpson served as adjutant general of Missouri from 1865-1869 and was promoted to brevet brigadier general. He died on August 3, 1905, in Leavenworth, Kansas.[65]

35. William Wade
Colonel, C.S.A.
Block 84, Lot 445

Born in Maryland in 1819, Wade moved to St. Louis to make his fortune and became active in the local militia. On May 10, 1861, Wade was among those captured at Camp

Jackson. After his parole, he entered the Missouri State Guard and, after organizing a battery of artillery, was elected its captain. Wade and his battery served with General Sterling Price in numerous engagements, including Pea Ridge, Farmington, Iuka, and Corinth. In December 1863 Wade was promoted to colonel for his accomplishments.

On April 29, 1863, Wade was killed while directing his guns on the fortifications of Grand Gulf, Mississippi. He was struck in the head by a fragment of shot from a Federal gunboat. Wade was initially buried near Corinth, Mississippi, but was reinterred after the war.[66]

36. John M. Wimer
Mayor, St. Louis
Colonel, C.S.A.
Block 83, Lot 284

Born near Charlottesville, Virginia, on May 10, 1810, John Wimer moved with his family in 1828 to St. Louis, where he found work with a blacksmith. Within a few years he owned a blacksmith shop at Fourth and Chestnut.

Wimer became an active political leader from St. Louis' Fifth Ward. In the next thirty years, he was elected constable, alderman, sheriff, superintendent of the waterworks, and county judge. Between two terms as mayor of St. Louis (1843-1844 and 1857-1858), Wimer served as the city's postmaster. The most important accomplishment of his second mayoral term was the establishment of a regular paid fire department. Wimer proved to be a commercial success as well as a political one, serving as president of the Pacific Railroad and of the Commercial Insurance Company.

After the Camp Jackson incident, former mayor Wimer was among the most outspoken critics of Federal intervention in Missouri. In the spring of 1862, he was arrested and imprisoned in the Gratiot Street Prison for his sympathies. He was transferred to the Alton Prison in August but escaped in December, making his way to join Confederate cavalry south of Springfield, Missouri.

In the early hours of January 11, 1863, Wimer was killed in action near Hartville, Missouri, while leading a detachment of Burbridge's cavalry regiment. Wimer's body and the body of Colonel Emmett MacDonald, killed in the same action, were returned to St. Louis for burial. During the wake the Federal provost marshal broke into the homes of the mourners, took the bodies, and buried them in unknown and unmarked locations. Wimer's body was located after the war in the old Wesleyan Cemetery (near Grand and Olive) and reinterred at Bellefontaine Cemetery.[67]

John M. Wimer. *Oil on canvas. Missouri Historical Society Art Collection.*

37. Roswell Martin Field
Dred Scott's attorney
Block 73, Lot 611

Born in Vermont on February 22, 1807, Field was admitted to the bar by the time he was eighteen. He served as state's attorney for his county from 1832 to 1835. After a decision by the Vermont Supreme Court went against an emotionally involved Field, he swore never again to practice law in his native state.

Field arrived in St. Louis in 1839. After several difficult years, his fortune began turning in 1853 when he took on the suit of Dred Scott. In the next few years, his efforts and Scott's cause brought him to prominence.

Field married Miss Frances Reed in 1846 and had six children in the ten years before her death. Only two of the children, the famous poet Eugene and Roswell, Jr., lived past infancy. During the Civil War, Field was a strong Union supporter but took no active role other than the maintenance of his law practice. He died in St. Louis in 1869.

The home in which Field lived still stands at 634 South Broadway.[68]

38. James S. Thomas
Mayor, St. Louis, 1864-1869
Block 168, Lot 2158

Thomas was born in Maryland on May 25, 1802. He came to St. Louis in 1825 and opened the city's first bank. In 1838 he entered a banking partnership with L. A. Benoist, which continued until Thomas withdrew in 1850.

During the Civil War, Thomas held a number of civil appointments while the city was under martial law. In April 1864 he was elected mayor to complete the term of Chauncey I. Filley. He continued in office until 1869. One of Mayor Thomas' greatest interests was the development of Tower Grove Park from land donated by Henry Shaw. Thomas died in St. Louis on September 26, 1874.[69]

39. Charles G. Stifel
Colonel, U.S.A.
Block 168, Lot 2158

Stifel was born in the Kingdom of Württemberg on January 28, 1819. After his education, he determined to pursue his fortune in America, arriving in New York in 1837. He worked in Newark, Wheeling, New Orleans, and Nashville before returning to Germany in 1845 with enough money to bring his father back with him to the United States. He established himself first in Cincinnati but moved to St. Louis in 1849.

In St. Louis Stifel engaged in the brewing business and met with sufficient success to build his own brewery in 1859 at Fourteenth and Chambers Streets. The brewery had a capacity of eighty barrels of beer a day, and by the 1860s it had made Stifel very prosperous. In 1861, in anticipation of events, Stifel purchased muskets and began drilling recruits in the malthouse of his brewery.

On May 11, 1861, Stifel was appointed colonel of the 5th Regiment, United States Reserve Corps. That same day, the day after the capture of Camp Jackson, his soldiers were attacked on Walnut Street while marching home from the St. Louis Arsenal. Stifel and his men served briefly at Boonville and later tried to take Confederate colonel Joseph Shelby by surprise near Lexington, Missouri. Stifel also participated in the engagement at Blue Mills, near Independence. He returned to St. Louis with his command at the expiration of their ninety-day enlistments and commanded the reorganized and reenlisted regiment for the next six months before resigning from the service to return to the brewing business.

In 1889 Stifel sold most of his brewing interests, although he continued to manage his brewery until his retirement in 1892.[70]

40. William Ward Childs
Sergeant, C.S.A.
Block 165, Lot 2236

Born December 6, 1843, Childs was the great-great-grandson of Betty Washington, sister of President George Washington. Childs enlisted in Landis' Missouri Confederate artillery on December 8, 1861, and served with it throughout the war. He was with the battery company when it surrendered at Vicksburg on July 4, 1863, and was later exchanged. Serving until the end of the war, Childs signed his parole on May 1, 1865.

After the war Childs returned to St. Louis and in 1870 married Miss Mary Fairfax Berkley. In 1891 he moved to New York to work for the American Manufacturing Company on Wall Street. He died in Brooklyn on March 22, 1911.[71]

41. Julius Pitzman
Major, U.S.A.
Block 318, Lot 4844

Pitzman was born in Halberstadt, Prussia, on January 11, 1837, and was brought to the United States in 1854 by his widowed mother. Pitzman came to St. Louis that fall to work with his brother-in-law, Charles E. Salomon, formerly an engineer officer in the Prussian army. By 1859 Pitzman was in business for himself as a surveyor and engineer.

When General Frémont arrived in St. Louis in 1861, Pitzman volunteered his services and was appointed first lieutenant, Topographical Engineers. In April 1862 he accompanied General Halleck to Shiloh, Tennessee, where he created the topographical map to accompany the official report just four days after the battle. Working through the stench of the barely buried corpses, Pitzman completed his work but then collapsed with typhoid fever. After his recovery in July, he returned to duty with General Grant, taking part in the crossing of the Mississippi River

Julius Pitzman as First Lieutenant, U.S.A. Carte de visite photograph, ca. 1863. Missouri Historical Society Photograph and Print Collection.

and the advance on Vicksburg. In May 1863 he was badly wounded in the hip while conducting a survey of the Vicksburg siege lines and was returned to St. Louis for recuperation. There he accepted nomination for county surveyor. He was elected in October 1863.

In the fall of 1864, Pitzman voluntarily returned to duty as a major during General Sterling Price's raid into Missouri and supervised the construction of fortifications near Washington, Missouri, before returning to civilian life. In the nearly sixty years between his military service and his death, Pitzman was a successful architect and engineer in St. Louis. Among his many contributions are Benton Place (1866), Forest Park (1870s), and Westmoreland and Portland Places (1888). Pitzman died in St. Louis in 1923.[72]

42. Joseph Pesch
Private, U.S.A.
Medal of Honor
Block 281, Lot 4537

Born in Prussia on July 18, 1835, Joseph Pesch was awarded the Medal of Honor for his bravery at Grand Gulf, Mississippi, on April 28-29, 1863, when, as a private in Company A, 1st Missouri Light Artillery, he and two comrades took position on the steamer *Cheeseman* and manned the guns despite the fact that the steamer had become unmanageable and was exposed to a heavy enemy fire.[73]

43. John Willock Noble
Brevet Brigadier General, U.S.A.
Block 281, Lot 3769

Born in Lancaster, Ohio, on October 26, 1831, John Noble was educated at Miami University, Yale University, and the Cincinnati Law School, where he graduated in 1852.

Noble's Civil War service began as first lieutenant and aide to General Samuel Curtis. Later he was promoted to colonel, 3rd Iowa Cavalry. On March 13, 1865, he was promoted to brevet brigadier general for his "faithful and meritorious services."

After the war he resumed his occupation as a lawyer and, in time, became U.S. Secretary of the Interior, 1889-1893. Noble died in St. Louis on March 22, 1912.[74]

44. Chauncey I. Filley
Mayor, St. Louis, 1863
Block 282, Lot 3914

Born in Lansingburg, New York, on October 17, 1829, Chauncey Filley attended law school in Saratoga County, New York, before coming to St. Louis in 1850 as a clerk in his relatives' china business.

Filley supported Whig and Republican candidates in most elections and consequently was a strong Unionist during the Civil War. He attended the Republican National Convention in 1860 at which Abraham Lincoln was nominated for president. Four years later, he was a delegate to the convention in Baltimore that renominated Lincoln.

Filley was elected mayor of St. Louis in 1863 but served only one year of his two-year term because of poor health. During his brief tenure his attempts at restoring commerce and city services were generally successful. He continued to be active in politics after his resignation, serving as an elector on the U. S. Grant presidential ticket in 1868 and as a delegate to all Republican National Conventions from 1868 to 1892.

Filley died in Overland, Missouri, on September 24, 1923, at the age of ninety-three. Chauncey Filley was the brother of Oliver Dwight Filley, also a wartime mayor of St. Louis.[75]

John W. Noble as Colonel, U.S.A. *Cabinet card copy photograph by Mosher Gallery, Chicago, ca. 1895. Missouri Historical Society Photograph and Print Collection.*

45. Henry D. O'Brien
Lieutenant, U.S.A.
Medal of Honor
Block 292, Lot 4482

A native of Maine, O'Brien entered the Union army at St. Anthony Falls, Minnesota. By the time of the battle of Gettysburg, O'Brien was a corporal in Company E, 1st Minnesota Infantry. Having survived the horrific losses to his regiment on July 2, 1863, O'Brien was among the remnant of the 1st Minnesota which found itself defending against "Pickett's Charge" on July 3. As the Confederates neared the Union lines, O'Brien's regiment, with the others in its brigade, attacked the Confederate flank. The 1st Minnesota's color bearer was shot down, the flagstaff broken in two by the gunfire. O'Brien picked up the flag by its remaining staff and, in the words of a comrade, "with his characteristic bravery and impetuosity" led his regiment into hand-to-hand combat with the 28th Virginia Infantry. O'Brien, now severely wounded, yielded the colors to another member of the 1st Minnesota. For his bravery he was awarded the Medal of Honor on April 9, 1890.

O'Brien was promoted to lieutenant after Gettysburg and was wounded in the chest at Petersburg in 1864. His wound forced his withdrawal from active service.

After the war, O'Brien served for a time as postmaster of St. Anthony Falls before moving to St. Louis to become a government pension agent.[76]

Fitz Guerin. Detail of group portrait by Guerin Studio, 1895. Missouri Historical Society Photograph and Print Collection.

46. George Graham Vest
Congressman, Senator, C.S.A.
Senator, U.S.A.
Block 283, Lot 4468

Born in Frankfort, Kentucky, on December 6, 1830, Vest graduated from Center College in Danville, Kentucky, in 1848. After graduation from the Transylvania Law School in Lexington he began a journey west that he hoped would end in California. While delayed by a stage accident in Georgetown, Missouri, he undertook the defense of a young black accused of murder. After Vest secured the youth's acquittal, the young man was seized by a mob and burned at the stake. Threats against Vest made him determined to stay in Missouri.

Vest had great success in his profession and in politics. By 1860 he was a presidential elector and a representative in the state legislature. In 1861 he chose to support the South and served with General Price as judge advocate general. In the fall he was elected a member of the Confederate Congress. He served in both the regular Congresses of the Confederate States, including one year as senator.

After the war Vest returned to private practice, first in Sedalia and later in Kansas City, Missouri. He was elected to the United States Senate for the term beginning March 18, 1879, and served until 1903. He died at his home in Sweet Springs, Missouri, on August 9, 1904.[77]

47. Fitz W. Guerin
Private, U.S.A.
Medal of Honor
Block 155-157, Lot 4001

While a private in Company A, 1st Missouri Light Artillery, Guerin and two other artillerymen voluntarily took position on board the steamer *Cheeseman* at Grand Gulf, Mississippi, on April 28-29, 1863. They took charge of the guns and ammunition of the battery for a considerable time while the steamer was unmanageable and subjected to heavy fire from the enemy.

For their gallantry Guerin and his two comrades, Henry A. Hammel and Joseph Pesch, were awarded the Medal of Honor on March 10, 1896. Curiously, all three men are buried in Bellefontaine Cemetery.[78]

48. Edward Cunningham, Jr.
Major, C.S.A.
Block 37, Lot 2938

Born in Cumberland County, Virginia, on August 21, 1841, Cunningham was educated at the Virginia Military Institute and graduated in

1860. In May and June of 1861, Cunningham served briefly on the staffs of Generals Thomas J. Jackson and Joseph E. Johnston. Commissioned a lieutenant of artillery in the Confederate army, he was transferred to New Orleans. In 1864 he was promoted to major and served as chief of artillery for General E. Kirby Smith. Cunningham surrendered at Shreveport, Louisiana, in 1865.

Cunningham took up teaching as his postwar occupation, including three years as professor of physics at Louisiana State University (1870-1872). During this time he also studied law. He was admitted to the St. Louis Bar Association in 1873, and in 1889 he joined in partnership with former fellow Confederate Alphonso C. Stewart. Cunningham practiced in St. Louis for three decades. After a lingering illness he died in St. Louis on October 18, 1904.[79]

49. Thomas Clement Fletcher
Brevet Brigadier General, U.S.A.
Governor, Missouri
Block 161, Lot 2772

Fletcher was born in Herculaneum, Missouri, on January 22, 1827. In his profession as a lawyer, he was involved in the formation of the Republican Party and attended the 1860 Republican National Convention. Fletcher's first military assignment came on October 7, 1862, as colonel of the 31st Missouri Infantry, leading the regiment throughout the Vicksburg campaign. Two years later he became colonel of the 47th Missouri Infantry.

On November 18, 1864, ten days after being elected governor of Missouri, Fletcher resigned his commission. During his 1865-1869 term he supervised the adjustment of the state to emancipation. Fletcher was breveted to brigadier general on March 13, 1865, for his services at Pilot Knob, Missouri.

Fletcher died in Washington, D.C., on March 25, 1899. He was the brother-in-law of General Madison Miller, who is also buried in Bellefontaine Cemetery.[80]

50. Joseph N. McDowell, M.D.
Colonel, Surgeon, C.S.A.
Block 161, Lot 1604

Born in Fayette County, Kentucky, on April 1, 1805, Joseph Nash McDowell first practiced medicine at Cincinnati, Ohio. He came to St. Louis in 1840 and soon afterward founded the medical department of Kemper College, later known as McDowell Medical College. In 1847 he erected the McDowell Medical College building at the corner of Eighth and Gratiot Streets. That year, it became the medical department of Missouri State University (now the University of Missouri) and continued in that capacity until 1857.

At the beginning of the war, Dr. McDowell made no secret of his Southern sympathies, and his building was soon confiscated and used first as a barracks and then as the infamous Gratiot Street Prison. During the war Dr. McDowell served as medical director for General Sterling Price's command in the Department of the Trans-Mississippi.

In 1865 he returned to St. Louis to reestablish the college, but he died three years later on September 18, 1868.[81]

51. Trusten Polk
Governor, Senator, U.S.A.
Colonel, C.S.A.
Block 55/56, Lot 1736

Trusten Polk was born in Delaware on May 29, 1811, a relative of President James K. Polk. He was educated at Cambridge, Maryland, and graduated from law school at Yale in 1831. In 1835 Polk moved to Missouri. By the 1840s he was active in politics, serving as city counselor (1843), delegate to the state Constitutional Convention (1845), and presidential elector (1848).

Polk was inaugurated as Missouri's governor on January 5, 1857, but resigned after being elected by the Missouri General Assembly as United States Senator in March of the same year. When war came Polk followed other Southern Democrats and resigned his Senate seat on January 10, 1862. Joining the Confederate army, the newly elected Colonel Polk served the Confederacy as judge

Dr. Joseph Nash McDowell. *Photograph of daguerreotype, ca. 1859. Missouri Historical Society Photograph and Print Collection.*

advocate general of the Department of the Trans-Mississippi. In 1864 he was captured and imprisoned at Johnson's Island for several months before being exchanged.

Polk followed Generals Price and Shelby to Mexico after the war but soon returned to St. Louis to continue the practice of law. He died in the city on April 16, 1876.[82]

52. Thomas Lowndes Snead
Colonel, Congressman, C.S.A.
Block 65, Lot 1926

Born in Henrico County, Virginia, on January 10, 1828, Snead graduated from Richmond College in 1846 and continued his education at the University of Virginia Law School. In 1850 he was admitted to the bar in Virginia, but later that year moved to St. Louis and went into law partnership with Judge John Wickham. In 1860 he acquired the *St. Louis Bulletin,* a "states' rights" newspaper.

In 1861 Snead became an aide to Governor Jackson and then assistant adjutant general to General Price in the Missouri State Guard and in the Confederate service. On May 25, 1864, Colonel Snead became Congressman Snead and left for Richmond where he served until the surrender.

After the war Snead and his family moved to New York City, where he worked for the *New York Daily News.* He authored several articles for *Century* magazine, which were later included in *Battles and Leaders of the Civil War*. He also authored a book-length account of his experiences entitled *The Fight for Missouri.* Snead died of heart failure in New York on October 17, 1890, and was returned to St. Louis for burial.[83]

53. Frank Carter
Major, C.S.A.
Block 65, Lot 1926

Born on July 25, 1838, Carter received his education in Palmyra, Missouri, at St. Paul's College. When the war broke out, he was a student at the University of Virginia. After enlisting in the Virginia State Army, Carter was transferred to staff duty with General John Bowen. After the surrender of Vicksburg, Carter was exchanged and transferred back to Virginia where he served in the Army of Northern Virginia.

After the war Carter was a businessman in St. Louis, first as a steamboat agent and then in real estate and insurance. He died in St. Louis on April 28, 1896.[84]

54. Hugh A. Garland
Colonel, C.S.A.
Block 75, Lot 244

Born in 1835 in Lynchburg, Virginia, Garland was working as a lawyer in St. Louis in 1861. As captain of Company F (the Jackson Grays), 2d Regiment, Missouri Volunteer Militia, he was among those taken prisoner at Camp Jackson on May 10, 1861.

After his parole, Garland joined the Confederate service and became a captain in the 1st Missouri Infantry, participating in the battles of Shiloh, Corinth, Grand Gulf, Port Gibson, and Champion Hill. Elected major on May 26, 1862, he advanced to lieutenant colonel on May 1, 1863. After the surrender of Vicksburg, Garland was on recruiting duty at Richmond until February 1864, when he returned to field service. He succeeded to command of the consolidated 1st/4th Missouri Infantry after the death of Colonel Amos Riley at New Hope Church, Georgia, in May 1864. Colonel Garland was killed in the assault on Franklin, Tennessee, on November 30, 1864. He was buried on the battlefield and later reinterred at Bellefontaine Cemetery.[85]

55. Wells Howard Blodgett
Colonel, U.S.A.
Medal of Honor
Block 67, Lot 2947

Blodgett was born on December 29, 1839, at Downer's Grove, Illinois. He entered the service in August 1861 as first lieutenant, 37th Illinois Infantry. On September 30, 1862, near Newtonia, Missouri, Blodgett and a lone orderly captured an armed picket of eight men and marched them in as prisoners. In January 1863 he was promoted to captain in his regiment, and he was promoted again in March and assigned as judge advocate of the Army of the Frontier. In late 1864 Blodgett was promoted to lieutenant colonel and colonel in the 48th Missouri Infantry.

For the action at Newtonia, Blodgett was awarded the Medal of Honor on February 15, 1894. He died on May 8, 1929.[86]

56. Alphonso Chase Stewart
Lieutenant, C.S.A.
Block 48, Lot 2922

The son of future Confederate general A. P. Stewart, Alphonso Stewart was born in Lebanon, Tennessee, on August 27, 1848. In 1863, though only fifteen years old, Stewart enlisted in the 4th Tennessee Cavalry, C.S.A. He was in action at the battle of Saltsville, Virginia, but shortly afterward he was transferred to his father's staff, where he served for the rest of the war.

In 1867 Stewart graduated from Cumberland University (Tennessee) with a law degree and was admitted to the bar at the age of nineteen. He practiced law in Tennessee and Mississippi until 1872 when he, his wife, and their son moved to St. Louis. In 1873 he joined former circuit judge and Missouri congressman Andrew King and former Union cavalry officer John W. Phillips in partnership as "King, Phillips, and Stewart," the ancestor law firm of the modern Bryan, Cave. Stewart was active in the city's business, social, and religious circles until his death in 1916.[87]

57. Alexander Peter Stewart
Lieutenant General, C.S.A.
Block 48, Lot 2922

Born in Rogersville, Tennessee, on October 2, 1821, Alexander Stewart would become one of only seventeen officers to hold the rank of lieutenant general in the Confederate army. A graduate of West Point in 1842, he resigned from the U.S. Army shortly thereafter to teach. When war came, he helped organize and train troops and then served as an artillery officer at Belmont, Missouri.

Promoted to brigadier general in November 1861, Stewart commanded an infantry brigade in the Army of Tennessee and fought well in all the army's battles. He was promoted to major general in June 1863 and to lieutenant general a year later when he took over command of General Leonidas Polk's corps one month after Polk's death. He led this corps to the end of the war, surrendering with General Joseph Johnston's troops at Greensboro, North Carolina, in May 1865.

From 1870 to 1874, Stewart made his living as a businessman in St. Louis, but returned to his calling as an educator in 1875 when he was elected chancellor of the University of Mississippi. Stewart died in Biloxi, Mississippi, on August 30, 1908, and was returned for burial to St. Louis, where his son was an active businessman.[88]

58. Francis E. Brownell
First Lieutenant, U.S.A.
Medal of Honor
Block 40, Lot 2316

Brownell enlisted in Company A, 11th New York Infantry, on April 20, 1861. Without doubt he was drawn to the colors by the unit's commander, Colonel Elmer Ellsworth, and Ellsworth's passion for Zouave uniforms and drill. In May, Ellsworth's Zouaves were among the first Union volunteers to arrive in Washington, D.C., to guard it from anticipated Confederate incursions.

On May 20, 1861, the 11th New York was

Colonel Hugh Garland, C.S.A. *Photograph, ca. 1862. Missouri Historical Society Photograph and Print Collection.*

part of a force ordered to Alexandria, Virginia, a Washington suburb, to help secure the Potomac River for navigation. Ellsworth spied a Confederate flag flying prominently from atop the Marshall House, a hotel, and decided to remove it. While descending the staircase from the rooftop, Colonel Ellsworth was confronted by the hotel's proprietor, James T. Jackson. Brownell tried unsuccessfully to deflect Jackson's shotgun, but Jackson fired point-blank into Ellsworth's chest, killing him instantly. Brownell fired, hitting Jackson in the forehead, and then finished him with the bayonet.

Brownell was soon after commissioned directly into the regular service as a second lieutenant of the 11th U.S. Infantry. He was promoted to first lieutenant on October 24, 1861, and served in that rank until leaving the army on November 4, 1863. For his bravery in Ellsworth's defense, he was awarded the Medal of Honor on January 26, 1877, sixteen years after the event.

Francis Edwin Brownell, Ellsworth's avenger, died in St. Louis on March 15, 1894.[89]

59. Thomas W. Freeman
Congressman, C.S.A.
Block 49, Lot 1513

Freeman was born in Anderson County, Kentucky, in 1824 and educated in the public schools there. After studying law in Lawrenceburg, Kentucky, he was admitted to the bar in 1847. Two years later, Freeman followed the gold rush to California, where he practiced as a criminal lawyer. In 1851 he moved to Bolivar, Missouri, and was soon elected circuit attorney.

In 1861 he was elected by Missouri's Confederate legislature to the Congress of the Confederate States of America. He served two terms in Richmond but after the war returned to St. Louis, where he died on October 24, 1865.[90]

60. Albert Gallatin Edwards
Brigadier General, Missouri, U.S.A.
Block 50, Lot 280

Born in October 1812, Edwards grew up in Illinois, where his father was active in politics. He graduated from West Point in 1832 and was assigned to duty at Jefferson Barracks. On April 28, 1835, he married Louise Cabanne, a descendant of the Chouteau family. He then resigned his commission and entered the mercantile trade. In 1850, nine years after his wife's death, Edwards married Mary Ewing Jencks and moved from St. Louis to Kirkwood.

At the outbreak of the Civil War, Edwards had strong political connections and was an ardent Union sympathizer. He was appointed a brigadier general of Missouri militia and given responsibility for the St. Louis area. During the war he also served at Governor Gamble's request as the bank examiner for the state. On April 9, 1865, his service and his abilities in finance led to his appointment as assistant secretary of the United States Treasury for the subtreasury bank in St. Louis, a position he held until March 1887. At that time, he entered into partnership with his son to establish the brokerage service of A. G. Edwards & Son. Edwards died in April 1892.[91]

61. James Buchanan Eads
Inventor
Block 59, Lot 217

Eads was born on May 23, 1820, in Lawrenceburg, Indiana. He came to St. Louis as a young teenager and took odd jobs to sustain himself. Though Eads' formal schooling ended before he was fourteen, he learned mathematics and the sciences on his own. Eads' energy and inventiveness resulted in his becoming a prominent riverine engineer by the time of the Civil War.

In 1861 Eads won a contract from the Federal government for the construction of seven ironclad gunboats to be completed within one hundred days. Eads' gunboats were used to help capture Forts Henry and Donelson in February 1862, one month before the more famous USS *Monitor* and CSS *Virginia* exchanged fire at Hampton Roads, Virginia. During the war he continued to construct gunboats and mortarboats for use on the Mississippi River.[92]

In 1867 he began work on the steel-arch bridge across the Mississippi River at St. Louis that still bears his name. The bridge was opened with great ceremony on July 4, 1874. For the next decade, Eads consulted on a wide range of projects in the United States and internationally. His last great plan was for the construction of a ship railway across the Isthmus of Tehuantepec in Central America. In 1884 Eads moved from St. Louis to New York, but he was in Nassau, Bahama Islands, at the time of his death on March 8, 1887.[93]

62. James E. Yeatman
Western Sanitary Commission
Block 60, Lot 72

James Yeatman was born in Bedford County, Tennessee, on August 27, 1818. After working for some years with an iron foundry in Cumberland, Tennessee, Yeatman moved to St. Louis in 1842 to establish a branch of a Nashville iron manufacturing facility. In 1850 he opened a commission house and became one of the founders of the Merchants' Bank. In 1860 he dropped his other business interests to become the bank's president. Throughout his career, Yeatman was actively involved in philanthropic pursuits. Among his many accomplishments were the presidency of the St. Louis Mercantile Library Association and a leadership role in the establishment of the Bellefontaine Cemetery.

Yeatman, though once a slaveholder, was a strong supporter of the Union cause during the Civil War. In early 1861 he accompanied Hamilton Gamble on a visit to President Lincoln to persuade him to continue with General William Harney's conciliatory policies in St. Louis. They failed in their mission, Lincoln listening instead to the arguments of Frank Blair. In September 1861 Yeatman became president of the Western Sanitary Commission. The commission established hospital steamers, founded soldiers' homes, and took steps to provide relief for freedmen and former slaves. Yeatman died in St. Louis in 1901.[94]

63. Wilson McGunnegle
Lieutenant, U.S.N.
Block 70, Lot 1167

On May 18, 1862, Wilson McGunnegle was ordered to take command of the gunboat USS *St. Louis,* then near Memphis, Tennessee, on the Mississippi River. On June 16, 1862, he found himself in charge of a small squadron of gunboats operating on the White River in Arkansas. This came about when the squadron commander's gunboat, USS *Mound City*, suffered a direct hit that burst the steam drum, killing many of the crew and killing or disabling all but two of the gunboat's officers.

Born in 1829, McGunnegle died of consumption while on assignment to Annapolis, Maryland, in 1863.[95]

64. William Mackey Wherry
Brevet Brigadier General, U.S.A.
Medal of Honor
Block 51, Lot 627

William Mackey Wherry was born in St. Louis on September 13, 1836. He was educated at the University of Missouri in Columbia.

Wherry's Civil War service began as first lieutenant, 3d Regiment, U.S. Reserve Corps, and on the staff of General Nathaniel Lyon. At Wilson's Creek on August 10, 1861, Wherry rallied troops recoiling under heavy fire. For his "conspicuous coolness and heroism" in this action, he was awarded the Medal of Honor on October 30, 1895.

After Wilson's Creek, Wherry served as a first lieutenant in the 13th United States Infantry and as major on the staff of General John Schofield. He received his promotion to brevet brigadier general of U.S. Volunteers on March 13, 1865, and continued to serve until retiring from the Regular Army as a brigadier general in 1899. He died in Cincinnati on November 3, 1918.

General Wherry was the author of "Wilson's Creek and the Death of Lyon," which appears in *Battles and Leaders of the Civil War.*[96]

65. Henry Hitchcock
Major, U.S.A.
Block 51, Lot 320

Hitchcock was born on July 3, 1829, near Mobile, Alabama, where his father, a Vermonter, and mother, a native of Ireland, were living while his father pursued a career in law. Hitchcock graduated from the University of Nashville and from Yale before moving to St. Louis, where he was admitted to the bar in 1851. There he pursued a long and distinguished career, including the postwar establishment of the law school of Washington University.

Hitchcock's military service began in October 1864 when he was appointed to the staff of General William T. Sherman as a legal adviser. The letters and diaries that Hitchcock wrote between November 1864 and May 1865

were compiled in book form and published after his death as *Marching with Sherman.* They have become one of the most important firsthand accounts of Sherman's march to the sea.

Hitchcock died in St. Louis on March 18, 1902.[97]

66. Henry Almstedt
Colonel, U.S.A.
Block 42, Lot 1941

A native of Germany, Almstedt was one of numerous foreign-born St. Louisans whose prior military experience was called upon in the early days of the Civil War. Almstedt was unusual, however, in that his training was received in the United States.

Almstedt's military experience was gained first in Missouri, where he served as a lieutenant in the St. Louis Legion in 1846. In 1847 he entered the United States Army as a lieutenant and served with the 2d and 12th Infantry Regiments during the Mexican War.

Almstedt was elected colonel of the 1st Regiment, United States Reserve Corps, on May 7, 1861, and led his regiment in the capture of Camp Jackson. On September 19, 1861, he took command of the 2d Missouri Light Artillery, a position he held until his resignation from active service on August 27, 1863. From 1864 until January 1, 1868, Almstedt served in the paymaster's department of the U.S. Army. He died in St. Louis on November 24, 1884.[98]

67. William M. McPheeters, M.D.
Major, Surgeon, C.S.A.
Block 41, Lot 415

McPheeters was born in Raleigh, North Carolina, on December 3, 1815, and attended the state university at Chapel Hill. In 1840 he completed his studies of medicine in Philadelphia and in 1841 began his residence and practice in St. Louis. Dr. McPheeters served on the staff of the St. Louis Medical College from 1843 until 1861.

In early 1862 the McPheeters family was among the numerous prominent St. Louis families of Southern sympathies who were forced to pay fines, supposedly to be used for the relief of refugees from southwest Missouri. Refusing to take an oath of loyalty to the Union, Dr. McPheeters left his family and his practice on June 20, 1862, and made his way to Richmond to tender his services to the Confederacy. On July 8 he was commissioned a major and surgeon. His initial assignment was as medical director for General Price's command at Tupelo, Mississippi. He continued to serve with Price for most of the war.

After his parole at Monroe, Louisiana, Dr. McPheeters returned to St. Louis on June 17, 1865. He resumed his practice and, until 1874, his professor's role at the medical college. For many years he was an editor or contributor to the *St. Louis Medical and Surgical Journal.* McPheeters died in St. Louis on March 15, 1905.[99]

68. Lewis Baldwin Parsons
Brevet Major General, U.S.A.
Block 40, Lot 667

Born in western New York in 1818, Parsons graduated from Yale in 1840, taught school in Mississippi, and returned to Harvard to study law. He began his practice in Alton, Illinois, but moved to St. Louis in 1854 and soon after became chief executive officer of the Ohio and Mississippi Railroad. In 1861 he served as aide to Frank Blair during the capture of Camp Jackson. In October he was made an assistant quartermaster of volunteers with the rank of captain.

Parsons' contributions to Federal success all stemmed from his unusual competence with transportation. In his initial assignment in St. Louis, he held responsibility for all military river and rail transport from Pittsburgh west to Montana and south to New Orleans. In August

1864 Parsons was moved to Washington, D.C., and put in charge of all river and rail transportation. On May 11, 1865, he was commissioned brigadier general and was breveted major general on the day he mustered out: April 30, 1866.

For the next twenty-five years, Parsons was a director of several railroads and corporations and was president of a St. Louis bank. He died in Flora, Illinois, on March 16, 1907.[100]

69. Philip Perry Brown, Jr.
Brevet Brigadier General, U.S.A.
Block 29, Lot 2678

Born on October 8, 1823, in Smithfield, New York, Brown attended Shurtleff College in Alton, Illinois, and Madison (Colgate) University in Hamilton, New York, graduating in 1855. His career as teacher and merchant was interrupted by his service as colonel, 157th New York Infantry; colonel and provost marshal general, Department of the South; and colonel, 7th U.S. Veteran Volunteer Infantry.

Brown was breveted brigadier general on March 13, 1865, for "gallant and meritorious services." He died on April 9, 1881, in St. Louis.[101]

70. Madison Miller
Brevet Brigadier General, U.S.A.
Block 21/30, Lot 3906

Miller was born in Mercer, Pennsylvania, on February 6, 1811. In the Mexican War, he commanded a company in the 2d Illinois Infantry and was wounded at Buena Vista. Following that, he became successful in Missouri in both politics and business. He served as mayor of Carondelet, president of the St. Louis and Iron Mountain Railroad, and in 1860 was elected to the Missouri General Assembly.

Miller's initial service in the Union army was as captain, 1st Missouri Infantry, followed by the same rank in the 1st Missouri Light Artillery. Having come to the attention of General John Schofield, Miller was appointed colonel, 18th Missouri Infantry, on January 31, 1862, a position he held until 1864 when he became a brigadier general in the Missouri militia. He was promoted to brevet brigadier general on March 13, 1865, for "gallant and meritorious services in the battle of Shiloh."

Miller, the brother-in-law of General (later Governor) Thomas Fletcher, died in St. Louis on February 27, 1896.[102]

**71. Francis P. Blair, Jr.
Congressman, Senator,
Major General, U.S.A.
Block 13, Lot 298**

Francis Preston Blair, Jr. was born in Lexington, Kentucky, on February 19, 1821. After graduating from Princeton and law school, he took up practice with his brother in St. Louis in 1842. He was elected to Congress in 1856 and again in 1860. His organizational ability in creating the Union Party in Missouri, his active opposition to Governor Jackson and other Southern sympathizers, and his family's political influence were instrumental in holding Missouri for the Union.

Blair was appointed a brigadier general of volunteers in August 1862 after he had successfully organized seven Union regiments. He was promoted to major general that same year. By the end of his military career, he had led both the XV and XVII Corps of Sherman's army in Georgia and the Carolinas. He resigned in November 1865, having spent his entire fortune in support of the Union.

Blair reentered Missouri politics on a moderate platform with limited success, but he became unpopular with the Radical Republicans for his interest in restoring the former Confederate states to the Union on lenient terms. He served as U.S. Senator from Missouri from 1871-1873 to fill an unexpired term and retired because of poor health. He died in St. Louis on July 8, 1875.[103]

Stops in Tour of Calvary Cemetery (In alphabetical order)	
Name	**Tour No.**
Clemens, Sherrard	9
Cobb, Major Seth W.	1
Cooke, William M. Flynn	8
Flynn, Sergeant James E.	10
Frost, General Daniel M.	13
Guibor, Captain Henry	5
Knapp, Colonel John	12
Morrison, General Pitcairn	4
Reynolds, Thomas	11
Scott, Dred	7
Sherman, General William T.	2
Taylor, Daniel G.	6
Turner, General John W.	3

Calvary Cemetery

From Interstate 70 in north St. Louis, take the West Florissant exit north approximately 1.1 miles to Calvary Cemetery at 5239 West Florissant. The cemetery gates are open every day from 8:00 A.M. until 5:00 P.M. The office is open Monday through Friday from 8:30 A.M. to 4:30 P.M. and on Saturday from 8:30 A.M. to 12:30 P.M. The office is closed on Sundays, holidays, and holy days. For information call 314-381-1313.

The first step in creating Calvary Cemetery was taken in 1867 by Archbishop Peter Richard Kenrick. Archbishop Kenrick enlisted eleven prominent Catholic citizens to help him organize a cemetery association. Numerous tracts of land north of Bellefontaine Cemetery were purchased until an area of some 450 acres was enclosed. Some of the most well-known St. Louisans of the Civil War era are buried there.

1. Seth Wallace Cobb
Major, C.S.A.
Congressman, U.S.A.
Section 18, Lot 246

Seth Wallace Cobb was born in Southampton County, Virginia, on December 5, 1838, to Margaret Wallace and Benjamin Cobb. When Virginia's governor Letcher called for volunteers in 1861, Cobb entered the military service in one of the first companies to be formed. He served in the artillery of the Army of Northern Virginia during the entire war, rising to the rank of major.

In December 1867 Cobb came to St. Louis to start over. After an extensive apprenticeship with a grain commission firm, Cobb opened his own company in 1875. A year later, on October 4, 1876, he married Zoe Desloge, a daughter of one of the pioneer French families of Missouri.

By the turn of the century, Seth W. Cobb & Company would become one of the city's leading enterprises. In 1889 Cobb's commercial success carried over to politics; he was elected to the first of three consecutive terms in the U.S. House of Representatives as a Democrat from Missouri's Twelfth District. Declining to run for a fourth term, Cobb returned to St. Louis, where he died in 1909.[104]

Calvary Cemetery. *Map by Pat Baer, 1994.*

2. William Tecumseh Sherman
General, U.S.A.
Section 17, Lot 8

William T. Sherman was born on February 8, 1820, in Lancaster, Ohio, one of eleven children. After his father's death in 1829, Sherman found a home with Senator Thomas Ewing, whose daughter he would later marry. Ewing obtained an appointment for Sherman to West Point. From the time of his graduation in 1840 until 1853, Sherman served on routine service with the U.S. Army, receiving a brevet promotion to captain for his contributions in California during the Mexican War.

Sherman left the army in 1853 to try the banking business in San Francisco and the practice of law in Kansas before accepting the position of superintendent of the Louisiana State Seminary, the ancestor of Louisiana State University, in 1859. In January 1861 he refused to become involved in acts "hostile to the United States" and resigned. He came to St. Louis a few weeks later to become president of the St. Louis Railroad Company, a streetcar line.

Sherman reentered the U.S. Army in May 1861 as colonel, 13th United States Infantry. He commanded a brigade at First Bull Run in Virginia and was promoted to brigadier

general of volunteers on August 7, 1861. Sherman was then sent west to help hold Kentucky but was later relieved of command by Don Carlos Buell because of his purported instability. For a brief period Sherman supervised Benton Barracks in St. Louis but was soon back in action, commanding a division at the battle of Shiloh, Tennessee, on April 6-7, 1862. He was promoted to major general of volunteers to rank from May 1, 1862.

After Shiloh, Sherman's history is the history of the Civil War in the Western Theater. He led troops at Chickasaw Bluffs, Arkansas Post, throughout the Vicksburg campaign, and in the relief of Rosecrans at Chattanooga. After Grant's promotion to command of all the Union armies, Sherman took command of most of the troops in the Western Theater. Launching his campaign from Chattanooga, Sherman captured Atlanta in late 1864, for which he was rewarded with promotion to major general. He then astonished his enemies by cutting loose from his supply lines and tearing through Georgia in the "March to the Sea." He continued north through the Carolinas where, two weeks after Appomattox, he received the surrender of the South's only remaining significant field force.

In 1866 he was promoted to lieutenant

general and in 1869 became a full general, reporting to the new commander in chief, President Grant. Sherman retired from the army on February 8, 1884, but was beset by offers to run for president. After 1886 he made his home in New York City, where he died on February 14, 1891. His funeral procession in St. Louis was the largest the city had ever witnessed.[105]

3. John Wesley Turner
Brevet Major General, U.S.A.
Section 13, Lot 13

Born in New York on July 19, 1833, Turner moved with his parents to Chicago as a youth. At eighteen, he entered West Point, graduating in the class of 1855. Turner's Civil War service began in August 1861 on the staff of General David Hunter in Kansas and then on the staff of General Benjamin Butler in New Orleans. He was promoted to brigadier general of volunteers to rank from September 7, 1863, and in 1864 he led a division of the XVIII Corps in action at Petersburg, Virginia. Turner commanded a division in General Gibbon's XXIV Corps in the Appomattox campaign.

Turner was promoted to brevet major general of volunteers in 1864. In March 1865 he was awarded brevets of brigadier general and major general, U.S. Army. From June 1865 until April 1866, he commanded the District of Henrico (Richmond). Turner resigned from the army in 1871 and remained in St. Louis, where he had been serving as depot commissary. He died of pneumonia at his home on April 8, 1899.[106]

4. Pitcairn Morrison
Brevet Brigadier General, U.S.A.
Section 13, Lot 128

Morrison was born in New York City on September 18, 1795. An army officer since 1820, Morrison and his wife were living at Jefferson Barracks in early 1861. His Civil War service began as lieutenant colonel of the 7th U.S. Infantry. As colonel, he commanded the 8th U.S. Infantry and later Camp Butler Military Prison in Springfield, Illinois. He retired from the Regular Army in the rank of colonel in 1863. His promotion to brevet brigadier general came on March 13, 1865, for long and faithful services in a career spanning forty-five years. Morrison died in Baltimore, Maryland, on October 5, 1887.

Morrison was the father-in-law of Lewis Henry Little, who resigned his commission in the U.S. Army in early 1861, joined the Missouri State Guard, and later became the first commander of the First Missouri Brigade and a Confederate general.[107]

Henry Guibor.
*Photograph, ca. 1895.
Missouri Historical
Society Photograph and
Print Collection.*

5. Henry Guibor
Captain, C.S.A.
Section 17, Lot 71

Henry Guibor was arguably the most accomplished artilleryman from Missouri to serve the Confederacy. Guibor was born in Alsace, France, in 1823 and was brought to St. Louis with his family. As a young adult, Guibor worked as a carpenter until he enlisted for service in the Mexican War. His personal reputation was such that by 1861 Guibor had become deputy marshal of the criminal court in St. Louis.

In the fall of 1860, Guibor was a part of the militia expedition to drive the "jayhawkers" of Kansas from western Missouri. During this assignment, Guibor organized and led his first artillery battery. His battery was present at Camp Jackson, where its members were taken prisoner by Federal forces on May 10, 1861.

After his release, Guibor organized a battery for the Missouri State Guard. It served with General Price's army in the battles of Carthage, Wilson's Creek, Lexington, Pea Ridge, Iuka, and Corinth, and in the process won an outstanding combat reputation. Guibor was badly wounded on March 30, 1863, during the Vicksburg campaign when a nearby cannon exploded. After the surrender of Vicksburg, Guibor's battery was consolidated with two other Missouri batteries, and he retained command of the combined unit. With this battery, Guibor served with the Army of Tennessee and fought at Resaca, Kingston,

Cassville, Lost Mountain, New Hope Church, and Kennesaw Mountain in the campaign for Atlanta. He was again wounded at Kennesaw Mountain and remained convalescent for several months. Guibor was present with General Johnston's army when it surrendered in North Carolina.

Guibor returned to St. Louis, where he was for some time the superintendent of the House of Refuge, occasionally instructing the boys in drill while wearing his Confederate gray. After a long battle with cancer, Guibor died on October 17, 1899.[108]

6. Daniel G. Taylor
Mayor, St. Louis, 1861-1863
Section 17, Lot 4

Daniel Taylor was born in Cincinnati, Ohio, on November 15, 1819, nine years after his parents immigrated from Scotland. After a public school education, Taylor worked on steamboats on the Ohio and Mississippi Rivers. He became a captain and was master of the steamer *Clairmont,* which traveled the Yellowstone River for a fur-trading expedition of Pierre Chouteau in 1845.

In 1849 Taylor established the steamboat agency of Taylor and Hopkins. He served as a member of the St. Louis City Council in 1852, 1854, and 1855. Taylor was married twice. His first wife, Angelique Henri, died in a riverboat explosion in 1858. He married Emilie Lebeau in 1860.

In 1861 Taylor was elected mayor on the "Union Anti-Black Republican" ticket. Taylor's time in office was turbulent. On May 11, 1861, he made an appeal for peace after citizens had ambushed a Union Home Guard unit in St. Louis. During his administration, a dispensary was set up to provide free medical advice and medicine to the indigent. When the courthouse was completed in 1862, Taylor supervised the movement of the city's offices to the new building's north wing.

After the Civil War, Taylor served as city treasurer in 1870 and 1872. He was also president of the Boatmen's Insurance and Trust Company. Taylor died in St. Louis on October 8, 1878.[109]

His grave is marked with a small stone to the right rear of the family plot.

7. Dred Scott
Former Slave
Section 1, Lot 77

Dred Scott was born a slave in Southampton County, Virginia, the property of Peter Blow, a tobacco grower. Scott's precise birthdate is unknown, but he was at least twenty when Blow and his family and five slaves moved to St. Louis in 1830. Shortly thereafter, Scott was sold to army surgeon John Emerson. He then lived with Emerson at his posts in Illinois and the Wisconsin Territory (modern Minnesota), both areas where slavery was prohibited.

While in the Wisconsin Territory, Scott married Harriet Robinson, also a slave. In 1838 Harriet gave birth to Eliza and the small family returned to St. Louis with Emerson in 1842, where a second daughter, Lizzie, was born to the Scotts in 1846. By the time of Lizzie's birth, Emerson had died, and ownership of the Scotts had passed to his wife, then living in New York. White friends of Scott urged him to sue for freedom on the grounds of prolonged residence on free soil. Several precedents were in his favor, so no one anticipated the eleven-year struggle that would result from Scott's desire to gain his freedom.

On March 6, 1857, the United States Supreme Court ruled against Scott's bid for freedom. After the decision, Scott and his family were passed by inheritance to Calvin C. Chaffee, a member of Congress from Massachusetts. Chaffee then passed ownership to Taylor Blow of St. Louis, who freed the Scotts on May 26, 1857. Dred Scott, then in his sixties, died on September 17 of the following year.

Scott was first buried in the Wesleyan Cemetery at Grand and Laclede Avenues, but when that site was abandoned in 1867 Blow had Scott's body removed to its present location. No stone marked his burial place until 1957 when, on the one hundredth anniversary of the Supreme Court's decision, the present modest monument was put in place.[110]

8. William Mordecai Cooke
Staff Officer, Congressman, C.S.A.
Section 3, Lot 12

Born in Portsmouth, Virginia, on December 11, 1823, William Mordecai Cooke benefited from belonging to a family whose roots in Virginia went back to 1650. Cooke was educated at home by private tutors and then attended the University of Virginia, receiving his degree in law at age twenty. In 1843 he moved west to St. Louis to begin his practice. In 1846 Cooke married Eliza von Phul, daughter of prominent St. Louisan Henry von Phul.

Cooke moved to Hannibal in 1849 and was soon elected judge of the Common Pleas Court for that district. Family considerations caused him to return to St. Louis in 1854. Active in politics, Cooke was one of the leaders of the opposition to Francis P. Blair, Jr.

In March 1861 Cooke was sent to Richmond by Missouri governor Claiborne Jackson as a commissioner to the President of the Confederate States. He returned to Missouri to serve in a military capacity on Governor Jackson's staff and was present at the battles of Boonville, Carthage, and Wilson's Creek.

Cooke was elected to the Confederate Congress in the fall of 1861 and served in that body until his death on April 14, 1863. George Vest, then a member of the Confederate Congress and future United States Senator from Missouri, delivered Cooke's eulogy to the Congress. His body was returned to St. Louis for burial in Calvary Cemetery.[111]

9. Sherrard Clemens
Congressman, U.S.A.
Section 3, Lot 34

Born on April 28, 1820, Clemens was appointed a cadet at the United States Military Academy but resigned after six months to study law at Washington College, Pennsylvania. He was first elected to Congress in 1852 to fill a vacant Virginia seat for four months. He was reelected to the House of Representatives for two consecutive terms, serving 1857-1861. Opposed to secession, he was not a candidate for renomination in the fall of 1860. He resumed the practice of law in Virginia, later moving to St. Louis, where he died on May 30, 1880.[112]

10. James E. Flynn
Sergeant, U.S.A.
Medal of Honor
Section 7, Lot 465

Born in Pittsfield, Illinois, in 1843, Flynn saw Civil War service as a sergeant in Company G, 6th Missouri Infantry, U.S.A.

On the afternoon of May 21, 1863, the regimental commanders of Major General Frank Blair's division canvassed their soldiers, asking for unmarried men who would form a storming party or "forlorn hope" to lead an assault on the Confederate lines at Vicksburg, Mississippi. Flynn and 150 others from Blair's three brigades volunteered.

Around 10:00 A.M. the next day, the soldiers of the storming party surged forward, muskets slung to leave their hands free for carrying planks and ladders to scale the defenses. They advanced at a run to cross the open ground in front of the Confederate entrenchments, and nearly half were wounded or killed before nearing their objective. When the survivors arrived at the ditch at the base of the Confederate works, they discovered that so many planks and ladders had been dropped in the advance that it was impossible to build a bridge to cross the ditch. Their only choice was to jump in and seek shelter from the relentless fire being poured on them. The three infantry brigades following the storming party were stymied in their advance, the Confederate defenses proving too stout.

The men of the storming party remained under fire until well after dark, when they were able to slip back to the Union lines. At least 85 percent of the storming party was wounded or killed during its one day of combat.

For participation as a volunteer in this attack, Flynn and seventy-seven others were awarded the Medal of Honor on June 19, 1894. Flynn died in St. Louis on January 1, 1913.[113]

11. Thomas Reynolds
Governor, Missouri, C.S.A.
Section 1, Lot 231

Born in Charleston, South Carolina, on October 11, 1821, Reynolds graduated from the University of Virginia in 1842 and was admitted to the bar in 1844. A few years later, he opened a law office in St. Louis. From 1853-1857 he served as U.S. district attorney for Missouri and allied himself politically with Claiborne Jackson. Reynolds was chosen to be Jackson's running mate in the gubernatorial election of 1860 and soon found himself the lieutenant governor.

Jackson and Reynolds were forced from Jefferson City to Neosho by advancing Union forces. At Neosho they called the pro-Confederate legislators into session and passed an ordinance of secession for Missouri. On Jackson's death in December 1862, Reynolds became governor-in-exile.

Reynolds' "capital" migrated from Missouri to Arkansas to Texas based on the military fortunes of the Confederacy. He did return to Missouri during the war years as a volunteer in General Shelby's command during General Price's raid of 1864.

After the war Reynolds went to Mexico with Shelby, but Emperor Maximilian refused to hire the former Confederates as mercenaries. Reynolds found brief employment as a counselor to Maximilian before returning to Missouri in 1868, where he resumed the practice of law. On March 30, 1887, Governor Reynolds fell down the north elevator shaft of the Custom House (now the "Old Post Office" at Ninth and Olive) and was killed. In his pocket was a letter in his handwriting, which read, in part: "Troubled by insomnia and frequent nervousness, I suffer from persistent melancholy. My mind has begun to wander. I have hallucinations and even visions. When I am awake, [I see] materialized spirits of deceased relatives and friends urging me by signs to join them in their world. . . . I am now still in sound mind, and I wrote down this statement so that should I do anything rash my friends may feel assured that it was in some such temporary disorder of my mind."[114]

12. John Knapp
Lieutenant Colonel, Missouri
Colonel, U.S.A.
Section 1, Lot 46

Knapp was born in New York City on June 20, 1816, and was brought to St. Louis in 1820 by his father and mother. After his father's death, Knapp's family moved to Illinois, but John returned to St. Louis in 1831 as an apprentice to a tailor. Thirteen years later, Knapp married Virginia Wright, also of St. Louis. Over the years their family grew to include three sons and three daughters. Knapp prospered in the clothing business but lost heavily in the great fire of 1849. He then entered the wholesale grocery business, but in 1854 he purchased an interest in the *Missouri Republican* with his brother George and another partner. The *Republican* was fifty years old in 1858, and the Knapps continued its development into "the most powerful and influential journal of the Southwest."

General Daniel Frost. *Carte de visite photograph by J. A. Scholten, ca. 1861. Missouri Historical Society Photograph and Print Collection.*

Knapp's military service began in 1840 when he enlisted as a private in a St. Louis militia company. During the Mexican War, he served as captain, Company C, 1st Missouri Volunteers. After his return to St. Louis he remained active in militia service. In the fall of 1860 he commanded the 1st Regiment of Missouri militia as part of the Southwest Expedition to the Kansas border. Knapp also led his regiment at Camp Jackson in May 1861 when the command was captured by Federal forces under General Lyon.

After Camp Jackson, Knapp's service was to the Union cause. He was appointed by Governor Gamble to command the 8th Enrolled Missouri Militia and later by Governor Hall to lead the 13th Provisional Regiment. He supervised a brigade of Missouri Union militia in the pursuit of General Price during his Missouri raid in 1864.

Knapp died on November 11, 1888, having devoted his entire life to the success of the *Missouri Republican*.[115]

13. Daniel Marsh Frost
Brigadier General, C.S.A.
Section 18, Lot 48

Frost, born in New York in 1823, graduated from the United States Military Academy in 1844 and later won a brevet for gallantry in the Mexican War. Resigning from the army in 1853, he engaged in business in St. Louis and was active in the Missouri militia, holding the rank of brigadier general in 1861. Paroled after his capture at Camp Jackson on May 10, he was not exchanged until after Price's capture of Union officers at Lexington, Missouri, in September. In March 1862 he was promoted to the rank of brigadier general in the Confederate army.

Offered the command of a Missouri brigade in the battle of Pea Ridge, Frost "declined so small a command" and remained an observer of the battle. He subsequently served as a staff officer to General Bragg and under General Hindman in Arkansas at the battle of Prairie Grove. In the fall of 1863, Frost left the army for Canada as a result of the banishment of his wife and family from their home near St. Louis. Unfortunately for his military career, Frost left without bothering to advise the Confederate War Department and was dropped from the rolls on December 9, 1863. After the war he returned to St. Louis County, where he farmed until his death on October 29, 1900.[116]

Oak Hill Cemetery

From Interstate 44, take the Big Bend exit west to 10305 Big Bend. Oak Hill Cemetery is on the north side of the street. The telephone number of the cemetery office is 314-821-4511.

Oak Hill Cemetery predates the establishment of the town of Kirkwood. Originally called Oak Ridge Cemetery, it was surveyed and plotted in 1835. The first recorded burial occurred there in 1849. It is a beautiful and monument-laden cemetery, well worth visiting. The map shows the locations of the graves of three prominent veterans of the Civil War.

1. Lorraine Farquhar Jones
Captain, C.S.A.
Lot 270, Block 28/29, Section A,
Grave 10

Jones was born in Charles Town, (West) Virginia, on November 9, 1837. During the Civil War he was a captain in the second company of the Richmond Howitzers of the Confederacy's Army of Northern Virginia. The unit was formed in May 1861 and was assigned successively to the artillery battalions of J. T. Brown, R. A. Hardaway, and W. E. Cutshaw of General Robert E. Lee's army. As a result, Jones served in all the major battles of the Eastern Theater, from Seven Pines to Appomattox.

After the war, Captain Jones came to St. Louis from Appomattox with nothing but his demilitarized uniform, now on display at the Kirkwood Historical Society. Jones lived at first in a warehouse on the levee. He later became the organist at St. Peter's Episcopal Church in St. Louis and married one of the rector's daughters, Miss Matilda Fontaine Berkley, in 1870. In later life, Jones was one of the organizers and treasurer of the American Manufacturing Company and was later president of the State National Bank in St. Louis. By the turn of the century, Jones was one of Kirkwood's most prominent citizens and benefactors.

Jones died at his home, Ivy Lodge, in Kirkwood on October 19, 1920. The inscription on his tombstone eulogizes him as "one of God's noblemen."[117]

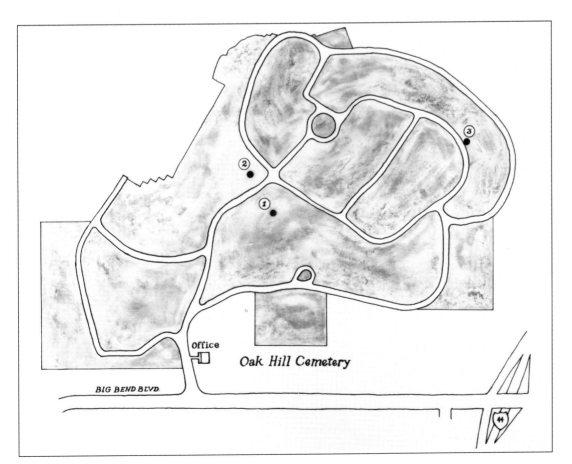

Oak Hill Cemetery.
Map by Jennifer Ratcliffe-Tangney, 1994.

2. Solomon George Kitchen
Colonel, C.S.A.
Lot 104, Block 28, Section J

Kitchen was born in Roane County, Tennessee, in 1820 and came to Missouri in his twenties. Not long after, he married Miss Martha Ann Giboney of Cape Girardeau County. Together they would raise seven children to adulthood. Kitchen first made a living as a surveyor but studied law and was admitted to the bar in 1842. He served as judge of Stoddard County (1845-1847) and as a state senator (1854-1858). He sought election to the Missouri Convention in 1861 as a secessionist but was defeated.

In June 1861 Kitchen organized a company of cavalry for the Missouri State Guard and rose to the rank of lieutenant colonel. When the State Guard's term of service expired, Kitchen enlisted in the Confederate service and soon commanded Company B, 2d Missouri Cavalry, serving east of the Mississippi River. Within a few months, Kitchen resigned his position and returned to Missouri to recruit a regiment. His recruiting mission done, Kitchen was promoted to colonel of Kitchen's Regiment, Missouri Cavalry, on July 9, 1863. The regiment was designated the 10th Missouri and then re-designated the 7th Missouri Cavalry Regiment. The regiment took an active part in the war in Arkansas and was part of General Sterling Price's raid into Missouri in 1864. Kitchen was wounded at the battle of Big Blue on October 23, 1864.

After the surrender in 1865, Kitchen returned to Cape Girardeau but then moved with his family to St. Louis. There he practiced law until 1877. Kitchen was active in the movement to have Kirkwood selected as the county seat of St. Louis County, but Clayton was chosen despite his efforts. After his wife's death in 1877, Kitchen remarried and returned to Stoddard County, where he continued to practice law. He returned to Kirkwood shortly before his death on April 10, 1891.[118]

3. Benjamin Gratz Brown
Colonel, U.S.A.
Senator, U.S.A.
Governor, Missouri
Lot 153/410, Block 35, Section I

B. Gratz Brown was born on May 28, 1826, in Lexington, Kentucky. He attended Transylvania University and Yale College, graduating from Yale in 1847. He was first admitted to the bar in Kentucky but moved to St. Louis soon afterward to join the law firm of his cousins, Frank and Montgomery Blair.

Except for three years, Brown held public office continually from 1852 to 1873. In these two decades, his party affiliation fluctuated with the times: Whig, Benton Democrat, Republican, Liberal Republican, and Democrat. Brown began his public service as a member of the Missouri General Assembly and worked there until 1859. During this period, Brown established himself as being firmly antislavery, but his reasoning was based on mercantile rather than humanitarian grounds. Brown believed emancipation would stimulate trade and commerce while it increased the population and the price of land. To complement his program, he recommended gradual emancipation with compensation to the slaveowners. This approach helped Brown secure the support of moderates in both parties while assuring him of the continued support of his German antislavery constituents.

At the beginning of the Civil War, Brown threw all his influence in favor of the Union. At the capture of Camp Jackson in St. Louis on May 10, 1861, then Colonel Brown commanded a regiment of Home Guards, the 4th Regiment of the U.S. Reserve Corps. His calling, however, was political rather than military. When General John Frémont issued a proclamation emancipating the slaves of Missourians who resisted Federal authority, Brown took up Frémont's cause. In doing so, he broke with the politically powerful Blairs, who had hoped to hold on to loyal, though proslavery, Missourians. Brown had become an abolitionist.

In 1863 Brown won a long battle for the United States Senate seat formerly occupied by Waldo P. Johnson, who had been expelled for treason. Once in the Senate, Brown continued his fight for total emancipation. He served in the Senate into 1866.

In 1871 Brown was elected governor of Missouri with the help of not only Carl Schurz and the Liberal Republicans but also the Democrats. He was the Liberal Republican-Democratic candidate for vice president in 1872, along with Horace Greeley for president. The ticket was soundly defeated by the Republican ticket headed by Ulysses S. Grant. After his retirement as governor, Brown resumed his law practice in St. Louis until his death on December 13, 1885.[119]

Quinette Cemetery

From Oak Hill Cemetery, continue west on Big Bend Road to the intersection with Old Big Bend Road. Turn right on Old Big Bend and follow it to the cemetery on the left side of the street at 12200 Old Big Bend.

At first glance, the visitor will have difficulty distinguishing Quinette Cemetery from a vacant lot. Businesses on either side of the cemetery crowd its limits. The cemetery itself offers no place to park, not even for a hearse. The "entrance" is marked by two relatively recent brick columns about four feet high. The columns hold up a small iron arch, which in turn holds a wooden sign marking "Quinette Cemetery, Established 1873." The words are visible despite the peeling white paint of the sign. On the left brick column is a small marker that tells the history of Quinette Cemetery:

The historical beginnings of Quinette Cemetery date back to the time of the Civil War. According to one tradition, the area was first federally owned and used for the burial of prisoners of war. There is, however, no documentation to verify this usage.

The first recorded owner of the property was Luke Brockway, who allowed his slaves, and others living nearby, to use this parcel of land as a cemetery. He sold the property in 1866 to William Martin, Henry Nash and George Sleet. In 1873 Olive Chapel A.M.E. obtained the title to the cemetery and retains it to this day. The church, founded in 1853 and one of the oldest in Kirkwood, is located at 301 S. Harrison.

Quinette Cemetery is comprised of 2.7 acres. The actual number of graves is unknown. It is believed to be the site of over 100 burials. Except for the few remaining headstones exact grave locations cannot be determined.
The area was previously surrounded by a decorative wrought iron fence: however, none of this fence survives. Various specialized plantings indicate that the cemetery was formerly used and maintained.

The most recent burial was in 1973.

Olive Chapel, mentioned in this description, stands at the corner of Harrison and Monroe in Kirkwood. It has been described as "the most affecting public structure in Kirkwood." The church was built for a German congregation in 1896. It was later purchased by the African Methodist Episcopal Church.[120]

Quinette Cemetery is a stark contrast to its not-too-distant neighbor, Oak Hill Cemetery. Few stones remain intact. The broken stones give evidence of years of neglect; the rough edges have rounded in response to the elements. The cemetery grounds slope downhill away from Old Big Bend. The front third is at least still green. All ground cover from the rear of the property has been removed. The tracks of the bulldozers that presumably performed this "maintenance" are readily visible in the dirt.

Jefferson Barracks National Cemetery

From the intersection of Interstate 270 and Telegraph Road in south St. Louis County, take Telegraph Road north, following the signs to Jefferson Barracks National Cemetery.

If visiting from Jefferson Barracks County Park, exit the park on South Broadway back to Kingston. Turn left (south) on Kingston until reaching Telegraph Road. Follow Telegraph Road south, watching for signs directing the visitor east to Jefferson Barracks National Cemetery.

Jefferson Barracks National Cemetery is open to visitors every day from 9:00 A.M. until 4:00 P.M. The Administrative Office at the entrance to the cemetery can help visitors locate individual graves, but it is only open Monday through Friday. No information of a historical nature is maintained here other than individual grave site data. For information call 314-263-8691 or 314-263-8692.

The Jefferson Barracks National Cemetery was established in 1863 under authority of an Act of Congress passed on July 17, 1862. Major General Henry W. Halleck, then commanding general of the Department of the Missouri with headquarters in St. Louis, initiated the action to designate Jefferson Barracks as the site for a national cemetery. Four factors combined to make the post an obvious choice for a cemetery: its strategic location, the large concentration of troops in the area, the availability of docking facilities for river steamers bearing wounded, and the presence of a recently completed hospital.[121]

Jefferson Barracks National Cemetery is an extension of the Old Post Cemetery at Jefferson Barracks. Thirteen months after the establishment of Jefferson Barracks in 1826, the need for the first burial arose. Elizabeth Ann Lash, the eighteen-month-old daughter of a garrison officer, was buried on August 5, 1827, on ground that with time would become known as the Old Post Cemetery.[122]

The bodies of Union and Confederate soldiers came to Jefferson Barracks National Cemetery from a variety of sources. In 1862 the wounded from the battles of Forts Henry and Donelson, Shiloh, and Pea Ridge were sent to Jefferson Barracks for care at its hospital. Those who did not survive were buried in the nearby cemetery.[123]

In July 1865 General William T. Sherman arrived in St. Louis to command the Department of the West. Complying with a recent General Order, Sherman directed that the Union dead in temporary sites and battlefield cemeteries in twenty-nine counties in Missouri and Arkansas be reinterred at Jefferson Barracks National Cemetery.

At the time of the Civil War, Quarantine Island (also called Arsenal Island) existed in the Mississippi River opposite St. Louis. The island was used as a quarantine location for soldiers with contagious diseases, most notably smallpox. With time, the island became the burial place for 470 soldiers, but repeated flooding washed away the graves' wooden headboards. When the remains were relocated from Arsenal Island to the National Cemetery in April 1876, they were reburied in Sections 63, 64, and 68 and marked "Unknown."[124]

Not until 1873 did Congress appropriate money for marble headstones for Union veterans and then only to replace the wooden grave markers that had become nearly unreadable or dislodged. Confederate veterans had to wait until 1906 for Federal funding that allowed cemetery officials to mark their graves with marble headstones. The Union and Confederate headstones are nearly identical in size and shape, though the Union headstone has the traditional rounded top and the Confederate headstone comes to a point. An unrepentant Rebel has suggested that this is to provide an eternal indication of the direction in which the soul of the Confederate veteran traveled.

Jefferson Barracks National Cemetery today comprises more than 300 acres, 165 of which are developed. The cemetery lies entirely within the limits of the original Jefferson Barracks military reservation. Though Jefferson Barracks itself was deactivated in 1946, the National Cemetery remains an active facility. More than 103,000 men and women are buried there, including more than 12,000 Union and 1,000 Confederate victims of the Civil War.[125]

As you enter the cemetery, the Administration Building will be on your right. On Monday through Friday, you may ask the staff for assistance in locating individual graves. If you do not need to stop at the Administration Building, continue forward and around the Flag Circle to Longstreet Drive. Follow Longstreet Drive to Bundy Street. Turn left on Bundy. Turn right at the first opportunity on First Drive South and stop. On your left is Section 57 and:

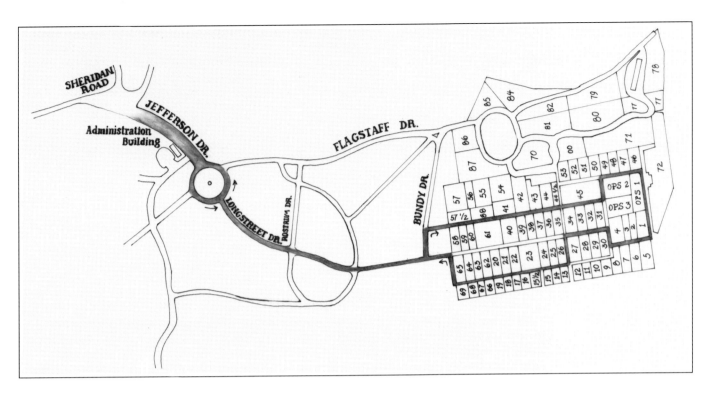

Monument to the 56th Infantry Regiment, United States Colored Troops. An obelisk in Section 57 at Grave 15009 honors the memory of the 175 soldiers of the 56th United States Colored Infantry who died of cholera in August 1866. In 1939 the monument and the remains were removed from "Quarantine Station, Missouri" by authority of the War Department in collaboration with a citizens' committee chaired by Mr. Joseph E. Mitchell. Graves 15008 and 15010 (on either side of the monument) are dedicated to "Unknown soldiers, 56th U.S. Colored Infantry."

The 56th Regiment was originally organized at St. Louis on August 12, 1863, as the 3d Arkansas Infantry Regiment (African Descent). The 3d Arkansas was ordered from St. Louis to Helena, Arkansas, and served on post duty there and at Little Rock until March 1864. On March 11, 1864, the designation of the unit was changed to 56th Infantry Regiment, U.S. Colored Troops.[126]

At one point, an inspector found the 56th Regiment to be "unsoldierlike" but went on to report that the regiment had "good material, and its bad condition was the fault of its company officers."[127] With a few notable exceptions, all officers of the U.S. Colored Troops were white.

A brass plaque on the east face of the monument proclaims "Their memory will not perish," a quotation attributed to Brigadier General N. B. Buford on July 27, 1864.

The unit's connection with Napoleon Bonaparte Buford, half-brother of Union cavalry leader and Gettysburg hero John Buford, began in January 1864. The regiment was one of fourteen units in the District of Eastern Arkansas that Buford commanded. On July 26, 1864, the day before Buford's quotation, the 56th was in action with two other black units (Co. E, 2d Cavalry and the 60th Infantry) and the 15th Illinois Cavalry against Confederate forces at Wallace's Ferry and Big Creek, Arkansas. Union losses in the battles were twenty killed, forty wounded, and four missing.[128]

General Buford and the 56th Regiment remained together until March 1865, when he was transferred to other duties. In August the 56th Regiment became part of the Department of Arkansas until it was mustered out of the service on September 15, 1866. Before the unit mustered out, the tragedy occurred that contributed to the reason for this monument.

The 56th was traveling aboard two steamers from Helena to St. Louis to be mustered out. During the trip several soldiers died of an undiagnosed illness. When the steamers reached Quarantine Station near St. Louis, Colonel Charles Bentzoni, the regimental commander, asked a surgeon to inspect the men. The surgeon reported no cholera among them. The regiment continued to St. Louis and arrived at night, but Bentzoni kept the men on board rather than allowing them to roam the town. The next morning, it

Jefferson Barracks National Cemetery. *Map by Jennifer Ratcliffe-Tangney, 1994.*

was clear the 56th Regiment had cholera. Ordered back to Quarantine Station, the unit lost 178 enlisted men and one officer to cholera in the next few weeks. If Bentzoni had allowed the men into the city on the night of their arrival, the results could have been as devastating to St. Louis as they were to the 56th Regiment, U.S. Colored Troops.[129]

During its service the 56th Regiment lost a total of 674 men. Four officers and 21 enlisted men were killed in action or died of wounds. Two officers and 647 enlisted men were killed by disease, 96 percent of their regiment's losses.[130]

Proceed east on First South Drive. Most of the sections on the right include the graves of Union veterans. Cross Monument Drive. On the right, there are more Union graves in Sections 34, 33, 32, and 31.

Turn left at the end of the drive and then right at the T-intersection onto Old Post North Drive. On the right in Sections OPS2 and OPS1 are the graves of five Union brevet brigadier generals and two brevet major generals.

Section OPS1, Grave 2175: Brevet Brigadier General Edwin Burr Babbitt was born on January 8, 1804, in Connecticut. He was an 1826 graduate of the United States Military Academy and a veteran of the Mexican War. His Civil War service consisted of duty as colonel and chief quartermaster, Department of the Pacific. His brevet promotion to brigadier general was awarded on March 13, 1865, for faithful and meritorious service. Babbitt retired from the Regular Army in 1866 and died at Fortress Monroe, Virginia, on December 10, 1881.[131]

Section OPS1, Grave 2172: In 1861 Friedrich Schaefer was a major in the militia of the First Military District of Missouri, General Daniel Frost's command. In April, after Governor Jackson's refusal to provide troops in response to Lincoln's call, Major Schaefer boldly resigned from the state militia. In his letter of resignation he stated: "I cannot reconcile it with my ideas of military discipline that a part of your command has hoisted another flag than the only true flag of these United States." Frost ordered Schaefer's arrest and court-martial, but Schaefer refused to honor it. He soon became an officer in the Union army.[132]

The grave of Colonel Friedrich Schaefer is unusual for Jefferson Barracks in that its inscription is in German. The weather-worn white obelisk reads: "Hier ruht Colonel Friedrich Schaefer, Nov. 11, 1808, gefallen in der Schlacht bei Murfresboro, Dec. 31, 1862." Colonel Schaefer was killed while commanding the Second Brigade of Brigadier General Philip's division at the battle of Murfreesboro, Tennessee.

Section OPS1, Grave 2180: Charles McDougall served the United States Army as a major and surgeon with appointments as medical director in the Departments of Virginia, the Mississippi, and the East. He was promoted to brevet brigadier general on March 13, 1865, for faithful and meritorious services during the war. He was the father-in-law of Confederate brigadier general John Adams. McDougall died in Berryville, Virginia, on July 25, 1885, at the age of eighty.[133]

Section OPS1, Grave 2210: Gustav Heinrichs, a native of Germany, was born on May 18, 1828. His Civil War service was all with Missouri units, first as a first lieutenant, 3d Missouri Infantry, then as a major in the 5th and 4th Missouri Cavalry Regiments, and finally as lieutenant colonel in the 41st Missouri Infantry. Heinrichs was awarded a brevet promotion to brigadier general on March 13, 1865. He died in St. Louis on January 20, 1874.[134]

Section OPS1, Grave 2276: William Augustus Nichols, a graduate of the United States Military Academy in 1838, devoted his adult life to the military. His Civil War service was performed as assistant adjutant general in Washington, D.C. For his contributions he received two brevet promotions. The first, to brigadier general, came on September 24, 1864. The second, to major general, came on March 13, 1865. Nichols died in St. Louis on April 8, 1869, while still serving as a colonel in the Regular Army.[135]

Section OPS1, Grave 2288F: Though a brevet brigadier general, the tombstone of Chester Harding, Jr., reads simply "Colonel, 25th Missouri Infantry." A graduate of Harvard University Law School in 1849, Harding's first Civil War service was on the staff of Brigadier General Nathaniel Lyon. He also served as adjutant general of Missouri in 1861-1862 and as colonel of the 10th and 43d Missouri Infantry Regiments. The son of noted artist Chester Harding, he died in St. Louis on February 10, 1875.[136]

Section OPS2, Grave 2096A: Amos Beckwith retired from the Regular Army as a colonel in 1889 after a highly rewarding military career. A graduate of the United States Military Academy in 1850, Beckwith began his Civil War service as a first lieutenant in the 1st U.S. Artillery. He later served as chief commissary of subsistence for the Washington, D.C., Depot and for Major General William T. Sherman's army. Beckwith was promoted to brevet brigadier general of U.S. Volunteers on January 12, 1865, and to brevet brigadier general in the Regular Army two months later for "gallant and meritorious services in the campaign terminating with the surrender of the insurgent army under General Joseph E. Johnston." On March 13, 1865, he was promoted to brevet major general of U.S. Volunteers for his service in the Subsistence Department. He died in St. Louis on October 26, 1894.[137]

Continue ahead on this circular drive until you reach a T-intersection. Section 4 will be on your right. Stop to visit the graves of two Medal of Honor winners.

Section 4, Grave 12342: Lorenzo D. Immel was awarded the Medal of Honor for his bravery in action at the battle of Wilson's Creek, Missouri, on August 10, 1861. At the time, he was a corporal in Battery F, 2d U.S. Artillery (Totten's Battery).[138]

Section 4, Grave 12310: Martin Schubert won his Medal of Honor as a private in Company E, 26th New York Infantry. At the battle at Fredericksburg, Virginia, on December 13, 1862, Schubert came back to his regiment from a furlough granted because of his wounds and entered the battle, where he "picked up the colors after several bearers had been killed or wounded and carried them until himself again wounded."

Turn right and move forward a few yards before taking the first left (Longstreet Drive). On the left in Section 29 is the founder of a little-known veterans organization.

Section 29, Grave 12060: George E. Dolton was born in Illinois in 1840. A schoolteacher when war broke out, he enlisted in Battery M, 1st Illinois Light Artillery on August 11, 1862, and served with the battery continuously until discharged on July 24, 1865. Dolton returned to Illinois after the war, but he moved with his wife and two children to St. Louis in 1873 and went into business selling carriages, sewing machines, organs, and other items. While in St. Louis Dolton founded a little-known veterans group called "Comrades of the Battlefield."

A member of a St. Louis post of the Grand Army of the Republic, Dolton took a dim view of the influence some veterans with dubious military records were exerting over this popular Union veterans group. Somewhat in jest, in September 1877 Dolton proposed a fraternal order for combat veterans that in time became formalized as Comrades of the Battlefield. Union soldiers and sailors had to prove that they had served at least ninety days under fire before they could be admitted to membership. Chapters of the organization were called "battlefields" and named after the fields of conflict. The St. Louis chapter, Chickamauga, was created on January 30, 1891, and founder George Dolton was soon elected "Commanding General" of the national order. How many chapters were formed and how many veterans became Comrades of the Battlefield are not known, but veterans were still applying for membership as late as 1906, the year of Dolton's death.[139]

Continue straight ahead to the intersection of Longstreet Drive and Monument Drive. At the intersection stop and view:

The Minnesota Monument. On May 15, 1922, the State of Minnesota dedicated this monument in memory of her 164 Civil War veterans buried at Jefferson Barracks.

According to the report of the Minnesota Monument Commission, the memorial consists of "a bronze female figure of heroic size, holding in her hands a wreath, and of expression representing memory, and firmly fixed upon a massive granite pedestal." The monument stands on a concrete foundation six feet deep. In 1921, the monument cost $6,500.[140]

The inscription on the monument reads: "Erected A.D. 1921 by the State of Minnesota in memory of her soldiers here buried who lost their lives in the service of the United States in the war for the preservation of the Union A.D. 1861-1865."

During the war, about six thousand Minnesota soldiers were on duty at one time or another in the lower Mississippi Valley, and many of them passed through St. Louis. Six regiments of Minnesota infantry did important service in Missouri. The 4th Infantry was on duty at Benton Barracks in April 1862. The 7th, 9th, and 10th Infantry began provost and garrison duty in St. Louis in October 1863. The 7th and 10th Infantry left the area in April 1864; the 9th Infantry departed a month later. The 5th Minnesota Infantry played a role in defending against

General Price's raid into Missouri in 1864. The 6th Infantry arrived in St. Louis in October 1864, to recuperate from the effects of "malaria and kindred diseases" encountered during the summer around Helena, Arkansas, "a country reeking with miasma." The 6th Infantry performed provost duty in St. Louis into 1865.[141]

The 164 soldiers buried here represent all of Minnesota's first ten infantry regiments, an infantry battalion, a cavalry regiment, a cavalry battalion, and one heavy and one light artillery unit. All but three of the burials were during the war years. Nearly all the wartime deaths were the result of disease. Among the dead are 8 sergeants, 15 corporals, 139 privates, and 2 wagoners. The 6th Infantry was particularly hard hit; 45 of the 164 soldiers are from its ranks. The 7th Regiment yielded 30 from its ranks, and the 1st Minnesota Light Artillery Battery buried 10 men here, a high proportion considering the smaller size of a battery.[142]

One soldier, Sergeant Major Edward S. Past (Section 3, Grave 6891AA), represents the 1st Minnesota Infantry Regiment. On July 2, 1863, his regiment was called on to make an attack at Gettysburg in an attempt to stop Confederate pursuit following the rout of the Federal III Corps. It cost the regiment 215 of its 262 men engaged, the highest casualty rate (82 percent) of any Union regiment in any battle of the war. Of the attack, General Winfield Hancock is reported to have said: "There is no more gallant deed recorded in history." Past was buried here on November 13, 1914.[143]

From the Minnesota monument, go south (left) on Monument Drive one block. Turn right on South Drive. Stop at Section 14 to view:

Memorial to the Unknown Dead, 1861-1865. This memorial to the unknown soldiers of the Civil War was dedicated in Section 14 by the Annie Whittenmeyer Tent No. 3, Daughters of Veterans U.S.A. The inscription reads:

On fame's eternal camping ground
Their silent tents are spread
While glory guards with solemn sound
The bivouac of the dead.

Row after row of unknown American soldiers populate Sections 14, 15, 15 1/2, 16, and 22 near the memorial.

Proceed along South Drive until you notice the headstones with pointed tops. They will appear first on the right in Sections 21 and 20 and then on the left in Sections 19, 66, and 67. The pointed headstones mark Confederate graves.

On the left in Section 66 is:

The Confederate Monument. On May 1, 1988, this monument was dedicated to the memory of Confederate veterans. It was donated by the Sons of the Confederate Veterans, the Jefferson Barracks Civil War Historical Association, and the Military Order of the Stars and Bars.

The inscription on the Monument reads:

To the Confederate dead, 1861-1865

Who knows but it may be given to us, after this life, to meet again in the old quarters, to play chess and draughts, to get up soon to answer the morning roll call, to fall in at the tap of the drum for drill and dress parade and again to hastily don our war gear while the monotonous patter of the long roll summons to battle? Who knows but again the old flags, ragged and torn, snapping in the wind, may face each other and flutter, pursuing and pursued, while the cries of victory fill a summer day? And after the battle, then the slain and wounded will arise, and all will meet together under the two flags, all sound and well, and there will be talking and laughter and cheers, and all will say: "Did it not seem real? Was it not as in the old days?"

The words of the inscription were written in the postwar years by First Sergeant Berry Greenwood Benson of the 1st South Carolina Battalion of Sharpshooters.[144]

There are 1,104 Confederate dead in the cemetery, all but a few located in these six sections. Among the dead are 824 soldiers, 161 civilian men, 2 civilian women, 1 gunboat crewman, 1 identified only as a "conscript," and 116 not identified as soldier or civilian. Only 15 Confederates are unknown, most of these having been originally buried on Quarantine Island.[145]

Some Confederate graves of interest:

Section 22, Grave 5257: John Lyden served as a fireman aboard the gunboat *Star of the West* on the Mississippi River and its tributaries.

Section 21, Grave 4841: Samuel Marion Dennis was born at Richmond, Alabama, on December 24, 1834. While a student at the University of Alabama, he was one of the founders of Sigma Alpha Epsilon fraternity. He completed his studies at Princeton and, when war came, was practicing law in Columbus, Texas. Dennis enlisted in the 8th Texas Cavalry, or "Terry's Texas Rangers," and rode with this elite Confederate cavalry regiment until his capture at Stone's River, Tennessee. While being transported to St. Louis on a river steamer, he was forced by overcrowded conditions to sit on deck during a violent rainstorm. Still in wet garments, Dennis was put into prison, where he contracted pneumonia. He died on January 28, 1863.[146]

Section 21, Grave 4815: One of only two women buried in the Confederate sections is Nancy Jane Vaughan. Nancy's husband, Dan, was a noted member of Quantrill's guerrilla band. Nancy, her mother-in-law, and her sister-in-law were interrogated while in Gratiot Street Prison. All three showed the stress and strain of their circumstances. In an attempt to please Union authorities, Nancy identified nine men of her area who had become bushwhackers and two neighbor women whom she identified as "bad rebels." After Nancy's death on March 17, 1865, her frightened mother-in-law took advantage of Nancy's "immunity" to testify against her as an aid to the guerrillas.[147]

Section 20, Grave 4613: The other woman buried in the Confederate sections is Mrs. Jane N. Foster from Randolph County, Arkansas, who died on November 4, 1864.

Section 20, Graves 4601 and 4602: Confederates Stephen R. Smith and William Moore, convicted of being guerrillas, were hanged by the Union army in St. Louis on September 9, 1864.

Smith, age thirty-seven, was a native of Tennessee but had lived for many years with his wife and two children in Oregon County, Missouri. He was an elder in the Campbellite denomination and "a preacher of no mean repute in his neighborhood." On August 27, 1863, Smith enlisted as a private in Major Lee Crandall's battalion. Though Smith maintained that the area in which he campaigned was claimed by both sides, Union authorities argued that he "did lurk and travel about" within their lines armed as "an outlaw and guerrilla." They also decided that his "unit" was not a lawful military organization but one whose purpose was to engage in "petty warfare" through "raids, extortion, destruction and oppression."

Moore, age twenty-two, was born in Kentucky, but his parents moved the family to Texas County, Missouri, where his father and mother still lived at the time of his execution. Moore enlisted in Colonel White's infantry regiment on August 29, 1862. He was convicted of operating "armed and disguised" within the Union lines and was also found guilty of robbing Nathaniel Shavers, a citizen of New Madrid County, of two dollars. Moore was captured on May 7, 1864, at the New Madrid home of James W. Cresap, whom he was threatening to kill if he did not volunteer for the Confederate service.

Although no apparent attempt was made at secrecy, the execution almost passed without notice. On September 9, 1864, the captives were driven in an ambulance from Gratiot Street Prison to a gallows erected near the intersection of Poplar and Eleventh Streets. The gallows used was a recent technological improvement in the administration of death sentences: it used only one rope to hang two people. Smith was a large man, weighing more than 230 pounds, but Moore was much smaller, weighing "scarcely more than half" of Smith. Attendants were certain that the disparity in weights would be no problem on the new gallows.

In previous days, Smith had converted his fellow prisoner Moore to the Christian faith and conducted his baptism inside Gratiot Street Prison. Now Smith and Moore were attended by Reverend Philip McKim, the prison's chaplain. After a lengthy prayer, white caps were placed over the heads of the condemned, and their hands were tied behind their backs. The trigger on the gallows was sprung at 2:45 P.M.

Smith's weight, however, proved to be too much for the rope, breaking it as he fell through the trap door to the ground. Some of the slack rushed to Moore's side of the contraption, causing his feet to stop only a few inches from the ground. Moore at least died quickly and without further struggle. Smith lay on the ground, his neck broken, his white cap showing "gouts of blood." The attending physicians watched Smith struggle spasmodically for five minutes before they could pronounce him dead. The bodies were taken to Jefferson Barracks for burial.[148]

Section 20, Graves 4605-4610: In these graves lie the bodies of six Confederate prisoners selected at random and executed by firing squad in St. Louis on October 29, 1864, in retaliation for the execution of

Union Major James Wilson and six enlisted men by Confederate guerrillas. The soldiers were Asa V. Ladd, George T. Bunch, James W. Gates, Charles W. Minnekin, John A. Nichols, and Harvey H. Blackburn.

As you move west through the Confederate sections, you will come again to Union graves:

Section 62, Grave 11903: James H. Coates was born in Norristown, Pennsylvania, on November 27, 1829. For his service during the Civil War as colonel of the 11th Illinois Infantry, Coates was promoted to brevet brigadier general on March 13, 1865. After the war he worked as a grain merchant. Coates died in St. Louis on May 17, 1902.[149]

Sections 63, 64, and 68: On either side of the drive, these three sections contain the graves of 470 unknown Union soldiers, all of them moved from Quarantine Island in 1876.

Follow South Drive around the corner and stop. On your right is Section 65 and the grave of another Medal of Honor winner.

Section 65, Grave 11798: A monument marks the grave of "Late Color Sergeant" Henry M. Day. The inscription describes the event: "A devoted husband and father, a loyal citizen and a gallant soldier, to whom was awarded a Medal of Honor for planting the colors on Ft. Gregg between two contending armies, April 2, 1865." Fort Gregg was part of the Confederate fortifications at Petersburg, Virginia. The north face of Day's monument has a raised replica of the Medal of Honor as it appeared at the time.

Turn left on Longstreet Drive and follow it back to the Administration Building and the cemetery exit.

Appendix A
Alton, Illinois

1. The Alton Museum of History and Art

In north St. Louis County, take Interstate 270 to State Highway 367. Follow Highway 367 north to its convergence with U.S. Route 67 and continue on U.S. 67 across the Missouri and Mississippi Rivers to Alton, Illinois.

Immediately after crossing the Mississippi on the Clark Bridge, turn left on Piasa. The best first stop for a tour of Alton's Civil War-related sites is the Alton Museum of History and Art. The museum was moved to its present location in late 1994, and it will be open to the public in February 1995. If the museum is not open when you are touring, the Greater Alton Visitors Bureau should be your first stop.

At Piasa's intersection with Ridge Street, turn right. Continue to East 4th Street. Turn right and stop at 829 East 4th Street, the new home of the Alton Museum of History and Art. As this book went to press, hours for the new museum had not yet been established; however, the museum can be opened by appointment. Donations are welcome. For current hours and other information call 618-462-2763.

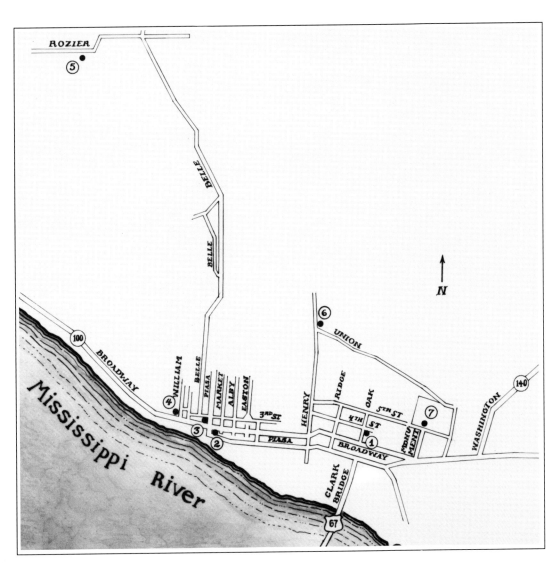

Alton, Illinois. *Map by Jennifer Ratcliffe-Tangney, 1994*

The Alton Museum of History and Art is an important starting point for a tour of Alton because it provides an instructive preview of the sites to be visited in the area. The museum moved into new quarters in November 1994, and the exhibits are unsettled. One of the more impressive exhibits, the Elijah Lovejoy press room, contains a replica of the press smashed by Lovejoy's murderers in 1837. Numerous artifacts from the printing trade during the prewar period are on display

The museum also owns an extensive collection of materials relating to the Alton Prison used to house Confederate prisoners of war. Unfortunately, the collection is not on display at this time.

One note about the staff: they are all volunteers, and they enjoy seeing visitors in their museum. If they cannot answer your questions, they will give you the name of someone who can.

2. The Lincoln-Douglas Debate

From the Alton Museum, go left on East 4th to Ridge. Turn left on Ridge to Broadway and turn right. Follow Broadway to the intersection with Market Street. On reaching this intersection, Lincoln-Douglas Square will be facing you on the front left.

Abraham Lincoln and Stephen A. Douglas opposed each other for the United States Senate seat from Illinois in 1858. To make their positions clear to the voting public, the two candidates agreed to a series of seven debates, the last of which was conducted in Alton on October 15, 1858. The candidates were tired and worn from the course of the campaign, and by this time they had little new to add to their presentations. Nevertheless, a crowd of some six thousand citizens assembled along Market Street to listen to Lincoln and Douglas speak from a temporary platform built in front of where the city hall then stood. The site of the speakers' platform is now within Lincoln-Douglas Square.

On this day, it was Douglas' turn to go first. He took the podium around 2:00 P.M. and spoke for nearly an hour. Lincoln followed with a ninety-minute presentation. Douglas returned for a thirty-minute rejoinder.

The 1858 senatorial race had been a difficult campaign. For Lincoln, the integrity of the fledgling Republican party seemed to hinge on the outcome. For Douglas, the 1858 election was perhaps the most significant of his career to that time. He was competing not only with the Republicans but also with discordant factions of the Democratic party. After the votes were counted, the Republicans swept the state offices as they had two years before, but Illinois sent Democrat Stephen A. Douglas to the United States Senate.[1]

3. Greater Alton Visitors Bureau

The Visitors Bureau is a short distance ahead at Broadway and Piasa. For free parking cross Piasa Street and turn right into a parking lot directly behind (west) of the Visitors Bureau.

The Greater Alton/Twin Rivers Convention and Visitors Bureau is open weekdays from 8:30 A.M. to 5:00 P.M., on Saturdays from 9:00 A.M. until 5:00 P.M., and on Sundays from 9:00 A.M. until 4:30 P.M. For information call 1-800-258-6645 or 618-465-6676.

The Greater Alton Visitors Bureau is a convenient spot to pick up brochures on the various Alton area attractions. Maps and historical booklets are also on sale there. The Visitors Bureau offers cold drinking water and clean rest rooms for the weary campaigner.

4. The Alton Prison

Continue west on Broadway to Williams Street. Turn right on Williams. A short distance ahead on the left (west) side of the street is the memorial to the Alton Prison.

The Federal Prison at Alton, Illinois, had a brief but infamous history. Originally the first state penitentiary to be built in Illinois, the prison was located on a seven-acre tract bounded by Wall Street (now Forsyth) on the north, Second Street (now Broadway) on the south, Williams Street on the east, and Mill Street on the west. Construction began in 1831. After the construction of the initial building, which contained twenty-four cells, other structures were built. The buildings were constructed of stone, oak timbers, and iron. They were on different levels and surrounded by stone walls thirty feet tall.

The first prisoners were received in August 1833. It was soon determined that the penitentiary was totally inadequate. The location was unsatisfactory. Water threatened to undermine the foundations. Living conditions were deplorable. The hospital was underground and rat infested. Three prisoners were assigned to a cell only large enough for one. Inmates slept on straw. Cells were not heated. There were no bathing facilities.

In 1847 Dorothea Dix and her penitentiary reform group urged that the prison be closed down. Finally, in 1857, the Illinois General Assembly decided the prison should be sold or razed and that prisoners should be relocated to a new state penitentiary at Joliet, Illinois. The last of the state prisoners was moved from Alton to Joliet in June 1860.[2]

On December 30, 1861, Major General Henry W. Halleck, commander of the Department of Missouri in St. Louis, ordered Lieutenant Colonel James B. McPherson to go to Alton and "examine the prison buildings, yards and other property in reference to its suitableness for a military prison." The decision to explore the possibility of the use of the former state penitentiary as a prison for prisoners of war was necessitated by the overcrowding of the Gratiot Street and Myrtle Street prisons in St. Louis.[3]

McPherson reported back almost immediately. In a lengthy letter on January 2, 1862, he advised Brigadier General George W. Cullum, chief of staff and chief engineer, of the general conditions of the prison, the number and size of the buildings, how they could be best used, and what needed to be done to make them suitable for use as a military prison. He estimated that 1,750 prisoners, including officers (who were normally kept in separate quarters), could be accommodated. He also reported that "the expense of fitting up the buildings to answer this purpose will be $2,415.00."[4]

Though McPherson reported that the property had been sold by the State of Illinois, it was actually under a long-term lease to Samuel A. Buckmaster, so the War Department completed an agreement with him. Security for the prison would be provided by the army, but Buckmaster was to be paid twenty thousand dollars annually to maintain the prison and feed, clothe, and care for the prisoners. Any funds left over after Buckmaster had complied with the terms of the agreement were to go to Buckmaster, providing him an incentive to cut costs at every opportunity. Buckmaster is reported to have become a wealthy man while the prisoners suffered.[5]

The first prisoners of war arrived at Alton on February 9, 1862, transferred from the Gratiot Street Prison in St. Louis. Soldiers of the 13th United States Infantry were transferred to Alton to serve as guards. By the time the war ended, the 77th Ohio, 3d United States, 37th Iowa, 10th Kansas, and 144th Illinois regiments had served as guards at the Alton Prison. The 144th Illinois Infantry was organized expressly for this purpose and was composed of men primarily from small communities in the Alton area. Mustered into service at Alton on October 21, 1864, the 144th Illinois had 1,159 officers and men. It was mustered out in St. Louis on July 14, 1865.[6]

By April 1862, 791 men were imprisoned at Alton. While it is difficult to determine the exact numbers with any certainty, it has been estimated that more than 9,000 Confederate and civilian prisoners were confined there during its three years of operation.

There were numerous attempts to escape. Details of one escape are described in a letter of July 26, 1862, from Union Major F. F. Flint. Flint tells how thirty-six prisoners, led by Colonel Ebenezer Magoffin, the ranking Confederate officer in the prison, escaped the day before by digging a trench "some fifty or sixty feet in length and must be several feet below the surface to pass under the foundation of the wall." Only two of the escapees were recaptured.[7]

The combination of malnutrition, exposure, overcrowding, and horrible sanitary conditions began to exact its toll. As many as five thousand prisoners were jammed into buildings that were adequate to accommodate approximately fifteen hundred. Scurvy and smallpox ravaged the prisoners; smallpox reached epidemic proportions, and there was no way to stop it. In an attempt to quarantine victims, the army forcibly moved smallpox victims to McPike's Island in the Mississippi River. A small hospital was set up, but reportedly none of the sick returned alive. The island became known as Smallpox Island. Because of the current location of the Alton dam and the higher level of the waters, the island is no longer visible. Gradually the smallpox epidemic was brought under control. By June 1864 burials were again being made in Alton's Confederate Cemetery.

The end of the war brought an end to the need for Alton Prison. Special Orders No. 165, June 20, 1865, from J. W. Barnes, Commissary-General of Prisoners, ordered that prisoners be removed from Alton to the Gratiot Street Prison in St. Louis. Further use of the prison was no longer required.[8]

The precise number of prisoners who died at Alton Military Prison will never be known. Estimates of the death toll range as high as five thousand inmates. The Confederate Cemetery in Alton contains the remains of 1,354 Confederate soldiers. The Alton Cemetery holds the graves of more than 200 Union soldiers, many of whom died while in service at the prison.[9]

Closed in 1865, the prison was later razed and the stones used in the construction of many buildings around Alton. One section of the cell block was left standing, but over the years this section fell into poor condition. In 1973 the Peavey Company moved the remaining sections of the prison wall to another location on what had been the prison grounds. It stands now at Williams Street between Broadway and Fourth Streets, a grim reminder of a sad and troubled past.[10]

5. The Confederate Cemetery

Return to Broadway and turn east to the intersection with Piasa Street (the Visitors Bureau). Turn left (north) on Piasa and left one block later onto 3d Street. Follow 3d one block to Belle and turn right. Follow Belle 2.1 miles to the intersection with Rozier Street. Turn left on Rozier Street and drive west 0.2 miles into a residential area. The Confederate Cemetery is on the left.

When the Alton Prison was a state penitentiary, this plot in an area of Alton known as "Buck Inn" was purchased for burial of convicts. Some thirty criminals had been interred there by the time of the Civil War. Shortly after the prison was converted into a military facility, this field began to be used to bury Confederate prisoners of war. Each prisoner's grave was to be marked with a headboard giving the initials of their names. Civilian undertakers and military surgeons were expected to keep records of the name, unit, cause of death, grave number, and other details. Unfortunately, undertakers were hired by contract, and each time the contract changed hands, a new numbering system was initiated. Records quickly became confused and confusing.[11]

In the forty years after the war, the Confederate cemetery became a cow pasture. Though one attempt was made to record the grave markers in 1867, with time the neighbors used up the wooden markers for firewood. In 1905 the Sam Davis Chapter of the United Daughters of the Confederacy was formed in Alton and petitioned the Federal Government for aid. The group's activist stance produced results: the United States purchased the property and surrounded it with an iron fence.[12]

Entering the cemetery the visitor passes first through a gate built in 1910 by Alton's United Daughters of the Confederacy. On the left column of the gateway, in weathered letters difficult to see, is the following exhortation:

> Soldiers rest! Thy warfare o'er,
> Sleep the sleep that knows not breaking!
> Dream of battlefields no more.
> Days of danger, nights of waking.

The forty-foot-tall granite shaft marks the burial place of the Confederates who died in Alton Prison and at the smallpox hospital established on a Mississippi River island. At the base of the shaft are six bronze tablets giving the name and unit of each of the 1,354 individuals buried there from 1862 through 1865. The memorial omits the names of 230 civilian prisoners, 7 soldiers removed to their homes, and 50 unknowns who died at Alton Military Prison or on Smallpox Island in the Mississippi River.[13]

From the back side of the memorial, two individual grave markers can be seen near the far edge of the fenced cemetery. The nearer of the two stones was placed in memory of Moses A. Collins, Company B, 2d Arkansas Cavalry, who died on December 24, 1864. Collins' name is among those given on the memorial's tablets. The second marker was placed to the memory of Third Sergeant Joseph Pearson Julian of Company E, 10th Texas Infantry. Sergeant Julian was born on January 6, 1828, and died on January 27, 1863.

6. The Lyman Trumbull House

Return to Broadway and turn east, continuing to Henry Street. Turn left on Henry (away from the river) and continue for several blocks to the intersection of Henry and Union Streets. Immediately on the right at 1105 Henry Street is the Lyman Trumbull home. It is in private hands and not open to the public.

United States senator Lyman Trumbull, a Democrat from Illinois and an ardent abolitionist, was instrumental in the creation and passage of the Thirteenth Amendment to the United States Constitution, which abolished slavery throughout the United States.

Trumbull was born in Colchester, Connecticut, on October 12, 1813, and was educated in local schools. He was admitted to the bar at age twenty-three and shortly thereafter set up practice with his brother in Belleville, Illinois. The house at 1105 Henry Street, soon to become his home, was built in 1837.

Trumbull was active in Illinois politics, serving in the state legislature (1840), as secretary of state (1841-1843), and as a state supreme court justice (1848-1854). He was appointed to the United States Senate as a Democrat in 1855, but in 1861 was elected to the Senate as a Republican because of his antislavery beliefs. In 1864 Trumbull was the chairman of the Senate Judiciary Committee, providing him with a powerful platform from which to champion the 13th Amendment.

After the Civil War, Trumbull moderated his views toward the South and resisted the vindictive efforts of the Radical Republicans, voting against the impeachment of President Andrew Johnson in 1868. In 1873 he retired from the Senate and moved to Chicago, where he practiced law until his death there on June 25, 1896.[14]

The Lyman Trumbull House was designated a National Historic Site in 1975.

7. The Lovejoy Monument and Alton Cemetery

Return by Henry Street to Broadway. At Broadway turn left and proceed east several blocks to the intersection with Monument Avenue. Turn left on Monument and proceed up the hill to the Alton Cemetery and the Lovejoy Monument.

The Lovejoy Monument was dedicated on November 8, 1897, by the citizens of Illinois in memory of Elijah Parish Lovejoy, abolitionist editor and one of the first white martyrs in resistance to slavery. As the visitor approaches the imposing, ninety-foot-high monument, it is easy to overlook the two stones flanking the entrance, which briefly tell the story of this important figure of the era immediately preceding the Civil War.

Elijah Lovejoy was born in Albion, Maine, on November 8, 1802. He graduated from Waterville College in 1823 and came to St. Louis in 1827. For a short while he taught school and worked for a Whig journal called *The Times.* After his conversion to Presbyterianism, he attended Princeton Theological Seminary and was licensed to preach in 1832. Instead, he returned to St. Louis and, with friends, established a religious newspaper, *The St. Louis Observer.* Antislavery articles began appearing in the newspaper in 1834, and, despite warnings from prominent citizens, they continued into 1835.[15]

Anti-abolitionist sentiment ran high in St. Louis in 1835. Many citizens were convinced that abolitionists were plotting to encourage slave rebellions within the city's black population. Free blacks were watched with suspicion and fear. In October 1835, after two Illinois men helped several slaves from St. Louis escape across the Mississippi River, Lovejoy's press was threatened with destruction. Only the threat of force in defense of the press against the mob saved Lovejoy's newspaper.[16]

Lovejoy misread his opposition. In an editorial of November 5, 1835, he lashed out against the Roman Catholics, which caused him to be held in increased disrepute. Eventually the furor abated, and soon St. Louisans, including many with no direct involvement in the slavery controversy, were coming to the defense of Lovejoy's civil rights. Though sympathy toward Lovejoy's stand for freedom of speech and freedom of the press produced a lull in the violence, it did not eliminate his opposition. Prominent Presbyterians took Lovejoy to task in the city's newspapers for his actions, which promoted "neither the harmony nor respectability of the Presbyterian Church in Missouri."[17]

In February 1836 Lovejoy took the ultimate position in his antislavery crusade, announcing in the *Observer:* "Our creed is that slavery is a sin—now, heretofore, hereafter, and forever, a sin.... Consequently," he argued, "it follows that whoever has participated, or does now participate, in that sin, ought to repent without a moment's delay." After announcing this position, his newspaper remained quiet on the subject, and as a result, Lovejoy, his wife, and their new son enjoyed a peaceful spring. In April they traveled to Pittsburgh for a meeting of the general assembly of the Presbyterian Church.[18]

When the Lovejoys returned to St. Louis, the city was in the grip of racial hysteria from the events of the preceding day. Francis McIntosh, a black cook on one of the steamboats, had intervened in a scuffle between two of his friends and two deputies. His friends escaped, but he was arrested for interfering with the officers in the conduct of their duties. As McIntosh walked with the officers toward jail, he learned that his likely punishment would be twenty-five or thirty lashes. Deciding to make his escape, McIntosh produced a knife and in the struggle with his captors killed one and severely wounded the other. McIntosh was jailed, but a mob, insisting on revenge, overcame the resistance of a few defenders. He was soon chained to a tree and forced to watch as a fire was built at his feet. The crowd watched as the flames rose around him. No one responded to his pleas for someone to shoot him.[19]

Lovejoy walked to the scene the next day. McIntosh's charred body was still bound to the tree. The corpse had been stoned. The head was missing. Outraged, Lovejoy returned to his office and set his thoughts in type. Not long after, the Lovejoy family left again for Pittsburgh, bearing a heavy burden of guilt for the atrocity that Elijah Lovejoy's abolitionist stand had apparently helped produce. While he was away, his press was heavily damaged by intruders in several incidents. At about the same time, Lovejoy's friend, fellow Presbyterian minister and strident abolitionist Reverend David Nelson, was forced from his pulpit in northern Missouri to safe haven in Quincy, Illinois.[20]

Lovejoy decided that St. Louis would no longer tolerate him. After sending his wife and son to her mother's home in St. Charles, he began making plans to move his newspaper to Alton. Lovejoy's last editorial blast at the city's leaders produced a crowd of two hundred people at his office. They watched as some twenty men broke down the doors and wrecked much of Lovejoy's materials, although the press itself was not harmed. Lovejoy was finished in St. Louis.[21]

He arrived in Alton in late July 1836, hoping that the free soil of Illinois would be a better environment for himself, his wife Celia, and their young son as it had for Nelson. The Presbyterian reformer was wrong. On Sunday, July 23, the steamboat *Palmyra* delivered his printing press from St. Louis to the Alton wharf, contrary to Lovejoy's instructions. Unwilling to move his press on the Sabbath, Lovejoy allowed it to remain on the wharf. Shortly before dawn on Monday morning, a group of men, reportedly from Missouri, damaged the press and pushed it into the river. As Lovejoy would soon learn, his difficulties would only intensify while he was in Alton.[22]

On the night of November 7, 1837, Lovejoy and a few friends held vigil in an Alton warehouse guarding yet another press to be delivered to his newspaper. A crowd grew around the warehouse. Alton's mayor tried to persuade those inside to abandon the press and avoid violence, but the men refused to budge. Soon the crowd set fire to the roof of the warehouse, and while Lovejoy and a friend tried to put out the fire, Lovejoy was struck by the load of a double-barreled shotgun. He died with five wounds. The defenders of the press were allowed to leave while the crowd searched out the press, broke it, and sank the broken parts in the Mississippi River.[23]

Lovejoy's body remained in the warehouse overnight. The next day, on what would have been his thirty-fifth birthday, he was buried in an unmarked grave in Alton Cemetery. His body was reinterred in 1852 at its present site some seventy-five yards north of the Lovejoy Monument. The iron fence surrounding his burial place was added in 1969. A marker in memory of Celia Ann French Lovejoy (born August 1813 in Salisbury, Vermont; died July 11, 1870, in Weaverville, California) was placed on November 9, 1987. Mrs. Lovejoy's burial location is unknown.[24]

Walk to the east side of the cemetery to visit the small National Cemetery established here in 1938.

Official records for the Alton Cemetery began in 1835, though burials may have begun there more than twenty years earlier. During the Civil War, Union soldiers were buried in the Citizens' Ground section of the cemetery. In 1938 these were removed to the National Cemetery established on the east side of the cemetery. Of the two hundred or more graves, most belong to soldiers from Kansas, Missouri, Iowa, and Illinois. Many of these individuals died while serving as guards at the Alton Prison.[25]

Appendix B
The Civil War in St. Louis
A Chronology

August 10, 1821	The Missouri Compromise allows Missouri to enter the Union as a slave state while Maine is admitted as a free state to maintain legislative balance in the United States Congress.
1826	Jefferson Barracks is established, and construction begins on the courthouse (now the "Old Courthouse") in St. Louis.
July 21, 1836	Violence is reported at the abolitionist newspaper operated in St. Louis by Elijah P. Lovejoy.
November 7, 1837	Lovejoy is killed in Alton, Illinois, while defending his printing press.
1847	The slave Dred Scott sues for freedom at the courthouse in St. Louis.
August 1852	Sterling Price, future Confederate general, is elected governor of Missouri to serve 1853-1856.
August 1856	Trusten Polk, St. Louis County, is elected to serve as governor beginning in 1857. Shortly after inauguration, Polk is elected to the United States Senate by the Missouri General Assembly. He loses the seat in 1862 as a result of his secessionist sympathies.
1857	The United States Supreme Court rules against Dred Scott and his petition for freedom.
October 16, 1859	John Brown raids the U.S. Arsenal at Harpers Ferry, Virginia, with the intention of starting a slave rebellion.
August 1860	Claiborne Fox Jackson, Saline County, is elected governor.
November 6, 1860	Abraham Lincoln and Hannibal Hamlin are elected president and vice president of the United States. Missouri is the only state carried by Lincoln's Democratic opponent, Stephen A. Douglas. Lincoln carries only two Missouri counties, Gasconade and St. Louis.
November 1860	In the last weeks of his term, Governor Robert M. Stewart orders the Missouri militia to the state's western border to defend against the depredations of abolitionists and jayhawkers from Kansas.
December 20, 1860	South Carolina is the first state to secede from the Union.
January 1, 1861	The last slave auction to be held at the courthouse in St. Louis is thwarted by a crowd of citizens.
January 12, 1861	A rally in support of the Union is held at the courthouse.
February 8, 1861	Alabama, Florida, Georgia, Louisiana, Mississippi, and South Carolina adopt a constitution for the provisional government of the Confederate States of America in Montgomery, Alabama. North Carolina, Tennessee, Texas, and Virginia join the Confederacy during the next two months. Arkansas does not secede until May.
February 9, 1861	Jefferson Davis is elected president of the Confederate States of America.
February 13, 1861	Abraham Lincoln is officially elected president of the United States.
March 4, 1861	The state Constitutional Convention meeting in the Mercantile Library Hall, St. Louis, votes against secession.
March 13, 1861	Captain Nathaniel Lyon takes command of troops at the United States Arsenal at St. Louis.
April 13, 1861	Fort Sumter at Charleston, South Carolina, surrenders to Confederate forces.
April 15, 1861	Lincoln issues call for seventy-five thousand militia for three months' service for the purpose of suppressing insurrection and "to cause the laws to be duly executed." Missouri's quota is four regiments of infantry and one brigadier general.
April 17, 1861	From Jefferson City, Governor Claiborne Jackson replies to Secretary of War Simon Cameron: "Your requisition, in my judgement, is illegal, unconstitutional, and revolutionary in its object, inhuman and diabolical, and can not be complied with. Not one man will the State of Missouri furnish to carry on any such unholy crusade."
April 20, 1861	The United States Arsenal at Liberty, Missouri, is seized by Southern sympathizers.

April 21, 1861	Captain Lyon is designated to muster in Federal troops in St. Louis. The city's German population is especially responsive to the call for volunteers. Four regiments, each one thousand men strong, are filled immediately, and the five regiments of the United States Reserve Corps are created to enlist the overflow.
May 4, 1861	U.S. ordnance stores at Kansas City are seized by pro-Confederates forces.
May 6, 1861	The state militia force of St. Louis County is mustered at Lindell Grove on the western edge of St. Louis. The encampment is named Camp Jackson in honor of Missouri's governor.
May 10, 1861	Camp Jackson is captured by Union forces under Lyon.
May 11, 1861	Rowdies at Fifth and Walnut Streets ambush the 5th Regiment, U.S. Reserve Corps.
May 14, 1861	Missouri's pro-Southern General Assembly creates the Missouri State Guard with one division for each congressional district. St. Louis County (which at this time includes the city of St. Louis) and the counties of Washington, Franklin, Jefferson, and Crawford compose the Ninth Division, Missouri State Guard.
May 15, 1861	General William S. Harney, commander of the U.S. Department of the West, advises the War Department to raise an all-Irish regiment in St. Louis to alleviate prejudice against the predominantly German Federal troops.
May 18, 1861	Former U.S. congressman and Missouri governor Sterling Price is appointed to command the Missouri State Guard.
May 21, 1861	Harney and Price reach an agreement to preserve order in the state.
May 31, 1861	Lyon replaces Harney as commander of the Department of the West.
June 11, 1861	Lyon and Francis P. Blair, Jr., meet with Price and Jackson at the Planters' House in St. Louis. Lyon repudiates Price's prior agreement with Harney and effectively declares war on Missouri.
June 14, 1861	Federal forces capture Jefferson City.
July 15, 1861	Confederate sympathizers skirmish with the 8th Missouri Infantry along the Northern Missouri Railroad near Wentzville. Seven Union soldiers are killed, one wounded.
July 22, 1861	With Jackson acting as the "Confederate" governor of Missouri, a loyal state convention in Jefferson City declares the executive offices to be vacated.
July 25, 1861	Major General John Charles Frémont arrives in St. Louis to take command of the Western Department and establishes headquarters at the Brant mansion, Eighth and Chouteau Streets.
July 31, 1861	Hamilton R. Gamble, St. Louis County, is elected governor by the pro-Union provisional government to replace Governor Jackson, now in open opposition to Federal authority.
August 7, 1861	Seven ironclad gunboats are ordered from St. Louisan James B. Eads.
August 10, 1861	Lyon is killed in the battle of Wilson's Creek (called "Oak Hills" by Confederates) near Springfield, Missouri.
August 24, 1861	Governor Gamble calls for the enrollment of forty-two thousand militia for a period of six months "to protect the lives and property of the citizens of the state."
August 30, 1861	Frémont declares martial law in Missouri and announces his intention to free the slaves of any who resist the Federal government. Lincoln later revokes Frémont's proclamation.
October 28, 1861	At a meeting at Neosho, Missouri, members of Missouri's General Assembly pass an ordinance of secession declaring that all political ties between the state and the government of the United States are dissolved and an act ratifying the provisional constitution of the Confederate States of America. Governor Jackson signs both on November 3 at Cassville, Missouri.
November 2, 1861	Frémont is relieved of command.
November 5, 1861	Missouri is accepted by the Confederate States of America as its thirteenth state.
November 7, 1861	Brigadier General U. S. Grant leads Union soldiers in an attack on the Confederate camp at Belmont, Missouri, opposite Columbus, Kentucky.
November 9, 1861	Major General Henry W. Halleck takes command of the Department of the Missouri, with headquarters in St. Louis.

November 21, 1861	John Schofield, brigadier general of U.S. Volunteers and brigadier general of Missouri militia, takes command of the Military District of St. Louis until April 10, 1862.
January 26, 1862	Halleck orders the officers and directors of the Mercantile Library Association and the St. Louis Chamber of Commerce to take an oath of allegiance to the United States or resign, thus identifying themselves as "disloyal." A week later the order is extended to include the staff of the University of Missouri, the railroads, Federal civil servants, and any merchant wishing to do business with the U.S. Government.
February 2, 1862	Several companies of the 4th Regiment, Missouri Volunteers, U.S.A., are disarmed in St. Louis and placed in confinement in Benton Barracks for mutinous behavior and disobedience of orders. The soldiers are later sent to Cairo, Illinois, to help build defenses.
February 16, 1862	Battle of Fort Donelson, Tennessee. Casualties are sent by steamer to Jefferson Barracks, beginning its role as a major military hospital.
March 7-8, 1862	Battle of Pea Ridge (Elkhorn Tavern) in northwest Arkansas. Among the Confederates are Price, the Missouri State Guard, and several Missouri infantry and artillery units recently transferred from state to Confederate service.
April 6-7, 1862	The battle of Shiloh, Tennessee, sends even more casualties northward to Jefferson Barracks and its hospital facilities.
June 5, 1862	Schofield commands the Department of the Missouri from St. Louis until September 24, 1862.
August 28, 1862	Schofield orders assessments against the Southern sympathizers and secessionists in St. Louis County for the purpose of equipping and maintaining the Missouri militia. The size of the assessments are based on the subject's wealth and the degree of sympathy for the South.
July 4, 1863	Vicksburg surrenders. St. Louisan John Bowen, now a Confederate major general, acts as General John Pemberton's go-between in negotiating with Bowen's former St. Louis acquaintance, General U. S. Grant.
July 13, 1863	William McKee, editor of the *Missouri Democrat*, is arrested for disloyal statements.
January 30, 1864	Major General William Rosecrans takes command of the Department of the Missouri from its headquarters in St. Louis.
February 1864	Willard P. Hall of Buchanan County, lieutenant governor to Hamilton Gamble, becomes governor upon Gamble's death.
May 17, 1864	The Grand Mississippi Valley Sanitary Fair opens in St. Louis.
July 28, 1864	The 40th and 41st Missouri Volunteers are organized at Benton Barracks to protect the populace from Confederate soldiers who "have been sent or permitted to come among [the citizens of St. Louis] to recruit, rob, plunder, and murder, as best they can, in violation of the laws of war and of humanity."
September 19, 1864	Price and a Confederate force of twelve thousand men in three cavalry divisions enter southeast Missouri. Over the preceding summer, Missouri had been stripped of Union troops. Rosecrans has only fourteen thousand Federal troops and twenty-six hundred militia scattered in more than fifty garrisons statewide.
September 24, 1864	Price's troops attack Fayette and skirmish at Jackson. On the next day, they engage Federal troops at Farmington and Huntsville.
September 26, 1864	Confederates advance to Ironton near the southern terminus of the St. Louis and Iron Mountain Railroad.
	In St. Louis, General Rosecrans issues an order directing that "all public business will be suspended after 12 m. tomorrow to enable us to complete our organizations for local defense, and so permit an active force to pursue the enemy." Citizens exempt from military service but "capable of defending their homes" are asked to organize under the direction of the mayor. More than five thousand men respond, including two companies of blacks.
September 27, 1864	Federal forces commanded by General Thomas Ewing, Jr., foster brother to General William T. Sherman, repulse Price's forces at Fort Davidson near Pilot Knob and then evacuate their position under cover of darkness. The Confederate incursion into the state creates serious alarm in St. Louis.

September 28, 1864	Price resumes his advance, but at Potosi the column turns northwest toward Cuba rather than northeast toward St. Louis.
September 29, 1864	Four Confederate riders assault the postmaster at Cheltenham Post Office. At Cuba, Price turns his raid west, following the south bank of the Missouri River. The last threat to St. Louis passes.
October 1864	General A. J. Smith's corps and a cavalry brigade are diverted from the pursuit of General Nathan B. Forrest in Tennessee and arrive in St. Louis by steamer in response to Price's threatening movements.
October 3, 1864	Price's invasion reaches Hermann and Miller's Station.
October 7, 1864	Price's column encounters Union forces near Jefferson City as it continues west.
October 29, 1864	Six Confederate prisoners held at Jefferson Barracks are executed near Lafayette Square in retaliation for the murder of Union major James Wilson, a noted guerrilla-hunter, and six of his soldiers.
November 1864	Thomas C. Fletcher, St. Louis County, is elected governor to serve 1865-1868.
November 8, 1864	Abraham Lincoln is reelected president of the United States with Andrew Johnson of Tennessee as vice president.
December 9, 1864	Major General Grenville Dodge is appointed to command the Department of the Missouri from St. Louis, serving until June 27, 1865.
December 19, 1864	Lincoln calls for additional troops. Governor Fletcher protests, claiming "our State will be depopulated unless something is done to prevent it." Fletcher argues that the loyal men "who have braved everything to stay in Missouri" will all be drafted and "all peaceful avocation be completely abandoned."
January 11, 1865	Spectators in the St. Louis Courthouse offer loud applause after the State Convention, meeting at the Mercantile Library, passes an ordinance of emancipation. Missouri, as a state loyal to the Union, had not been included in President Lincoln's Emancipation Proclamation two years earlier.
March 7, 1865	Martial law ends.
April 9, 1865	General Robert E. Lee surrenders his Confederate army to Grant at Appomattox, Virginia.
April 14, 1865	President Lincoln is assassinated in Washington, D.C.
April 17, 1865	A meeting is held at the Union Merchants Exchange in St. Louis to mourn the death of Abraham Lincoln.
April 26, 1865	General Joseph E. Johnston surrenders his Confederate army to former St. Louisan William T. Sherman at Bentonville, North Carolina.
April 29, 1865	Lieutenant Colonel Charles E. Davis and a detachment of the 17th Illinois Cavalry leave St. Louis to receive the surrender of M. Jeff Thompson's Confederate forces in southeast Missouri.
May 9, 1865	Thompson surrenders.
May 26, 1865	Missouri, with the rest of the Confederacy's Department of the Trans-Mississippi, is surrendered by General E. Kirby Smith.
June 6, 1865	Missouri's citizens ratify a new state constitution that includes the abolition of slavery.

Notes

1. Before the War

1. David D. March, *The History of Missouri*, 810. Michael Fellman, *Inside War: The Guerrilla Conflict in Missouri during the Civil War*, 7.

2. Fellman, *Inside War*, 7. Audrey L. Olson, "St. Louis Germans, 1850-1920: The Nature of an Immigrant Community and Its Relations to the Assimilation Process," 14.

3. Fellman, *Inside War*, 7.

4. Ibid., 5-8. Olson, "St. Louis Germans," 14.

5. Galusha Anderson, *A Border City during the Civil War*, 9. Fellman, *Inside War*, 7-8.

6. John McElroy, *The Struggle for Missouri*, 21.

7. James Neal Primm, *Lion of the Valley: St. Louis, Missouri*, 244. Fellman, *Inside War*, 5.

8. Primm, *Lion of the Valley*, 244.

9. Fellman, *Inside War*, 10.

10. Richard E. Mueller, "Jefferson Barracks: The Early Years," 11.

11. Ibid., 17. Promotions to brevet rank, an honorary title, were awarded for meritorious action in combat or for faithful service. Although brevet rank generally had no real significance under army regulations, it was recognized on occasion to settle questions of precedence. Abuses of promotion to brevet rank during the Civil War led to the abandonment of the brevet system in the postwar years. See Mark M. Boatner III, *The Civil War Dictionary*, 84.

12. Mueller, "Jefferson Barracks," 19. Ezra J. Warner, *Generals in Blue: Lives of the Union Commanders*, 209.

13. James Longstreet, *From Manassas to Appomattox*, 17-18.

14. Mueller, "Jefferson Barracks," 23. Warner, *Generals in Blue*, 231.

15. Lloyd Lewis, *Captain Sam Grant*, 100-101.

16. Glenn Tucker, *Hancock the Superb*, 46.

17. Grady McWhiney, *Braxton Bragg and Confederate Defeat*, vol. 1, 121, 128.

18. Christopher Phillips, *Damned Yankee: The Life of General Nathaniel Lyon*, 75.

19. Harold B. Simpson, *Cry Comanche: The 2d U.S. Cavalry in Texas, 1855-1861*, 21.

20. Ibid., 172-76.

21. Ibid., 42.

22. Ray W. Irwin, ed., "Missouri in Crisis: The Journal of Captain Albert Tracy, 1861," 18.

23. Ibid., 20-21.

24. Frederick H. Dyer, *A Compendium of the War of the Rebellion*, 1713. Mueller, "Jefferson Barracks," 28.

25. Peter Josyph, ed., *The Wounded River: The Civil War Letters of John Vance Lauderdale, M.D.*, 104.

26. Lewis, *Captain Sam Grant*, 100-102. William S. McFeely and Mary Drake McFeely, eds., *Personal Memoirs of U. S. Grant and Selected Letters, 1839-1865*, 36.

27. Lewis, *Captain Sam Grant*, 103.

28. Ibid., 104.

29. McFeely and McFeely, eds., *Memoirs of U.S. Grant*, 39.

30. Ibid., 1125.

31. Ibid., 1127.

32. Lewis, *Captain Sam Grant*, 340. Kimberly S. Little, *Ulysses S. Grant's White Haven*, 110.

33. Little, *Grant's White Haven*, 102-3.

34. John Y. Simon, ed., *The Personal Memoirs of Julia Dent Grant*, 75, 78.

35. John Y. Simon, "Grant at Hardscrabble," 192. Lewis, *Captain Sam Grant*, 340-41.

36. Simon, "Grant at Hardscrabble," 195.

37. Ibid., 196-97.

38. Simon, ed., *Memoirs of Julia Dent Grant*, 79-80. Thomas J. Keiser, "The St. Louis Years of Ulysses S. Grant," 15. Lewis, *Captain Sam Grant*, 343.

39. Keiser, "St. Louis Years of Ulysses S. Grant," 16.

40. Simon, ed., *Memoirs of Julia Dent Grant*, 80.

41. Lewis, *Captain Sam Grant*, 347-48.

42. Keiser, "St. Louis Years of Ulysses S. Grant," 17. Little, *Grant's White Haven*, 119. In the 1860s the street address changed to 219 Pine Street (Little, *Grant's White Haven*, 120).

43. Lewis, *Captain Sam Grant*, 363. Keiser, "St. Louis Years of Ulysses S. Grant," 17.

44. Lewis, *Captain Sam Grant*, 366. Keiser, "St. Louis Years of Ulysses S. Grant," 18.

45. Little, *Grant's White Haven*, 124. Julia's four slaves were hired out to St. Louis families who promised to take care of them (Little, *Grant's White Haven*, 126). One postwar visit occurred on October 9, 1874, to the home of Colonel Robert Campbell at 1508 Locust Street. Built in 1851, the home is the sole survivor of its neighborhood. It is now operated as the Campbell House Museum. For

information call 314-421-0325.

46. George McCue, *Sculpture City: St. Louis*, 36-37.

47. Ibid., 36.

48. John F. Marszalek, *Sherman: A Soldier's Passion for Order*, 16.

49. Ibid., 47. William T. Sherman, *Memoirs of General W.T. Sherman*, 28.

50. Sherman, *Memoirs*, 106, 109.

51. McWhiney, *Braxton Bragg*, vol. 1, 35.

52. William T. Sherman to Ellen Sherman, September 22, 1850, Sherman Family Papers, University of Notre Dame Archives.

53. William T. Sherman to Ellen Sherman, October 23, 1850, Sherman Family Papers.

54. Marszalek, *Soldier's Passion for Order*, 87. Sherman, *Memoirs*, 109.

55. Sherman, *Memoirs*, 110. Marszalek, *Soldier's Passion for Order*, 88. Candace O'Connor, "Sherman in St. Louis," 9.

56. Marszalek, *Soldier's Passion for Order*, 142. Lloyd Lewis, *Sherman: Fighting Prophet*, 151-52.

57. Ibid., 98.

58. Marszalek, *Soldier's Passion for Order*, 116-21. Warner, *Generals in Blue*, 442.

59. Sherman, *Memoirs*, 188-89.

60. Ibid., 212-14.

61. Warner, *Generals in Blue*, 442. Earl S. Miers, *The General Who Marched to Hell*, 16. At the time of his promotion on August 7, 1861, Sherman became the seventh-ranking brigadier general of volunteers in the U.S. service. Brigadier General Grant was eighteenth on the same War Department list.

62. Sherman, *Memoirs*, 1098. Miers, *General Who Marched to Hell*, 16-17.

63. Bruce Catton, *Mr. Lincoln's Army*, 65. Warner, *Generals in Blue*, 442.

64. J. Thomas Scharf, *History of St. Louis City and County*, 1834.

65. Anna McAllister, *Ellen Ewing, Wife of General Sherman*, 312. Katherine Burton, *Three Generations: Maria Boyle Ewing, Ellen Ewing Sherman, and Minnie Sherman Fitch*, 168.

66. McAllister, *Ellen Ewing*, 312. Burton, *Three Generations*, 168.

67. Burton, *Three Generations*, 169. William "Willie" Ewing Sherman was born on June 8, 1854, the Sherman's first son. He died of typhoid fever in Memphis on October 3, 1863, and was buried in Indiana. Charles "Charley" Celestine Sherman was born in Lancaster, Ohio, on June 11, 1864, and died the following December. His father never saw him. Both boys were initially buried in Lot 16, Section 17, at Calvary Cemetery.

68. McAllister, *Ellen Ewing*, 317. Burton, *Three Generations*, 174-75. Files, St. Bridget of Erin Church.

69. Sherman, *Memoirs*, 1112-13.

70. Richard Wheeler, *We Knew General William Tecumseh Sherman*, 115-16.

71. Files, Calvary Cemetery.

72. Burton, *Three Generations*, 282.

73. Marszalek, *Soldier's Passion for Order*, 496.

74. Thomas C. Fletcher, *Life and Reminiscences of General Wm. T. Sherman*, 177.

75. Ibid., 189.

76. Ibid., 183-87.

77. Ibid., 189-91.

78. W. B. Stevens Scrapbook, No. 100, 121, Missouri Historical Society (MHS).

79. Merlin E. Sumner, ed., *The Diary of Cyrus B. Comstock*, 50-51.

80. National Archives, Records Group 404, Series 172, Orders Received, Vol. 2, 1852. Sumner, *Diary of Comstock*, 60.

81. Stella M. Drumm, "The Kennerlys of Virginia," 108-13. George W. Cullum, *Biographical Register of the Officers and Graduates of the U.S. Military Academy at West Point, N.Y.,* vol. 2, 343.

82. Cullum, *Biographical Register,* vol. 2, 343. *St. Louis Directory for the Year 1857,* 31, 247.

83. Bowen Family Papers, MHS. *St. Louis Directory for the Year 1859,* 64, 333, 535.

84. Bowen Family Papers, MHS. U.S. Census of 1860, Town of Carondelet, 591.

85. Bowen Family Papers, MHS.

86. John S. Bowen, Compiled Service Records, General Officers (Confederate), National Archives.

87. Edwin C. Bearss, *The Vicksburg Campaign,* 314. Larry J. Daniel, "Bruinsburg: Missed Opportunity or Postwar Rhetoric?" 264.

88. Bearss, *Vicksburg Campaign,* 1284, 1306. Ezra J. Warner, *Generals in Gray: Lives of the Confederate Commanders,* 30.

89. McFeely and McFeely, eds., *Memoirs of U.S. Grant,* 375.

90. Ephraim McD. Anderson, *Memoirs: Historical and Personal; Including the Campaigns of the First Missouri Confederate Brigade,* 365.

91. Drumm, "Kennerlys of Virginia," 113. Sherman, *Memoirs,* 1022. Carondelet Historical Society Newsletter, "John S. Bowen House," 1-2.

2. The Coming of War

1. Lewis, *Captain Sam Grant,* 365. Curiously, Mrs. Julia Grant kept her four young slaves until they were freed by the Thirteenth Amendment after the Civil War (Simon, "Grant at Hardscrabble," 194). The St. Louis Railroad Company was often called by its more descriptive name, the Fifth Street Railroad.

2. Alice Hamilton Cromie, *A Tour Guide to the Civil War,* 185.

3. National Park Service publication, "The Old Courthouse."

4. Donald F. Dosch, *The Old Courthouse,* 80.

5. James M. McPherson, *Battle Cry of Freedom,* 170.

6. Marshall D. Hier, "A Hero's Death for a Lawyer, Hamilton Rowan Gamble," 51. For a recent review of the success of similar suits, see Robert Moore, Jr., "A Ray of Hope, Extinguished: St. Louis Slave Suits for Freedom."

7. McPherson, *Battle Cry of Freedom,* 171. *National Intelligencer,* December 24, 1856.

8. Dosch, *Old Courthouse,* 80.

9. See McPherson, *Battle Cry of Freedom,* 170-81, for a discussion of the implications of the Dred Scott decision.

10. Anderson, *Border City during the Civil War,* 29.

11. Ibid., 30.

12. Ibid. The slave's market value was probably between $500 and $800.

13. Ibid., 31.

14. Dosch, *Old Courthouse,* 80. Marshall D. Hier, "The Spellbinding Voice of Uriel Wright," 41. Ironically, Wright joined the Confederate army after the events of Camp Jackson in May 1861.

15. Dosch, *Old Courthouse,* 84-85.

16. John Scholz, "Notes on the Roswell Martin Field Home," 1.

17. Ibid., 2.

18. William Hyde and Howard L. Conard, *Encyclopedia of the History of St. Louis,* 741. W. V. N. Bay, *Reminiscences of the Bench and Bar of Missouri,* 236.

19. Bay, *Reminiscences of the Bench,* 237-39.

20. Ibid., 237.

21. Scholz, "Roswell Martin Field Home," 6. Bay, *Reminiscences of the Bench,* 240.

22. Melvin L. Gray, "Recollections of Judge Roswell M. Field," 129.

23. Scholz, "Roswell Martin Field Home," 4. Though he was only known as Samuel Clemens at the time, Mark Twain's brief experience in service to the Confederacy is recounted by his friend Absalom Grimes in M. M. Quaife, ed., *Absalom Grimes, Confederate Mail Runner,* 1-19. Twain told the story his way in "A Private History of the Campaign That Failed."

24. *St. Louis Post-Dispatch,* "Mercantile Celebrates Building's Century Mark," January 22, 1989.

25. Clarence E. Miller, "Edward William Johnston, Roving Scholar," 84-85.

26. William E. Parrish, *Turbulent Partnership: Missouri and the Union, 1861-1865,* 89. Miller, "Edward William Johnston," 85.

27. Report quoted in Parrish, *Turbulent Partnership,* 12.

28. *Missouri Democrat,* August 18, 1862.

29. Ibid., August 18 and 20, 1862.

30. Parrish, *Turbulent Partnership,* 200. *Missouri Democrat,* January 15, 1865. The Thirteenth Amendment was approved by the United States Congress on January 31, 1865, but not ratified by the states until December 18, 1865.

31. *St. Louis Post-Dispatch,* January 22, 1989.

32. Stella M. Drumm, "Historic Homes of Missouri: The Berthold Mansion," 290-92.

33. Basil W. Duke, *Reminiscences of General Basil W. Duke, C.S.A.,* 35, 37-38. The eight organizers were Overton W. Barrett, Rock Champion, Basil Duke, Samuel Farrington, Colton Greene, Arthur McCoy, James Quinlan, and James R. Shaler (*Duke, Reminiscences,* 37).

34. Ibid., 39.

35. Ibid. *St. Louis Daily Evening News,* March 4, 1861. *Missouri Republican,* March 5, 1861.

36. Drumm, "Historic Homes in Missouri," 293. *Missouri Democrat,* March 5, 1861.

37. *Missouri Democrat,* April 26, 1861.

38. Drumm, "Historic Homes in Missouri," 293-94.

3. The Camp Jackson Affair

1. At the time of the Civil War, there was no political or governmental distinction between St. Louis city and county as there is today. Lyon was promoted to brigadier general on May 17, 1861, one week after the capture of the Missouri militia. Despite the fact that his true rank was only captain, he is often referred to in nonmilitary accounts as "general."

2. The modern biography by Christopher Phillips, *Damned Yankee: The Life of General Nathaniel Lyon*, is recommended for the details of Lyon's life.

3. McCue, *Sculpture City*, 39. Walter B. Stevens, *St. Louis, The Fourth City, 1764-1909*, 837.

4. Hyde and Conard, *Encyclopedia of the History of St. Louis*, 1336.

5. For the story of Siebert and the Lyon monument, see McCue, *Sculpture City*, 39. Included among Holm's accomplishments is the design of the Missouri monument at Vicksburg National Military Park.

6. Richard Roberts, "How General Frost Won the High Ground at Grand & Lindell," 25.

7. Robert J. Rombauer, *The Union Cause in St. Louis in 1861*, 444, 446.

8. United States Army Corps of Engineers, St. Louis District, *Archaeological Investigations at the St. Louis Arsenal Site*, 4.

9. Ibid., 5.

10. Anderson, *Border City during the Civil War*, 63. Phillips, *Damned Yankee*, 138.

11. McElroy, *Struggle for Missouri*, 39-40. Father John Bannon, pastor of the Church of St. John the Apostle, is suspected of involvement in Frost's plot. A chaplain in the Missouri militia, Bannon was well known for his sympathy toward states' rights and secession. The Church of St. John the Apostle still stands on Chestnut Street between Fifteenth and Seventeenth Streets (it would be at the corner of Chestnut and Sixteenth Streets, but development has closed Sixteenth). Its cornerstone was laid by Kenrick and Bannon on May 1, 1859, and the building completed that November. It is one of the few Civil War-era buildings still extant in downtown St. Louis (*St. Louis Star*, April 10, 1933).

12. Scharf, *History of St. Louis City and County*, 485.

13. Phillips, *Damned Yankee*, 140.

14. Ibid., 141. McElroy, *Struggle for Missouri*, 54.

15. L. U. Reavis, *The Life and Military Service of Gen. William Selby Harney*, 353-54.

16. Thomas L. Snead, *The Fight for Missouri from the Election of Lincoln to the Death of Lyon*, 155.

17. Rombauer, *Union Cause in St. Louis*, 349. William G. Bek, trans., "The Civil War Diary of John T. Buegel, Union Soldier," 308-9.

18. Duke, *Reminiscences*, 44-45.

19. Phillips, *Damned Yankee*, 182-83.

20. U.S. Army Corps of Engineers, *Archaeological Investigations*, 8.

21. *Missouri Republican*, May 11, 1861.

22. United States War Department, *The War of the Rebellion: A Compilation of the Official Records of the Union and Confederate Armies*, ser. 1, vol. 3, 5. Hereafter cited as *Official Records*.

23. Stevens, *Fourth City*, 841.

24. Ibid., 841.

25. P. D. Stephenson, "My War Autobiography," Louisiana State University, 2.

26. Information concerning the routes of march is from Rombauer, *Union Cause in St. Louis*, 226-30. Robert Julius Rombauer served in the 1st Regiment, United States Reserve Corps.

27. Rombauer, *Union Cause in St. Louis*, 367. Heinrich "Henry" Boernstein, *The Mysteries of St. Louis*, vii-x.

28. Rombauer, *Union Cause in St. Louis*, 230.

29. Ibid., 200-205.

30. Phillips, *Damned Yankee*, 177-78.

31. *Missouri Republican*, May 7, 1861. *St. Louis Post-Dispatch*, "These Men Answered the Camp Jackson Roll Call," clip file, St. Louis Public Library, no date.

32. Hyde and Conard, *Encyclopedia of the History of St. Louis*, 2053-55. Elihu H. Shepard, *The Autobiography of Elihu H. Shepard*, 189-91. Shepard later declined offers of commissions from Nathaniel Lyon and Sterling Price for service in the Union and Confederate armies. He enlisted in a Union militia company in 1864 and served until war's end, retiring from military service at seventy years of age.

33. Sayers' postwar rendering of the survey is in the collections of the St. Louis Mercantile Library. During the Civil War, Sayers served as captain and chief engineer on the staff of General Leonidas Polk in the Army of Tennessee, C.S.A. A few days after the events of May 6, 1861,

General Harney attempted to legitimize Lyon's actions by offering as evidence of secessionist sympathies that one of the company streets was named "Davis" and the other "Beauregard" (*Official Records*, ser. 1, vol. 3, 372). In his postwar writings, Frost vehemently denied this claim.

34. Stephenson, "My War Autobiography," 3.

35. Phillips, *Damned Yankee*, 185. Duke, *Reminiscences*, 50-51. "Memoirs," William Bull Papers, MHS. Duke and Colton Greene did not stay to see what Frost would do. They decided to continue on to report to Governor Jackson in Jefferson City about their meeting with President Davis.

36. Camp Jackson Papers, MHS.

37. *Official Records*, ser. 1, vol. 3, 4.

38. Ibid., 7.

39. Phillips, *Damned Yankee*, 189-90.

40. *St. Louis Republic*, "'Volunteer' Reviews History of First Missouri Regiment," July 26, 1908, Camp Jackson Papers, MHS.

41. *St. Louis Republic*, July 26, 1908. *St. Louis Globe-Democrat*, May 10, 1909, Camp Jackson Papers, MHS.

42. Military Map of St. Louis, 1865, Map Collection, MHS. *Official Records*, ser. 1, vol. 3, 5. Sherman, *Memoirs*, 191. Sayers survey, Mercantile Library.

43. Hans Christian Adamson, *Rebellion in Missouri: 1861*, 60.

44. *Official Records*, ser. 1, vol. 3, 5. Accounts by militia members give the number of men as 635. *St. Louis Republican*, July 26, 1908. Heinrich Boernstein, *Funfundsiebzig Jahre in der Alten und Neuen Welt*, 299.

45. *Missouri Republican*, March 17, 1887.

46. Samuel Hemple Chauvenet, "St. Louis in the Early Days of the Civil War and the Capture of Camp Jackson," Camp Jackson Papers, MHS. William Chauvenet had accepted a position as professor of mathematics at Washington University in 1859. In 1862 he would become the school's second chancellor, serving until poor health forced his resignation in 1869. Chauvenet is buried in Bellefontaine Cemetery, St. Louis.

47. Rombauer, *Union Cause in St. Louis*, 233. Sherman, *Memoirs*, 191.

48. *Missouri Republican*, May 15, 1861.

49. *Westliche Post*, May 15, 1861, in Steven Rowan, ed. and trans., *Germans for a Free Missouri: Translations from the St. Louis Radical Press, 1857-1862*, 210.

50. Scharf, *History of St. Louis City and County,* 498-99.

51. Ibid., 500.

52. Sherman, *Memoirs,* 191-92.

53. *Westliche Post,* May 15, 1861, in Rowan, ed. and trans., *Germans for a Free Missouri,* 211.

54. *Missouri Democrat,* May 13, 1861.

55. Stephenson, "My War Autobiography," 6.

56. Ibid., 6-7.

57. Boernstein, *Funfundsiebzig Jahre in der Alten und Neuen Welt,* 301-2.

58. *Missouri Republican,* March 19, 1887.

59. Harvey L. Carter and Norma L. Peterson, eds., "William S. Stewart Letters, January 13, 1861, to December 4, 1862," 211.

60. *Missouri Republican,* May 11 and 15, 1861. *Westliche Post,* May 15, 1861, quoted in Rowan, ed. and trans., *Germans for a Free Missouri,* 211. Boernstein, *Funfundsiebzig Jahre in der Alten und Neuen Welt,* 287, 300. Icenhower (also identified as Eisenhardt) was a private in Company E, 2d Missouri Volunteer Militia. Doan (or Dean) was a member of the Southwest Battalion. Knobloch was an artilleryman in the same unit (M. Hopewell, M.D., *Camp Jackson: History of the Missouri Volunteer Militia of St. Louis,* 24. *Missouri Republican,* May 18, 1861). The available information on casualties among the Union troops is contradictory. Although they are incomplete, the compiled service records of the 2d and 3d U.S. Volunteers reveal no evidence of deaths other than Blandowski's.

61. Bek, trans., "Civil War Diary of John T. Buegel," 310. *Official Records,* ser. 1, vol. 3, 5. Otto C. Lademann, "The Capture of Camp Jackson," 72.

62. "Memoirs," William Bull Papers, MHS.

63. *St. Louis Republic,* "'Volunteer' Reviews History of First Missouri Regiment," July 26, 1908, Camp Jackson Papers, MHS.

64. McFeely and McFeely, eds., *Memoirs of U.S. Grant,* 157.

65. *St. Louis Republic,* July 26, 1908.

66. In re MacDonald [Case No. 8,751, E.D. Missouri, 1861, 9 Am. Law Reg. 661]. Leonard E. Dressel II, *A Self-Guided Tour of Confederate Graves at Bellefontaine Cemetery,* 12.

4. At War in Earnest

1. Dyer, *Compendium of the War of the Rebellion,* 1324.

2. *Mississippi Blaetter,* May 12, 1861. Anderson, *Border City during the Civil War,* 106. *Harper's Weekly,* June 1, 1861. *Missouri Republican,* May 12 and 15, 1861.

3. *Missouri Republican,* May 12 and 18, 1861. Writing in the confusion of the day following the event, the *Missouri Republican* identified the fatalities as William Cody, John Dick, John Gabnin, and Jerry Switzerlan. *Missouri Democrat,* May 20, 1861, reports Cody, Dick, Enright, Lappe, and Miller as casualties and adds William Hulenhorst (Hollinghast?), Jacob Niederheuter, and John Schanklen (Shaukbeer?) to the list of those killed on May 11, 1861.

4. Anderson, *Border City during the Civil War,* 107.

5. *Daily Missouri State Journal,* May 11, 1861.

6. *Missouri Democrat,* May 29, 1861. R. Ernest Dupuy and Trevor N. Dupuy, *The Encyclopedia of Military History,* 773-74.

7. Dupuy and Dupuy, *Encyclopedia of Military History,* 772.

8. Rick Stewart, Joseph D. Ketner II, and Angela L. Miller, *Carl Wimar: Chronicler of the Missouri River Frontier,* 80.

9. Ibid., 111-12.

10. St. Louis Genealogical Society, *Index of St. Louis Marriages, 1804-1876,* vol. 1. U.S. Census for 1860, St. Louis, 7th Ward.

11. *Missouri Democrat,* May 12, 1860. The reference to Blandowski's Crimean War service has not been substantiated.

12. *Missouri Democrat,* May 24, 1861. *Missouri Republican,* May 28, 1861.

13. *Missouri Democrat,* May 28, 1861.

14. Ibid. In this account, the Blandowskis have three children. To complicate matters further, contemporary accounts also refer to this cemetery as the Picotte Cemetery.

15. *Missouri Republican,* May 31, 1861.

16. Hyde and Conard, *Encyclopedia of the History of St. Louis,* 445-46.

17. St. Louis Genealogical Society, *Old Cemeteries of St. Louis County, Missouri,* vol. 3, 74. Though Blandowski was the first Union officer to be mortally wounded, he was not the first officer to die in suppressing the rebellion. That distinction belongs to Colonel Elmer Ellsworth, who was killed in Alexandria, Virginia, on May 24, 1861. Mrs. Blandowski remained a widow for less than three years. On March 22, 1864, she married Mr. John Holland of St. Louis (St. Louis Genealogical Society, *Index to St. Louis Marriages,* vol. 2).

18. Dorothy G. Holland, "The Planters' House," 110-11.

19. Ibid., 113.

20. Robert E. Shalhope, *Sterling Price: Portrait of a Southerner,* 164.

21. Ibid., 165.

22. Thomas L. Snead, "The First Year of the War in Missouri," 267. Shalhope, *Sterling Price,* 165-66.

23. Holland, "Planters' House," 114-17.

24. Dyer, *Compendium of the War of the Rebellion,* 1322.

25. *Missouri Democrat,* June 18, 1861. This same incident is reported in *Leslie's Illustrated Newspaper,* June 29, 1861, but the unit is described as "the regiment of Colonel John McNeil," which would have been the 3d Regiment, United States Reserve Corps.

26. *Missouri Democrat,* June 18, 1861.

27. In addition to Pratt and Frenzel, the dead included Keren Tracy, Charles Cella, and a man named Burns. *Missouri Republican* quoted in Scharf, *History of St. Louis City and County,* 523.

28. *Missouri Republican* quoted in Scharf, *History of St. Louis City and County,* 524.

29. *Missouri Democrat,* June 18, 1861.

30. Dyer, *Compendium of the War of the Rebellion,* 255.

31. Jessie Benton Frémont, *The Story of the Guard: A Chronicle of the War,* x. Jessie Benton Frémont, *Souvenirs of My Time,* 166.

32. Primm, *Lion of the Valley,* 359. Mary Bartley, "Palace to Warehouse." McElroy, *Struggle for Missouri,* 218. Pamela Herr, *Jessie Benton Frémont: A Biography,* 327.

33. Frémont, *Souvenirs of My Time,* 166. Jay Monaghan, *Civil War on the Western Border, 1854-1865,* 184.

34. Herr, *Jessie Benton Frémont,* 327-28. Frémont, *Story of the Guard,* 43.

35. McPherson, *Battle Cry of Freedom,* 352.

36. Ibid., 352-53.

37. Herr, *Jessie Benton Frémont,* 339-40.

38. Frémont, *Story of the Guard,* 198.

39. Frémont, *Souvenirs of My Time,* 202. Monaghan, *Civil War on the Western Border,* 204-6.

40. Bartley, "Palace to Warehouse."

41. *Official Records,* ser. 2, vol. 4, 94, 171. Francis A. Lord, *They Fought for the Union,* 319. Boatner, *Civil War Dictionary,* 270.

42. Nannie M. Tilley, ed., *Federals on the Frontier: The Diary of Benjamin F. McIntyre, 1862-1864,* 8.

43. Hyde and Conard, *Encyclopedia of the History of St. Louis,* 134-35.

44. Dyer, *Compendium of the War of the Rebellion,* 1303, 1321, 135, 1333-37.

45. Ibid., 1322-23. *Missouri Democrat,* January 20, 1864.

46. *Missouri Democrat,* January 19, 1864.

47. Hyde and Conard, *Encyclopedia of the History of St. Louis.* Robert Lauenstein, "Notes on the Fortifications of St. Louis."

48. Hyde and Conard, *Encyclopedia of the History of St. Louis.* Lauenstein, "Notes on Fortifications."

49. Mrs. Simon L. Boogher (Sophia Hogan Boogher), *Recollections of John Hogan,* 54-58.

50. Lauenstein, "Notes on Fortifications."

51. Hyde and Conard, *Encyclopedia of the History of St. Louis,* 628.

52. Edwin C. Bearss, *Hardluck Ironclad: The Sinking and Salvage of the "Cairo,"* 15.

53. Ibid., 17.

54. Ibid.

55. Ibid., 21-22. McCune Gill, *The St. Louis Story,* 188, describes a marine railway: "A marine railway is a device composed of great runways extending down into the river, on which runways there is a huge cradle or frame that is lowered under a steamboat as it floats in the river. . . . When a new boat is constructed it is built on the cradle and when finished is lowered into the river."

56. To see the sort of housing available to St. Louis' artisans during this period, follow Broadway south from Bellerive Park to its intersection with Marceau Street. Turn left on Marceau toward the river. At the southeast corner of the intersection of Marceau and Vulcan Street stands the Schlightig home. The stone structure was built in 1857, the frame addition obviously a later modification. The owner, Charles Schlightig, and his sons were ship's carpenters. No connection has been established between the family and Eads (Lauenstein, "Notes on Fortifications"). Bearss, *Hardluck Ironclad,* 24.

57. Bearss, *Hardluck Ironclad,* 25.

58. Ibid., 27. In August, Eads chose names for six of the seven gunboats: "J. C. Frémont," "Geo. B. McClellan," "N. P. Banks," "Nathaniel Lyon," "M. C. Meigs," and "John Rodgers." None of his suggestions were used (ibid., 22).

59. Scharf, *History of St. Louis City and County,* 537. Paul H. Silverstone, *Warships of the Civil War Navies,* 151.

60. Silverstone, *Warships of the Civil War Navies,* 152-53. Fortunately for

students of the Civil War, *Cairo* was recovered in 1965 and is on display at Vicksburg National Military Park, Vicksburg, Mississippi.

61. Marjorie E. Fox Grisham, "Joseph Nash McDowell and the Medical Department of Kemper College, 1840-1845," 370.

62. Ibid., 359-60. Anderson, *Border City during the Civil War,* 188-89.

63. Howard I. McKee, "The 'Swamp Fox,' Meriwether Jeff Thompson," 123-24. W. B. Hesseltine, "Military Prisons of St. Louis, 1861-1865," 382.

64. *Missouri Republican,* December 23 and 27, 1861.

65. *Missouri Democrat,* December 25, 1861.

66. Hesseltine, "Military Prisons of St. Louis," 383-84.

67. Bassford Scrapbook, MHS, 43. Hugh P. Williamson, "Military Prisons in the Civil War," 332. Anderson, *Border City during the Civil War,* 189.

68. Griffin Frost, *Camp and Prison Journal,* 28, 30.

69. Quaife, *Absalom Grimes,* 164-65.

70. *Missouri Democrat,* January 8, 1862. Vicki Vaughn Johnson, "War Comes to Main Street: The St. Louis Chamber of Commerce Election of 1862," 2.

71. Johnson, "War Comes to Main Street," 4-5. *Missouri Democrat,* January 9, 1862. *Missouri Republican,* January 9, 1862.

72. Johnson, "War Comes to Main Street," 5.

73. Ibid., 9.

74. *Missouri Democrat,* February 18, 1862. Scharf, *History of St. Louis City and County,* 427.

75. *Missouri Democrat,* February 27, 1862. Scharf, *History of St. Louis City and County,* 428.

76. *Missouri Democrat,* February 22, 1862.

77. "Em" to "My darling brother," May 17, 1862, Edward C. Robbins Papers, Mercantile Library.

78. Anderson, *Border City during the Civil War,* 290, 302.

79. Stephen Z. Starr, *Jennison's Jayhawkers: A Civil War Cavalry Regiment and Its Commander,* 28-32.

80. Ibid., 61-62.

81. *Official Records,* ser. 1, vol. 7, 449, 507. Albert Castel, *A Frontier State at War: Kansas, 1861-1865,* 61.

82. Starr, *Jennison's Jayhawkers,* 85. One of Jennison's many inconsistencies was that, although an ardent abolitionist during the war, he worked actively against Negro

suffrage in the postwar years (ibid., 384).

83. Ibid., 124-33.

84. Ibid., 134-36.

85. Ibid., 141.

86. Ibid., 142-43.

87. *Missouri Democrat,* April 28, 1862. Hesseltine, "Military Prisons of St. Louis," 381-88. Hyde and Conard, *Encyclopedia of the History of St. Louis,* 1333. Starr, *Jennison's Jayhawkers,* 148.

88. *Missouri Democrat,* April 22 and 24, 1862.

89. *Missouri Republican,* April 21 and 23, 1862.

90. *Missouri Democrat,* April 22, 24, and 25, 1862. Starr, *Jennison's Jayhawkers,* 145-51. Castel, *Frontier State at War,* 60. Formal charges had been prepared but were never used because Jennison was never brought to trial. They included charges of disrespectful language toward President Lincoln and Generals Halleck, Denver, Sturgis, and Mitchell and of encouraging soldiers to desert (Starr, *Jennison's Jayhawkers,* 147).

91. *Missouri Democrat,* April 28, 1862.

92. Starr, *Jennison's Jayhawkers,* 159-61.

93. Castel, *Frontier State at War,* 60.

94. *Missouri Democrat,* May 12, 1863. In 1865 Drake led the Missouri Constitutional Convention in imposing the harsh and vindictive "test oath" on former Confederates and suspected Southern sympathizers. Drake later represented Missouri in the United States Senate.

95. *Missouri Democrat,* May 14, 1863.

96. *Florissant Valley Reporter,* July 6, 1961, in Civil War Scrapbook, MHS.

97. Ibid.

98. United Daughters of the Confederacy, Missouri Division, *Reminiscences of the Women of Missouri during the Sixties,* 78-79.

99. *Missouri Republican,* May 14, 1863.

100. Joseph G. Knapp, *The Presence of the Past,* 2, 8. *Missouri Republican,* May 14, 1863.

101. *Missouri Democrat,* May 14, 1863.

102. *Missouri Republican,* May 14, 1863. *Missouri Democrat,* May 14, 1863. The thirteen men were Charles Clark, James S. Daugherty, Daniel H. Donovan, George W. Dutro, Henry N. Hart, Mortimer Kennett, Owen Mency, Dr. S. Gratz Moses, Isaac J. Pollard, Christian Pullis, Samuel Robbins, Linton Sappington, and Christian Shaffer.

103. *Missouri Democrat,* May 22, 1863.

104. *Missouri Republican,* May 18, 1863.

105. *St. Louis Daily Evening News,* July 6, 1863.

106. *Missouri Democrat,* July 6-10, 1863.

107. *Missouri Democrat,* September 14, 1863. On May 9, 1861, *J. C. Swon* had been used to transport munitions up the Mississippi for the Missouri Volunteer Militia assembled at Camp Jackson.

108. *Missouri Democrat,* September 29 and October 5, 1863. Felix G. Stidger, *Treason History of the Order of Sons of Liberty,* 12. Patricia Faust, ed., *Historical Times Illustrated Encyclopedia of the Civil War,* 322.

109. *Missouri Democrat,* October 5, 1863.

110. James D. Horan, *Confederate Agent: A Discovery in History,* 137-38. John B. Castleman, *Active Service,* 173. Castleman's presence in St. Louis during this time is established, but the precise dates are unknown. Greek fire was not used more widely during the Civil War era because of its well-deserved reputation for instability.

111. Horan, *Confederate Agent,* 225-27. There is considerable possibility that Jones was deliberately passing "disinformation." Jones, described as "well educated" and fluent in French, German, and Spanish, convinced his captors in Maine that he was the son of the president of St. Louis University, though all of the school's presidents have been Jesuit priests. Jones disclosed William Kendall and Captain Lewis Kennerly as operatives in St. Louis.

112. William A. Tidwell, James O. Hall, and David Winifred Gaddy, *Come Retribution: The Confederate Secret Service and the Assassination of Abraham Lincoln,* 166-67. *Official Records,* ser. 1, vol. 48, part 2, 194-95. In addition to Frazor, the St. Louisans identified were John R. Barrett (a former member of Congress from Missouri), S. B. Harwood, Harrison Fox, Robert Louden, and Peter Mitchell. Ex-St. Louisan Joseph W. Tucker, a Southern Methodist minister and one-time editor of the *Missouri State Journal,* was identified as "chief of this service under the Secretary of War."

113. *Official Records,* ser. 1, vol. 48, 194-96.

114. Stephen Z. Starr, *The War in the East from Gettysburg to Appomattox, 1863-1865,* 4.

115. Ibid. Scharf, *History of St. Louis City and County,* 445.

116. Military Map of St. Louis, 1865, Map Collection, MHS.

117. Scharf, *History of St. Louis City and County,* 445-46.

118. Starr, *War in the East,* 8, 9.

119. Ibid., 5.

120. Paula Coalier, "Beyond Sympathy: The St. Louis Ladies' Union Aid Society and the Civil War," 41-42.

121. Hyde and Conard, *Encyclopedia of the History of St. Louis,* 2494. Coalier, "Beyond Sympathy," 43.

122. Jasper W. Cross, "The Mississippi Valley Sanitary Fair, St. Louis, 1864," 238.

123. Ibid. Anderson, *Border City during the Civil War,* 311.

124. Cross, "Mississippi Valley Sanitary Fair," 243.

125. Ibid.

126. Anderson, *Border City during the Civil War,* 311-13.

127. Cross, "Mississippi Valley Sanitary Fair," 244.

128. Ibid., 244-46. Coalier, "Beyond Sympathy," 49.

129. Anderson, *Border City during the Civil War,* 314.

130. Dyer, *Compendium of the War of the Rebellion,* 1327.

131. Marcus O. Frost, *Regimental History of the Tenth Missouri Volunteer Infantry,* 201.

132. Ibid., 204.

133. Ibid., 205. Holmes commanded the regiment from April 1862 to June 1863.

134. Ibid., 208. Deimling had commanded the regiment since June 1863.

135. Ibid., 209.

136. Patrick J. O'Connor, *History of Cheltenham and St. James Parish, St. Louis, 1860-1937.*

137. *Missouri Republican,* October 1, 1864.

138. *Missouri Democrat,* October 5, 1864.

139. David Radcliffe, "Kirkwood and the Civil War," 1.

140. Stephen B. Oates, *Confederate Cavalry West of the River,* 144-45.

141. Record and Pension Office, War Department, *Organization and Status of Missouri Troops (Union and Confederate) in Service during the Civil War,* 187.

142. Paul B. Jenkins, *The Battle of Westport,* 38-39. Radcliffe, "Kirkwood and the Civil War," 1.

143. Oates, *Confederate Cavalry,* 145. Richard S. Brownlee, *Gray Ghosts of the Confederacy: Guerrilla Warfare in the West, 1861-1865,* 221-22.

144. John Margreiter, "Major James Wilson: 3d Cavalry, Missouri State Militia, U.S.A.," 1.

145. Reeves' name is also spelled "Reves" in contemporary accounts.

146. Mark Crawford to John Margreiter, July 21, 1992.

147. Fellman, *Inside War,* 182. Five of the six Union enlisted men were Corporal Gourly and Privates Grotts, Scaggs, and Shew from Company I, 3d Cavalry, Missouri State Militia, and Private Holabaugh from Company K of the same regiment (Dr. John Margreiter to Mr. Mark Crawford, July 25, 1992).

148. Margreiter, "Major James Wilson," 1.

149. *Florissant Valley Reporter,* February 1, 1862, in Civil War Scrapbook, MHS.

150. Tony Fusco, "Bloody Saturday," 7. At the time, Fort No. 4 was located near the northeast corner of Russell and Jefferson Streets. Street names in the area have since changed.

151. *Missouri Democrat,* October 31, 1864.

152. Ibid. The graves at Jefferson Barracks National Cemetery are in Section 40, Graves 4605-10.

153. Contrary to a claim in the information sheet provided for visitors to Jefferson Barracks National Cemetery, the Union veteran James Wilson buried there in Section 39, Grave 4319, is not the Major James Wilson of this incident. Muster rolls indicate that he is James Wilson of Company I, 9th Missouri Volunteer Cavalry, who died on February 8, 1863 (Margreiter, "Major James Wilson," 3).

154. Margreiter, "Major James Wilson," 4.

155. *Missouri Democrat,* December 28, 1864. Leonard E. Dressel II, "Major James Morgan Utz, C.S.A." Elinor M. Coyle, *Old St. Louis Homes, 1790-1865: "The Stories They Tell,"* 22.

156. Dressel, "Major James Morgan Utz." *Florissant Valley Reporter,* February 8, 1862, in Civil War Scrapbook, MHS.

157. *Missouri Republican,* December 28, 1864.

158. Dressel, "Major James Morgan Utz." *Missouri Democrat,* September 27, 1864.

159. *Missouri Republican,* December 28, 1864. Hyde and Conard, *Encyclopedia of the History of St. Louis,* 1086.

160. *Missouri Democrat,* December 28, 1864. *Missouri Republican,* December 28, 1864.

161. *Missouri Democrat,* December 28, 1864. Coyle, *Old St. Louis Homes,* 22.

162. Scharf, *History of St. Louis City and County,* 449. Joseph H. Crute, Jr., *Units of the Confederate States Army,* 202.

163. Scharf, *History of St. Louis City and County,* 449.

164. Ibid., 45

5. In Memoriam

1. Marshall D. Hier, "Attorney General Edward Bates, Lincoln's Conservative Counterweight," 44.

2. Caroline Loughlin and Catherine Anderson, *Forest Park*, 14-18, 252.

3. Marshal D. Hier, "Sir Charles Gibson: From Missouri Log Cabin to Imperial Counsel," 35. Gibson's wife was the daughter of Hamilton Gamble's brother. Loughlin and Anderson, *Forest Park*, 252.

4. McCue, *Sculpture City*, 35-36.

5. Stephen D. Engle, *Yankee Dutchman: The Life of Franz Sigel*, 2-26.

6. Ibid., 27-38.

7. Ibid., 42-43. Alfred von Rohr Sauer, "Sigel's Flanking Column: Costly Mistake at Wilson's Creek," 16. Just after Lincoln's election in 1860, for example, Sigel authored an article entitled "Can the United States Tolerate a Black Confederacy at Its Side?" (Engle, *Yankee Dutchman*, 45).

8. Warner, *Generals in Blue*, 477-78.

9. McCue, *Sculpture City*, 38. Loughlin and Anderson, *Forest Park*, 261.

10. Sauer, "Sigel's Flanking Column," 14.

11. Loughlin and Anderson, *Forest Park*, 133.

12. "Confederate Monument in St. Louis," 6, 515.

13. Ibid., 6.

14. Loughlin and Anderson, *Forest Park*, 253-54.

15. Faust, ed., *Historical Times Illustrated*, 64.

16. Warner, *Generals in Blue*, 36.

17. McFeely and McFeely, eds., *Memoirs of U.S. Grant*, 385.

18. Marshall D. Hier, "The Passion of Frank P. Blair," 56.

19. McCue, *Sculpture City*, 36. Loughlin and Anderson, *Forest Park*, 253.

20. W. T. Sherman quoted in Leo M. Kaiser, "Flood of Silver, Flood of Gold: Oratory in St. Louis," 320-21.

21. Leo M. Kaiser, "Symbolic Obelisk: The Hecker Monument in Benton Park," 353.

22. William L. Burton, *Melting Pot Soldiers: The Union's Ethnic Regiments*, 48-49, 73-74.

23. Ernest B. Furgurson, *Chancellorsville, 1863: The Souls of the Brave*, 183. "Opposing Forces in the Chattanooga Campaign," 728.

24. *St. Louis Globe-Democrat*, "Discovering a Heroic Hecker," December 2, 1906, Carl Schurz, Vertical File, MHS. Victor Wolfgang von Hagen, *The Germanic People in America*, 350.

25. Norbury L. Wayman, *History of St. Louis Neighborhoods: Lafayette Square and Benton Park*, 20. Kaiser, "Symbolic Obelisk," 355.

26. McCue, *Sculpture City*, 77.

27. Hyde and Conard, *Encyclopedia of the History of St. Louis*, 540, 1636-37. *Anzeiger des Westens* began publication in St. Louis on October 31, 1835.

28. Harvey Saalberg, "Dr. Emil Preetorius, Editor-in-Chief of the *Westliche Post*, 1864-1905," 103-6. Raymond F. Pisney, "Leadership and Service: The Presidents of the Missouri Historical Society, 1866-1983," 40.

29. Coy F. Cross II, "Carl Schurz: Reformer," 165-68.

30. Warner, *Generals in Blue*, 428. The other public memorial to Carl Schurz is a lengthy quotation carved in the north side, eastern end, of the Kiel Center on Market Street and Fourteenth Street in downtown St. Louis.

31. McCue, *Sculpture City*, 78.

32. Robert J. Rombauer, Vertical File, MHS.

33. Dressel, *Self-Guided Tour of Confederate Graves at Bellefontaine Cemetery*, 41. Hurst, *Nathan Bedford Forrest*, 379.

34. Stewart Sifakis, *Who Was Who in the Civil War*, 423. Warner, *Generals in Blue*, 306. Brownlee, *Gray Ghosts of the Confederacy*, 89-90.

35. Dressel, *Self-Guided Tour of Confederate Graves at Bellefontaine Cemetery*, 44. Stevens, *Fourth City*, 182-84.

36. United States Senate, Committee on Veterans' Affairs, *Medal of Honor Recipients, 1863-1973*.

37. Dressel, *Self-Guided Tour of Confederate Graves at Bellefontaine Cemetery*, 45. Civil War Scrapbook, MHS.

38. United States Senate, *Medal of Honor Recipients*.

39. Roger D. Hunt and Jack R. Brown, *Brevet Brigadier Generals in Blue*, 291.

40. Dressel, *Self-Guided Tour of Confederate Graves at Bellefontaine Cemetery*, 50.

41. Sifakis, *Who Was Who*, 124. Robert K. Krick, *Lee's Colonels: A Biographical Register of the Field Officers of the Army of Northern Virginia*, 412. Clark's dates of birth and death are taken from his tombstone. Krick gives Clark's dates of birth and death as January 16 and October 29.

42. Hier, "Sir Charles Gibson," 34-35. Gibson's imperial honors were stolen from the Missouri Historical Society during World War I.

43. Dressel, *Self-Guided Tour of Confederate Graves at Bellefontaine Cemetery*, 53. Stevens, *Fourth City*, 130-32.

44. Hier, "Attorney General Edward Bates," 42-44. Hyde and Conard, *Encyclopedia of the History of St. Louis*, 180-83.

45. Dressel, *Self-Guided Tour of Confederate Graves at Bellefontaine Cemetery*, 55. Hyde and Conard, *Encyclopedia of the History of St. Louis*, 292-93.

46. *Biographical Directory of the American Congress, 1774-1961*, 1573.

47. Warner, *Generals in Blue*, 476-77.

48. *Bulletin of the Missouri Historical Society*, January 1968, 186-87.

49. Walter Ehrlich, *They Have No Rights: Dred Scott's Struggle for Freedom*, 37-38. John Richard Anderson, Vertical File, MHS. *Missouri Democrat*, May 21-22, 1863. Anderson, *Border City during the Civil War*, 12-14.

50. William R. Vickroy, "The Sessinghaus Family."

51. Landmarks Association of St. Louis, Inc., *Tombstone Talks: Landmarks Tour of Bellefontaine Cemetery*, 2. Warner, *Generals in Blue*, 51-52.

52. Charles H. Cornwell, *St. Louis Mayors: Brief Biographies*, 16.

53. Dressel, *Self-Guided Tour of Confederate Graves at Bellefontaine Cemetery*, 12.

54. Hunt and Brown, *Brevet Brigadier Generals in Blue*, 690.

55. Ibid., 201. Sifakis, *Who Was Who*, 213.

56. Dressel, *Self-Guided Tour of Confederate Graves at Bellefontaine Cemetery*, 6.

57. Hunt and Brown, *Brevet Brigadier Generals in Blue*, 105.

58. Warner, *Generals in Blue*, 454-55.

59. Hier, "Hero's Death for a Lawyer," 51-53. Hyde and Conard, *Encyclopedia of the History of St. Louis*, 861-63.

60. Dressel, *Self-Guided Tour of Confederate Graves at Bellefontaine Cemetery*, 2. Shalhope, *Sterling Price*, 225-29, 287.

61. Shalhope, *Sterling Price*, 287-91. Warner, *Generals in Gray*, 246-47. Though the date of birth on Price's tombstone indicates September 14, 1809, his biographers indicate it as September 20, 1809.

62. Hunt and Brown, *Brevet Brigadier Generals in Blue*, 266.

63. Boatner, *Civil War Dictionary*, 658-60. Warner, *Generals in Blue*, 376-77.

64. Hunt and Brown, *Brevet Brigadier Generals in Blue*, 66.

65. Ibid., 560.

66. Dressel, *Self-Guided Tour of Confederate Graves at Bellefontaine Cemetery*, 13.

67. Cornwell, *St. Louis Mayors*, 7. Dressel, *Self-Guided Tour of Confederate Graves at Bellefontaine Cemetery*, 11. Clement A. Evans, *Confederate Military History—Extended Edition*, vol. 12, *Missouri*, 114.

68. Bay, *Reminiscences of the Bench*, 236-41. Hyde and Conard, *Encyclopedia of the History of St. Louis*, 740-43. Scholz, "Roswell Martin Field Home," n.p.

69. Cornwell, *St. Louis Mayors*, 19.

70. Hyde and Conard, *Encyclopedia of the History of St. Louis*, 2141-43.

71. Dressel, *Self-Guided Tour of Confederate Graves at Bellefontaine Cemetery*, 16.

72. Hyde and Conard, *Encyclopedia of the History of St. Louis*, 1739-42. Landmarks Association, *Tombstone Talks*, 17. Several of Pitzman's maps are included in the atlas to the *Official Records*.

73. United States Senate, *Medal of Honor Recipients*.

74. Hunt and Brown, *Brevet Brigadier Generals in Blue*, 449.

75. Cornwell, *St. Louis Mayors*, 18.

76. United States Senate, *Medal of Honor Recipients*. Richard Moe, *The Last Full Measure: The Life and Death of the First Minnesota Volunteers*, 289-91, 303-6.

77. Dressel, *Self-Guided Tour of Confederate Graves at Bellefontaine Cemetery*, 22.

78. United States Senate, *Medal of Honor Recipients*.

79. Dressel, *Self-Guided Tour of Confederate Graves at Bellefontaine Cemetery*, 24. Stevens, *Fourth City*, 810-12.

80. Hunt and Brown, *Brevet Brigadier Generals in Blue*, 207. Hyde and Conard, *Encyclopedia of the History of St. Louis*, 792-93. Sifakis, *Who Was Who*, 220. Fletcher's home, restored and furnished, still stands in Hillsboro, Missouri, at the southwest corner of 2d and Elm Streets. Tours can be arranged by contacting the Hillsboro Department of Parks and Recreation at 314-789-5335 or 314-942-4300 (Robert Lauenstein, "Notes on St. Louis Area Sites").

81. Hyde and Conard, *Encyclopedia of the History of St. Louis*, 1391-92.

82. Dressel, *Self-Guided Tour of Confederate Graves at Bellefontaine Cemetery*, 27. Hyde and Conard, *Encyclopedia of the History of St. Louis*, 1771-73. *Biographical Directory*, 1554.

83. Dressel, *Self-Guided Tour of Confederate Graves at Bellefontaine Cemetery*, 28.

84. Ibid., 29.

85. Ibid., 30.

86. United States Senate, *Medal of Honor Recipients*. Civil War Scrapbook, MHS.

87. Dressel, *Self-Guided Tour of Confederate Graves at Bellefontaine Cemetery*, 32. Robert H. McRoberts, *Bryan, Cave, McPheeters & McRoberts, 1873-1984*, 3-6.

88. Dressel, *Self-Guided Tour of Confederate Graves at Bellefontaine Cemetery*, 31. Warner, *Generals in Gray*, 293-94.

89. Ruth P. Randall, *Colonel Elmer Ellsworth*, 257-58. United States Senate, *Medal of Honor Recipients*.

90. Dressel, *Self-Guided Tour of Confederate Graves at Bellefontaine Cemetery*, 34.

91. Hugh Johns, "Albert Gallatin Edwards," 1-2.

92. The CSS *Virginia*, the Confederacy's first ironclad, was built on the captured hull of the USS *Merrimack*. Federal authorities continued to refer to her by that name.

93. Hyde and Conard, *Encyclopedia of the History of St. Louis*, 623-25.

94. Ibid., 2563-65.

95. Files, Bellefontaine Cemetery.

96. Hunt and Brown, *Brevet Brigadier Generals in Blue*, 663.

97. Malone, *Dictionary of American Biography*, vol. 10, 75-76. Hyde and Conard, *Encyclopedia of the History of St. Louis*, 1030-31.

98. Francis B. Heitman, *Historical Register and Dictionary of the United States Army*, vol. 1, 161.

99. Dressel, *Self-Guided Tour of Confederate Graves at Bellefontaine Cemetery*, 36. William McPheeters Papers, MHS.

100. Warner, *Generals in Blue*, 360-61.

101. Hunt and Brown, *Brevet Brigadier Generals in Blue*, 83.

102. Ibid., 414. Leslie Anders, *The Eighteenth Missouri*, 22. According to Anders, a sketch caption gives his name as "Peter Madison Miller."

103. Hier, "Passion of Frank P. Blair," 40-56. Warner, *Generals in Blue*, 35-37.

104. *Biographical Directory*, 712.

105. Faust, ed., *Historical Times Illustrated*, 681-83. Warner, *Generals in Blue*, 441-44. *St. Louis Globe-Democrat*, February 22, 1891. The device on Sherman's gravestone is a composite of the badges of the five Union army corps he led in the campaigns in Georgia and the Carolinas: XIV Corps (acorn), XV ("40 rounds"), XVII (arrow), XX Corps (star), and XXIII (shield). The phrase "40 rounds" is a reference to the standard contents of the Union soldier's cartridge box.

106. Warner, *Generals in Blue*, 512-13.

107. Evans, *Confederate Military History—Missouri*, 307-9. *St. Louis Globe-Democrat*, October 19, 1899.

108. Hunt and Brown, *Brevet Brigadier Generals in Blue*, 433. Irwin, ed., "Missouri in Crisis," 15.

109. Cornwell, *St. Louis Mayors*, 17.

110. Hyde and Conard, *Encyclopedia of the History of St. Louis*, 600-601. McPherson, *Battle Cry of Freedom*, 170-81. St. Louis Public Library, *The African-American Heritage of St. Louis: A Guide*, 3.

111. Hyde and Conard, *Encyclopedia of the History of St. Louis*, 481-82.

112. *Biographical Directory*, 751. This source gives Clemens' date of death as June 30, 1881, more than a year later than the date on his tombstone.

113. Bearss, *Vicksburg Campaign*, 816. W. F. Beyer and O. F. Keydel, eds., *Deeds of Valor*, 190-97.

114. Hyde and Conard, *Encyclopedia of the History of St. Louis*, 339-40. *St. Louis Globe-Democrat*, March 31, 1887.

115. Scharf, *History of St. Louis City and County*, 915.

116. Warner, *Generals in Gray*, 94-95.

117. Radcliffe, "Kirkwood and the Civil War," 1. Crute, *Units of the Confederate States Army*, 412. "Captain Lorraine F. Jones," 466.

118. Ray Nichols, "Solomon George Kitchen: Colonel, 7th Missouri Cavalry, C.S.A."

119. Hyde and Conard, *Encyclopedia of the History of St. Louis*, 250. Norma L. Peterson, "The Political Fluctuations of B. Gratz Brown: Politics in a Border State, 1850-1870," 23-26. Robert R. Archibald, "A Radical in the Center," 22-23.

120. Barringer Fifield and Keith Recker, *Seeing Beyond St. Louis*, 189.

121. Tony Fusco, *The Story of Jefferson Barracks National Cemetery*, 7.

122. Ibid., 4.

123. Ibid., 8.

124. Ibid., 13.

125. No current census of the Civil War graves at Jefferson Barracks National Cemetery has been located. Dyer, writing in 1908, credited the cemetery with 11,623 Union graves, of whom 2,906 were

unknown.

126. Dyer, *Compendium of the War of the Rebellion,* 1000, 1732.

127. Quoted in Joseph T. Glatthaar, *Forged in Battle: The Civil War Alliance of Black Soldiers and White Officers,* 106.

128. Dyer, *Compendium of the War of the Rebellion,* 685.

129. Glatthaar, *Forged in Battle,* 233-34.

130. Dyer, *Compendium of the War of the Rebellion,* 1732.

131. Hunt and Brown, *Brevet Brigadier Generals in Blue,* 21.

132. Scharf, *History of St. Louis City and County,* 490.

133. Hunt and Brown, *Brevet Brigadier Generals in Blue,* 399.

134. Ibid., 278.

135. Ibid., 448.

136. Ibid., 260.

137. Ibid., 43.

138. Boy Scouts of America, Troop 905, "Jefferson Barracks National Cemetery Pilgrimage."

139. John F. Powell, "George E. Dolton and the 'Comrades of the Battlefield.'" Dolton died on July 22, 1906.

140. Minnesota Monument Commission, *Report of the Minnesota Commission Appointed to Erect a Monument in the National Cemetery at Jefferson Barracks, Mo.,* 5-6.

141. Ibid., 13, 26.

142. Ibid., 35-38.

143. Faust, ed., *Historical Times Illustrated,* 498.

144. Bruce Catton, *Never Call Retreat,* 456.

145. Boy Scouts of America, "Jefferson Barracks Pilgrimage." Unfortunately the BSA transposed the digits in their pamphlet to get 1,140 Confederate dead rather than 1,104.

146. Correspondence between Mr. Joseph Moore, Civil War Round Table of St. Louis, and Sigma Alpha Epsilon fraternity headquarters, Evanston, Illinois. The fact sheet given out by Jefferson Barracks National Cemetery incorrectly places the seminal chapter of the fraternity at the University of Arkansas.

147. Fellman, *Inside War,* 197-98.

148. Fusco, "Bloody Saturday," 10. *Missouri Republican,* September 10, 1864.

149. Hunt and Brown, *Brevet Brigadier Generals in Blue,* 118.

Appendix A
Alton, Illinois

1. For analysis of the Lincoln-Douglas campaign of 1858, see Robert W. Johannsen, *The Frontier, the Union, and Stephen A. Douglas,* 228-45.

2. William E. Winter, "The Federal Prison at Alton, Illinois," 1.

3. Ibid.

4. Ibid.

5. Ibid., 1-2.

6. Williamson, "Military Prisons in the Civil War," 330. Winter, "Federal Prison," 2. Dyer, *Compendium of the War of the Rebellion,* 1102.

7. Winter, "Federal Prison," 2.

8. Ibid.

9. Ibid.

10. Ibid., 3.

11. United States Army Corps of Engineers, St. Louis District, *Alton Military Penitentiary in the Civil War: Smallpox and Burial on the Alton Harbor Islands,* 108-11.

12. Ibid., 111-12. Williamson, "Military Prisons in the Civil War," 331.

13. U.S. Army Corps of Engineers, *Alton Military Penitentiary,* 114.

14. Faust, ed., *Historical Times Illustrated,* 763-64.

15. Hyde and Conard, *Encyclopedia of the History of St. Louis,* 1313-14.

16. Merton L. Dillon, *Elijah P. Lovejoy: Abolitionist Editor,* 65.

17. Ibid., 69-71. *Missouri Republican,* December 8, 1835, quoted in Merton L. Dillon, *Elijah P. Lovejoy,* 73.

18. *Observer,* February 11, 1836, quoted in Dillon, *Elijah P. Lovejoy,* 75.

19. Dillon, *Elijah P. Lovejoy,* 82.

20. Ibid., 83-86.

21. Ibid., 88.

22. Ibid., 90.

23. Greater Alton/Twin Rivers Convention and Visitors Bureau, "Lovejoy: 'He Died a Martyr on the Altar of American Liberty.'"

24. Alton Cemetery Association, "Alton Cemetery."

25. Ibid.

Recommended for Further Study

The following list serves as a guide to some of the most useful, readily available books on Civil War St. Louis. For complete bibliographic details, see Works Consulted, following this section.

Burton, William L. *Melting Pot Soldiers: The Union's Ethnic Regiments.* (1988). An excellent overview of the problems of ethnic politics and military service. Chapter 5 discusses the German regiments, providing background for the situation in St. Louis in 1861.

Dillon, Merton L. *Elijah P. Lovejoy: Abolitionist Editor.* (1961). An important account for understanding prewar sentiments toward slavery in the St. Louis area.

Ehrlich, Walter. *They Have No Rights: Dred Scott's Struggle for Freedom.* (1979). A detailed lawyerly account of the Dred Scott decision.

Engle, Stephen D. *Yankee Dutchman: The Life of Franz Sigel.* (1993). Good overall in its discussion of the Germans and the Union, but little attention is given to Sigel's role at Camp Jackson.

Fellman, Michael. *Inside War: The Guerrilla Conflict in Missouri during the Civil War.* (1989). Of background interest for the ramifications on St. Louis as the state's urban center.

Herr, Pamela. *Jessie Benton Frémont: A Biography.* (1987). Chapters 22 and 23 discuss "General Jessie's" experiences in St. Louis.

Johannsen, Robert W. *The Frontier, the Union, and Stephen A. Douglas.* (1989). Indespensable for understanding Douglas' role in Democratic politics leading to the 1860 presidential election.

Little, Kimberly S. *Ulysses S. Grant's White Haven.* (1993). Thorough, innovative research marks this excellent account of the Grants' prewar life in St. Louis.

McFeely, William S., and Mary Drake McFeely, eds. *Personal Memoirs of U. S. Grant and Selected Letters, 1839-1865.* (1990). The chronology added to this edition makes it especially useful.

McPherson, James M. *Battle Cry of Freedom.* (1988). By far the best single-volume account of the Civil War era. Chapter 6 provides an excellent analysis of the Dred Scott decision.

Marszalek, John F. *Sherman: A Soldier's Passion for Order.* (1993). Useful concerning Sherman's life in St. Louis before and after the Civil War.

Monaghan, Jay. *Civil War on the Western Border, 1854-1865.* (1955). A very good beginning point for understanding the "border troubles" of Missouri and Kansas before the Civil War.

Parrish, William E. *Turbulent Partnership: Missouri and the Union, 1861-1865.* (1963). An authoritative account of the political difficulties of Missouri as a border state.

Phillips, Christopher. *Damned Yankee: The Life of General Nathaniel Lyon.* (1990). A critical examination of Lyon as ardent antisecessionist, indispensable to understanding events in St. Louis in 1861.

Primm, James Neal. *Lion of the Valley: St. Louis, Missouri.* (1981). The role of St. Louis in the Civil War is clearly told in chapter 7, supported by a wealth of local detail.

Rowan, Steven, ed. and trans. *Germans for a Free Missouri: Translations from the St. Louis Radical Press, 1857-1862.* (1983). Important to comprehension of the political sympathies and aspirations of the city's largest minority on the eve of the Civil War.

Shalhope, Robert E. *Sterling Price: Portrait of a Southerner.* (1971). Useful for the Southern view of events in Missouri.

Works Consulted

Unpublished Works

I am grateful to the following Friends and Members of the Civil War Round Table of St. Louis for allowing me to quote from their unpublished works.

Dressel, Leonard E., II. "Major James Morgan Utz, C.S.A."

Johns, Hugh. "Albert Gallatin Edwards."

Johnson, Vicki Vaughn. "Antebellum St. Louis."

———. "War Comes to Main Street: The St. Louis Chamber of Commerce Election of 1862." Paper presented at the Missouri Conference on History, St. Louis, March 25, 1994.

Lauenstein, Robert. "Notes on the Fortifications of St. Louis."

———. "Notes on St. Louis Area Sites."

Margreiter, John. "Major James Wilson: 3d Cavalry, Missouri State Militia, U.S.A."

Nichols, Ray. "Solomon George Kitchen: Colonel, 7th Missouri Cavalry, C.S.A."

Powell, John F. "George E. Dolton and the 'Comrades of the Battlefield.'"

Radcliffe, David. "Kirkwood and the Civil War."

Vickroy, William R. "The Sessinghaus Family."

Winter, William E. "The Federal Prison at Alton, Illinois."

Newspapers

Daily Missouri State Journal
Mississippi Blaetter
Missouri Democrat
Missouri Republican
National Intelligencer
St. Louis Business Journal
St. Louis Daily Evening News
St. Louis Globe-Democrat
St. Louis Post-Dispatch
St. Louis Star
Westliche Post

Archival Collections

Anderson, John R., Vertical File, Missouri Historical Society, St. Louis.

Bassford Scrapbook, Missouri Historical Society, St. Louis.

Bowen, John S., Compiled Service Records, National Archives.

Bowen Family Papers, Missouri Historical Society, St. Louis.

Bull, William, Papers, Missouri Historical Society, St. Louis.

Camp Jackson Papers, Missouri Historical Society, St. Louis.

Camp Jackson Survey, St. Louis Mercantile Library, St. Louis.

Civil War Scrapbook, Missouri Historical Society, St. Louis.

Files, Bellefontaine Cemetery, St. Louis.

Files, Calvary Cemetery, St. Louis.

Files, St. Bridget of Erin Church, St. Louis.

McPheeters, William, Papers, Missouri Historical Society, St. Louis.

Map Collection, Missouri Historical Society, St. Louis.

Osterhaus Memoirs, Belleville Public Library, Belleville, Illinois.

Robbins, Edward C., Papers, St. Louis Mercantile Library, St. Louis.

Rombauer, Robert J., Vertical File, Missouri Historical Society, St. Louis.

Schurz, Carl. Vertical File, Missouri Historical Society, St. Louis.

Sherman Family Papers, University of Notre Dame Archives, South Bend.

Stephenson, P. D., "My War Autobiography," Louisiana State University, Baton Rouge.

Stevens, W. B., Scrapbook, Missouri Historical Society, St. Louis.

Published Works

Adamson, Hans Christian. *Rebellion in Missouri: 1861.* Philadelphia: Chilton, 1961.

Alton Cemetery Association. "Alton Cemetery." Pamphlet, n.d.

Anders, Leslie. *The Eighteenth Missouri.* Indianapolis: The Bobbs-Merrill Co., 1968.

Anderson, Ephraim McD. *Memoirs: Historical and Personal; Including the Campaigns of the First Missouri Confederate Brigade.* 1868. Reprint, Dayton: Morningside House, 1972.

Anderson, Galusha. *A Border City during the Civil War.* Boston: Little, Brown and Co., 1908.

Archibald, Robert R. "A Radical in the Center." *St. Louis People Magazine,* January 1991, 22-23.

———. "St. Louis Editor Battled Slavery for Economic, Not Ethical Reasons." *St. Louis Business Journal,* September 3, 1990, 3B.

Bartley, Mary. "Palace to Warehouse." *West End Word,* March 20, 1986, 3.

Bay, W. V. N. *Reminiscences of the Bench and Bar of Missouri.* St. Louis: F. H. Thomas and Co., 1878.

Bearss, Edwin C. *Hardluck Ironclad: The Sinking and Salvage of the "Cairo."* Baton Rouge: Louisiana State University Press, 1980.

———. *The Vicksburg Campaign.* 3 vols. Dayton: Morningside House, 1985-86.

Bek, William G., trans. "The Civil War Diary of John T. Buegel, Union Soldier." *Missouri Historical Review* 40 (April 1946): 307-13.

Beyer, W. F., and O. F. Keydel, eds. *Deeds of Valor.* Detroit: The Perrien-Keydel Co., 1906.

Biographical Directory of the American Congress, 1774-1961. Washington, D.C.: GPO, 1961.

Blum, Virgil C. "The Political and Military Activities of the German Element in St. Louis, 1859-1861." *Missouri Historical Review* 42 (January 1948): 103-29.

Boatner, Mark M., III. *The Civil War Dictionary.* New York: David McKay, 1959.

Boernstein, Heinrich "Henry." *Funfundsiebzig Jahre in der Alten und Neuen Welt.* 1881. Reprint, New York: Peter Lang, 1986.

———. *The Mysteries of St. Louis.* Translated by Friedrich Muench. Edited by Steven Rowan and Elizabeth Sims. Chicago: Charles H. Kerr Publishing Co., 1990.

Boogher, Mrs. Simon L. (Sophia Hogan Boogher). *Recollections of John Hogan.* St. Louis: Privately printed, 1927.

Boy Scouts of America, Troop 905. "Jefferson Barracks National Cemetery Pilgrimage." N.d.

Bradley, James. *Confederate Mail Carrier*. Mexico, Missouri, 1894. Reprint, Bowie, Md.: Heritage Books, 1990.

Brownlee, Richard S. *Gray Ghosts of the Confederacy: Guerrilla Warfare in the West, 1861-1865*. Baton Rouge: Louisiana State University Press, 1958.

Burton, Katherine. *Three Generations: Maria Boyle Ewing, Ellen Ewing Sherman, and Minnie Sherman Fitch*. New York: Longmans, Green and Co., 1947.

Burton, William L. *Melting Pot Soldiers: The Union's Ethnic Regiments*. Ames: Iowa State University Press, 1988.

"Captain Lorraine F. Jones." *Confederate Veteran* (1920): 466-67.

Carter, Harvey L., and Norma L. Peterson, eds. "William S. Stewart Letters, January 13, 1861, to December 4, 1862." *Missouri Historical Review* 61 (January 1967): 187-228.

Castel, Albert. *A Frontier State at War: Kansas, 1861-1865*. Cornell: Cornell University Press, 1958. Reprint, Westport, Conn.: Greenwood Press, 1979.

Castleman, John B. *Active Service*. Louisville: Courier-Journal Job Printing Co., 1917.

Catton, Bruce. *Mr. Lincoln's Army*. New York: Doubleday & Co., 1962.

———. *Never Call Retreat*. New York: Doubleday & Co., 1965.

Coalier, Paula. "Beyond Sympathy: The St. Louis Ladies' Union Aid Society and the Civil War." *Gateway Heritage* 11 (Summer 1990): 38-51.

"Confederate Monument in St. Louis." *Confederate Veteran* (1915): 16.

Corbett, Katherine T. "Bellefontaine Cemetery: St. Louis City of the Dead." *Gateway Heritage* 12 (Fall 1991): 58-67.

Cornwell, Charles H. *St. Louis Mayors: Brief Biographies*. St. Louis: St. Louis Public Library, 1965.

Coyle, Elinor M. *Old St. Louis Homes, 1790-1865: "The Stories They Tell."* St. Louis: Folkestone Press, 1964.

Cromie, Alice Hamilton. *A Tour Guide to the Civil War*. 2d ed. New York: E. P. Dutton, 1975.

Cross, Coy F., II. "Carl Schurz: Reformer." In *Missouri Folk Heroes of the 19th Century*, edited by F. Mark McKiernan and Roger D. Launius, 165-80. Independence, Mo.: Independence Press, Herald Publishing House, 1989.

Cross, Jasper W. "The Mississippi Valley Sanitary Fair, St. Louis, 1864." *Missouri Historical Review* 46 (April 1952): 237-46.

Crute, Joseph H., Jr. *Units of the Confederate States Army*. Midlothian, Va.: Derwent Books, 1987.

Cullum, George W. *Biographical Register of the Officers and Graduates of the U.S. Military Academy at West Point, N.Y.* 3 vols. New York: Houghton, Mifflin and Co., 1891.

Daniel, Larry J. "Bruinsburg: Missed Opportunity or Postwar Rhetoric?" *Civil War History* 32 (September 1986): 256-67.

Dillon, Merton L. *Elijah P. Lovejoy: Abolitionist Editor*. Urbana: University of Illinois Press, 1961.

Dosch, Donald F. *The Old Courthouse*. St. Louis: Jefferson National Expansion Historical Association, 1979.

Dressel, Leonard E., II. *A Self-Guided Tour of Confederate Graves at Bellefontaine Cemetery*. St. Louis: Sons of Confederate Veterans, Sterling Price Camp No. 145, 1992.

Drumm, Stella M. "Historic Homes of Missouri: The Berthold Mansion." *Missouri Historical Society Collections* 4.3 (1914): 290-94.

———. "The Kennerlys of Virginia." *Missouri Historical Society Collections* 6 (October 1928): 98-123.

Duke, Basil W. *Reminiscences of General Basil W. Duke, C.S.A.* Garden City: Doubleday, Page & Co., 1911.

Dunson, A. A. "Notes on the Missouri Germans on Slavery." *Missouri Historical Review* 59 (April 1965): 355-66.

Dupuy, R. Ernest, and Trevor N. Dupuy. *The Encyclopedia of Military History*. New York: Harper & Row, 1970.

Dyer, Frederick H. *A Compendium of the War of the Rebellion*. Des Moines, Iowa: Dyer Publishing Co., 1908.

Edom, Clifton C. *Missouri Sketch Book: A Collection of Words and Pictures of the Civil War*. Columbia, Mo.: Lucas Brothers, 1963.

Ehrlich, Walter. *They Have No Rights: Dred Scott's Struggle for Freedom*. Westport, Conn.: Greenwood Press, 1979.

Engle, Stephen D. *Yankee Dutchman: The Life of Franz Sigel*. Fayetteville: University of Arkansas Press, 1993.

Evans, Clement A. *Confederate Military History—Extended Edition*. Vol. 12, *Missouri*. 1899. Reprint, Wilmington, N.C.: Broadfoot, 1988.

Faust, Patricia, ed. *Historical Times Illustrated Encyclopedia of the Civil War*. New York: Harper & Row, 1986.

Fellman, Michael. *Inside War: The Guerrilla Conflict in Missouri during the Civil War*. New York: Oxford University Press, 1989.

Fifield, Barringer, and Keith Recker. *Seeing Beyond St. Louis*. St. Louis: Washington University, 1991.

———. *Seeing St. Louis*. St. Louis: Washington University, 1987.

"Files of the *Westliche Post* Presented to the Society." *Bulletin of the Missouri Historical Society* 4 (October 1947): 47-48.

Fletcher, Thomas C. *Life and Reminiscences of General Wm. T. Sherman*. Baltimore: R. H. Woodward Co., 1891.

Frémont, Jessie Benton. *Souvenirs of My Time*. Boston: D. Lothrop Co., 1887.

———. *The Story of the Guard: A Chronicle of the War*. Boston: Ticknor and Fields, 1863.

Frémont, John C. "In Command in Missouri." In *Battles and Leaders of the Civil War.*, edited by Clarence Clough Buel and Robert Underwood Johnson, vol. 1, 278-88, 1887. Reprint, New York: Castle Books, 1956.

Frost, Griffin. *Camp and Prison Journal*. Quincy, Illinois: Quincy Herald Book and Job Office, 1867.

Frost, Marcus O. *Regimental History of the Tenth Missouri Volunteer Infantry*. Topeka, Kans.: M. O. Frost Printing Co., 1892.

Furgurson, Ernest B. *Chancellorsville, 1863: The Souls of the Brave*. New York: Alfred A. Knopf, 1992.

Fusco, Tony. "Bloody Saturday." *St. Louis Home Magazine*, June 1976, 7-10.

———. *The Story of Jefferson Barracks National Cemetery*. St. Louis, 1967.

Gill, McCune. *The St. Louis Story*. 3 vols. Hopkinsville, Ky., and St. Louis: Historical Record Association, 1952.

Glatthaar, Joseph T. *Forged in Battle: The Civil War Alliance of Black Soldiers and White Officers*. New York: The Free Press, 1990.

Gray, Melvin L. "Recollections of Judge Roswell M. Field." In *The History of the Bench and Bar of Missouri*. St. Louis, 1899.

Greater Alton/Twin Rivers Convention and Visitors Bureau. "Lovejoy: 'He Died a Martyr on the Altar of American Liberty.'" Illinois Department of Commerce and Community Affairs pamphlet, 1987.

Grisham, Marjorie E. Fox. "Joseph Nash McDowell and the Medical Department of Kemper College, 1840-1845." *Bulletin of the Missouri Historical Society* 12 (July 1956): 358-71.

Hannon, Robert E., comp. and ed. *St. Louis: Its Neighborhoods and Neighbors, Landmarks and Milestones*. St. Louis: St. Louis Regional Commerce and Growth Association, 1986.

Heitman, Francis B. *Historical Register and Dictionary of the United States Army*. 2 vols. Washington, D.C.: GPO, 1973.

Herr, Pamela. *Jessie Benton Frémont: A Biography*. New York: Franklin Watts, 1987.

Hesseltine, W. B. "Military Prisons of St. Louis, 1861-1865." *Missouri Historical Review* 51 (1957): 380-99.

Hier, Marshall D. "A Hero's Death for a Lawyer, Hamilton Rowan Gamble." *St. Louis Bar Journal* (Winter 1989): 51-53.

———. "Attorney General Edward Bates, Lincoln's Conservative Counterweight." *St. Louis Bar Journal* (Spring 1991): 42-44.

———. "The Passion of Frank P. Blair." *St. Louis Bar Journal* (Summer 1992): 40-56.

———. "Sir Charles Gibson: From Missouri Log Cabin to Imperial Counsel." *St. Louis Bar Journal* (Spring 1992): 34-35.

———. "The Spellbinding Voice of Uriel Wright." *St. Louis Bar Journal* (Spring 1991): 34-41.

Holland, Dorothy G. "The Planters' House." *Bulletin of the Missouri Historical Society* 28 (January 1972): 109-17.

Hopewell, M., M.D. *Camp Jackson: History of the Missouri Volunteer Militia of St. Louis*. St. Louis: George Knapp & Co., 1861.

Horan, James D. *Confederate Agent: A Discovery in History.* New York: Crown Publishers, 1954.

Howe, M. A. deWolfe, ed. *Home Letters of General Sherman*. New York: Charles Scribner's Sons, 1909.

Hunt, Roger D., and Jack R. Brown. *Brevet Brigadier Generals in Blue*. Gaithersburg: Old Soldier Books, 1990.

Hurst, Jack. *Nathan Bedford Forrest*. New York: Alfred A. Knopf, 1993.

Hyde, William, and Howard L. Conard. *Encyclopedia of the History of St. Louis*. New York: Southern History Co., 1899.

Irwin, Ray W., ed. "Missouri in Crisis: The Journal of Captain Albert Tracy, 1861." *Missouri Historical Review* 51 (October 1957): 8-21.

Jenkins, Paul B. *The Battle of Westport*. Kansas City, Mo.: Franklin Hudson Publishing Co., 1906.

Johannsen, Robert W. *The Frontier, the Union, and Stephen A. Douglas*. Urbana: University of Illinois Press, 1989.

"John S. Bowen House." Carondelet Historical Society Newsletter. Vol. 12, no. 4 (September 1981), 1-2.

Josyph, Peter, ed. *The Wounded River: The Civil War Letters of John Vance Lauderdale, M.D.* East Lansing: Michigan State University Press, 1993.

Kaiser, Leo M. "Flood of Silver, Flood of Gold: Oratory in St. Louis." *Bulletin of the Missouri Historical Society* 26 (July 1960): 303-21.

———. "Symbolic Obelisk: The Hecker Monument in Benton Park." *Bulletin of the Missouri Historical Society* 17 (July 1961): 352-56.

Keiser, Thomas J. "The St. Louis Years of Ulysses S. Grant." *Gateway Heritage* 6 (Winter 1985-1986): 10-21.

Knapp, Joseph G. *The Presence of the Past*. St. Louis: St. Louis University, 1979.

Krause, Bonnie J. "German Americans in the St. Louis Region, 1840-1860." *Missouri Historical Review* 83 (April 1989): 295-310.

Krick, Robert K. *Lee's Colonels: A Biographical Register of the Field Officers of the Army of Northern Virginia*. 4th ed., revised. Dayton, Ohio: Morningside House, 1992.

Lademann, Otto C. "The Capture of Camp Jackson." *War Papers of the Wisconsin Military Order of the Loyal Legion of the United States* (1914): 69-75.

Landmarks Association of St. Louis, Inc. *Tombstone Talks: Landmarks Tour of Bellefontaine Cemetery*. Reprint, 1975.

Loughlin, Caroline, and Catherine Anderson. *Forest Park*. Columbia: The Junior League of St. Louis and University of Missouri Press, 1986.

Lewis, Lloyd. *Captain Sam Grant*. Boston: Little, Brown and Co., 1950.

———. *Sherman: Fighting Prophet*. New York: Harcourt and Brace, 1932.

Little, Kimberly S. *Ulysses S. Grant's White Haven*. St. Louis: Historic Resource Study, Ulysses S. Grant National Historic Site, National Park Service, 1993.

Long, E. B., and Barbara Long. *The Civil War Day by Day: An Almanac, 1861-1865*. Garden City: Doubleday and Co., 1971.

Longstreet, James. *From Manassas to Appomattox*. Philadelphia: Lippincott, 1896. Reprint, Bloomington: Indiana University Press, 1960.

Lord, Francis A. *They Fought for the Union*. New York: Bonanza Books, 1960.

McAllister, Anna. *Ellen Ewing, Wife of General Sherman*. New York: Benziger Brothers, 1936.

McCue, George. *Sculpture City: St. Louis*. New York: Hudson Hills Press, 1988.

McElroy, John. *The Struggle for Missouri*. Washington, D.C.: The National Tribune Co., 1909.

McFeely, William S., and Mary Drake McFeely, eds. *Personal Memoirs of U. S. Grant and Selected Letters, 1839-1865*. New York: Library of America, 1990.

McKee, Howard I. "The 'Swamp Fox,' Meriwether Jeff Thompson." *Bulletin of the Missouri Historical Society* 13 (January 1957): 118-34.

McPherson, James M. *Battle Cry of Freedom*. New York: Oxford University Press, 1988.

McRoberts, Robert H. *Bryan, Cave, McPheeters & McRoberts, 1873-1984.* Privately printed, 1984.

McWhiney, Grady. *Braxton Bragg and Confederate Defeat*. Vol. 1. Tuscaloosa: University of Alabama Press, 1969.

March, David D. *The History of Missouri*. New York: Lewis Historical Publishing Co., 1967.

Marszalek, John F. *Sherman: A Soldier's Passion for Order*. New York: The Free Press, 1993.

Miers, Earl S. *The General Who Marched to Hell*. 1951. Reprint, New York: Dorset Press, 1990.

Miller, Clarence E. "Edward William Johnston, Roving Scholar." *Missouri Historical Review* 47 (October 1952): 81-87.

Minnesota Monument Commission. *Report of the Minnesota Commission Appointed to Erect a Monument in the National Cemetery at Jefferson Barracks, Mo.*, 1922.

Moe, Richard. *The Last Full Measure: The Life and Death of the First Minnesota Volunteers*. New York: Henry Holt and Co., 1993.

Monaghan, Jay. *Civil War on the Western Border, 1854-1865*. Lincoln: University of Nebraska Press, 1955.

Moore, Robert, Jr. "A Ray of Hope, Extinguished: St. Louis Slave Suits for Freedom." *Gateway Heritage* 14 (Winter 1993-1994): 4-15.

Mueller, Richard E. "Jefferson Barracks: The Early Years." *Missouri Historical Review* 67 (October 1972): 7-30.

Oates, Stephen B. *Confederate Cavalry West of the River*. Austin: University of Texas Press, 1961.

O'Connor, Candace. "Sherman in St. Louis." *St. Louis Post-Dispatch Magazine*, July 21, 1991, 8-11.

O'Connor, Patrick J. *History of Cheltenham and St. James Parish, St. Louis, 1860-1937*. St. Louis, 1937.

Olson, Audrey L. "St. Louis Germans, 1850-1920: The Nature of an Immigrant Community and Its Relations to the Assimilation Process." Ph.D. diss., University of Kansas, 1970.

"Opposing Forces in the Chattanooga Campaign." In *Battles and Leaders of the Civil War*, edited by Clarence Clough Buel and Robert Underwood Johnson, vol. 3, 728, 1887. Reprint, New York: Castle Books, 1956.

Parrish, William E. *Turbulent Partnership: Missouri and the Union, 1861-1865*. Columbia: University of Missouri Press, 1963.

Peckham, James. *General Nathaniel Lyon and Missouri in 1861*. New York: American News Co., 1866.

Peterson, Norma L. "The Political Fluctuations of B. Gratz Brown: Politics in a Border State, 1850-1870." *Missouri Historical Review* 51 (October 1956): 22-30.

Phillips, Christopher. *Damned Yankee: The Life of General Nathaniel Lyon*. Columbia: University of Missouri Press, 1990.

Pisney, Raymond F. "Leadership and Service: The Presidents of the Missouri Historical Society, 1866-1983." *Gateway Heritage* 4 (Fall 1983): 36-48.

Primm, James Neal. *Lion of the Valley: St. Louis, Missouri*. Boulder: Pruett Publishing Co., 1981.

Quaife, M. M., ed. *Absalom Grimes, Confederate Mail Runner*. New Haven: Yale University Press, 1926.

Randall, Ruth P. *Colonel Elmer Ellsworth*. Boston: Little, Brown and Co., 1960.

Ravenswaay, Charles Van. "Years of Turmoil, Years of Growth: St. Louis in the 1850s." *Bulletin of the Missouri Historical Society* 23 (July 1967): 303-24.

Reavis, L. U. *The Life and Military Service of Gen. William Selby Harney*. St. Louis: Bryan, Brand & Co., 1878.

Record and Pension Office, War Department. *Organization and Status of Missouri Troops (Union and Confederate) in Service during the Civil War*. Washington: Government Printing Office, 1902.

Roberts, Richard. "How General Frost Won the High Ground at Grand & Lindell." *Universitas* (Winter 1988): 22-25.

Roberts, Robert B. *Encyclopedia of Historic Forts*. New York: Macmillan Publishing Co., 1988.

Rombauer, Robert J. *The Union Cause in St. Louis in 1861*. St. Louis: Nixon-Jones Printing Co., 1909.

Rowan, Steven, ed. and trans. *Germans for a Free Missouri: Translations from the St. Louis Radical Press, 1857-1862*. Columbia: University of Missouri Press, 1983.

Saalberg, Harvey. "Dr. Emil Preetorius, Editor-in-Chief of the *Westliche Post*, 1864-1905." *Bulletin of the Missouri Historical Society* 24 (January 1968): 103-12.

St. Louis Directory for the Year 1857. St. Louis: R. V. Kennedy and Co., 1857.

St. Louis Directory for the Year 1859. St. Louis: R. V. Kennedy and Co., 1859.

St. Louis Directory for the Year 1860. St. Louis: R. V. Kennedy and Co., 1860.

St. Louis Genealogical Society. *Index of St. Louis Marriages, 1804-1876*. 2 vols. St. Louis: St. Louis Genealogical Society, 1973.

———. *Old Cemeteries of St. Louis County, Missouri*. Vol. 3. St. Louis: St. Louis Genealogical Society, 1984.

St. Louis Public Library. *The African-American Heritage of St. Louis: A Guide*. February, 1992.

Sauer, Alfred von Rohr. "Sigel's Flanking Column: Costly Mistake at Wilson's Creek." *Gateway Heritage* 7 (Fall 1986): 14-23.

Scharf, J. Thomas. *History of St. Louis City and County*. 2 vols. Philadelphia: Louis H. Everts and Co., 1883.

Scholz, John. "Notes on the Roswell Martin Field Home." The Eugene Field House and Toy Museum. Manuscript, n.d.

Shalhope, Robert E. *Sterling Price: Portrait of a Southerner*. Columbia: University of Missouri Press, 1971.

Shepard, Elihu H. *The Autobiography of Elihu H. Shepard*. St. Louis: G. Knapp & Co., 1869.

Sherman, William T. *Memoirs of General W. T. Sherman by Himself*. 1875. Reprint, New York: Library of America, 1990.

Sifakis, Stewart. *Who Was Who in the Civil War*. New York: Facts on File, 1988.

Silverstone, Paul H. *Warships of the Civil War Navies*. Annapolis: Naval Institute Press, 1989.

Simon, John Y. "Grant at Hardscrabble." *Bulletin of the Missouri Historical Society* 35 (July 1979): 191-201.

Simon, John Y., ed. *The Personal Memoirs of Julia Dent Grant*. New York: G. P. Putnam's and Sons, 1975.

Simpson, Harold B. *Cry Comanche: The 2d U.S. Cavalry in Texas, 1855-1861*. 2d ed. Hillsboro, Tex.: Hill College Press, 1988.

Snead, Thomas L. *The Fight for Missouri from the Election of Lincoln to the Death of Lyon*. New York: Charles Scribner's Sons, 1886.

———. "The First Year of the War in Missouri." In *Battles and Leaders of the Civil War*, edited by Clarence Clough Buel and Robert Underwood Johnson, vol. 1, 262-77. 1887. Reprint, New York: Castle Books, 1956.

Stadler, Mrs. Ernst A. "New Acquisitions: Manuscripts." *Bulletin of the Missouri Historical Society* 24 (January 1968): 186-87.

Starr, Stephen Z. *Jennison's Jayhawkers: A Civil War Cavalry Regiment and Its Commander*. Baton Rouge: Louisiana State University Press, 1973.

———. *The War in the East from Gettysburg to Appomattox, 1863-1865*. Vol. 2 of *The Union Cavalry in the Civil War*. Baton Rouge: Louisiana State University Press, 1981.

Stevens, Walter B. *St. Louis, The Fourth City, 1764-1909*. St. Louis: S. J. Clarke Publishing Co., 1909.

Stewart, Rick, Joseph D. Ketner II, and Angela L. Miller. *Carl Wimar: Chronicler of the Missouri River Frontier*. Fort Worth: Amon Carter Museum, 1991.

Stidger, Felix G. *Treason History of the Order of Sons of Liberty*. N.p. 1903.

Sumner, Merlin E., ed. *The Diary of Cyrus B. Comstock*. Dayton, Ohio: Morningside House, 1987.

Tidwell, William A., James O. Hall, and David Winifred Gaddy. *Come Retribution: The Confederate Secret Service and the Assassination of Abraham Lincoln*. Jackson: University Press of Mississippi, 1988.

Tilley, Nannie M., ed. *Federals on the Frontier: The Diary of Benjamin F. McIntyre, 1862-1864*. Austin: University of Texas Press, 1963.

Tucker, Glenn. *Hancock the Superb*. Indianapolis: The Bobbs-Merrill Co., 1960. Reprint, Dayton: Morningside Bookshop, 1980.

Tucker, Philip T. *The Confederacy's Fighting Chaplain: Father John B. Bannon*. Tuscaloosa: University of Alabama Press, 1992.

United Daughters of the Confederacy, Missouri Division. *Reminiscences of the Women of Missouri during the Sixties*. N.p. 1913. Reprint, Dayton: Morningside House, 1988.

United States Army Corps of Engineers, St. Louis District. *Alton Military Penitentiary in the Civil War: Smallpox and Burial on the Alton Harbor Islands*. Historic Properties Managment Report No. 36. November 1988.

———. *Archaeological Investigations at the St. Louis Arsenal Site*. Cultural Resource Management Report No. 22. March 1985.

United States Department of the Interior, National Park Service. *The Old Courthouse*. Jefferson Expansion Memorial, Missouri. N.d.

United States Senate. Committee on Veterans' Affairs. *Medal of Honor Recipients, 1863-1973*. Washington, D.C.: GPO, 1973.

United States War Department. *The War of the Rebellion: A Compilation of the Official Records of the Union and Confederate Armies*. 4 ser., 128 vols. Washington, D.C., 1881-1901.

von Hagen, Victor Wolfgang. *The Germanic People in America*. Norman: University of Oklahoma Press, 1976.

Warner, Ezra J. *Generals in Blue: Lives of the Union Commanders*. Baton Rouge: Louisiana State University Press, 1964.

———. *Generals in Gray: Lives of the Confederate Commanders*. Baton Rouge: Louisiana State University Press, 1959.

Wayman, Norbury L. *History of St. Louis Neighborhoods: Lafayette Square and Benton Park*. St. Louis: Civic Development Authority, 1980.

Wheeler, Richard. *We Knew General William Tecumseh Sherman*. New York: Thomas Y. Crowell, 1977.

Wherry, William M. "Wilson's Creek, and the Death of Lyon." In *Battles and Leaders of the Civil War*, edited by Clarence Clough Buel and Robert Underwood Johnson, vol. 1, 289-97. 1887. Reprint, New York: Castle Books, 1956.

Williamson, Hugh P. "Military Prisons in the Civil War." *Bulletin of the Missouri Historical Society* 16 (July 1960): 329-32.

Index

Holmes, Samuel A., 94
Holt, Joseph, 89
Home Guards, 39, 66, 69, 105; and Camp Jackson, 44-45, 142; and Nathaniel Lyon, 39, 44. *See also* United States Reserve Corps
Hood, John B., 7
Hotchkiss, Almerin, 110
Howard, Oliver O., 20
Hoyt, George, 84
Hughes, Harry H., 99
Hunter, David, 72, 137
Hunter, John, 16
Hutchinson, Robert Randolph, 115
Hyatt, Frederick, 99
Hyde Park, 87

Icenhower, William E., 53
Illinois units: 144th Infantry, 153
Immel, Lorenzo D., 147
Imperial (steamboat), 88
Independence, Mo., 83
Ironclad gunboats, 77-78, 130

J. C. Swon (steamboat), 88
Jackson, Claiborne Fox, 4, 30, 67-69, 121, 128, 133, 139, 146; and Camp Jackson, 35, 39, 47
Jackson, James T., 129
Jackson, Thomas J., 107, 122, 127
January, Derrick A., 81
Jayhawkers, 83-85
Jefferson, Thomas, 4, 100
Jefferson Barracks, 40, 42, 130; and the Civil War, 7, 63; and future military leaders, 4-7; and Jefferson Barracks National Cemetery, 7, 97, 144-50; and John S. Bowen, 21-22; and the Mexican War, 6; and Ulysses S. Grant, 9-10; and the U.S. Arsenal at St. Louis, 40, 42; and William T. Sherman, 14-16; *illus.*, 5
Jefferson Barracks County Park, 4, 7, 14, 144
Jefferson Barracks National Cemetery, 7, 97, 144-50
Jencks, Mary Ewing (Mrs. Albert Edwards), 130
Jennison, Charles Rainsford, 83-85
Jesse K. Polk (steamboat), 88
Johnson, J. B., 91
Johnson, Richard W., 7
Johnston, Albert Sidney, 5-6
Johnston, Edward William, 29
Johnston, Joseph E., 6-7, 110, 129, 147; and William T. Sherman, 19
Johnston, Mrs. Edward, 30
Jones, Francis, 89
Jones, Lorraine Farquhar, 141
Jones, William, 13
Journal of Army Life: and St. Louis, 3

Julian, Joseph Pearson, 154

Kallmann, Herman, 45
Kansas units: 7th Cavalry, 84-85; 10th Infantry, 97
Kautz, August, 90
Kearney, Stephen W., 14, 71, 117
Kennerly, Abbie Frances, 22
Kennerly, George Hancock, 21-22
Kennerly, Mary Lucretia Preston (Mrs. John S. Bowen), 21-23, 40
Kenrick, Peter Richard, 134
Kirkwood, Mo., 95
Kitchen, Solomon George, 142
Knapp, George, 42, 140
Knapp, John, 42, 48, 66, 140
Knoblock, Nicholas, 53
Kretschmar, Howard, 13, 106

Ladd, Asa V., 150
Lademann, Otto, 50, 53-54; *illus.*, 50
Lane, James, 85
Lappe, Conrad, 64
Lash, Elizabeth Ann, 144
Lawrence, Jacob, 64
Lebeau, Emilie, 138
Lee, Robert E., 5-7, 105, 122
Lincoln, Abraham, 25-26, 36, 77, 85, 91, 99, 101, 104-5, 107, 109, 116, 121, 125, 130, 146; and 1860 election, 4, 27, 101, 152; and John C. Frémont, 72-73
Lincoln-Douglas Square (Alton, Ill.), 152
Lind, Jenny, 67
Lindell Grove, 47, 49-50, 53, 85
Longstreet, James, 6, 122
Louisville (gunboat), 78; *illus.*, 78
Lovejoy, Celia Ann French, 156
Lovejoy, Elijah P., 25, 117-18, 155-56; monument to (Alton, Ill.), 155-56
Lowden, Mrs. R., 86
Lyden, John, 148
Lynch, Bernard M., 84
Lynch's Slave Pen, 25, 84. *See also* Myrtle Street Prison
Lyon, Nathaniel, 68, 115, 119, 121, 131, 140, 146; and battle of Wilson's Creek, 72; and Camp Jackson, 34, 36-37, 39-43, 45, 47, 50, 53-54; and Constantin Blandowski's funeral, 66; and defense of St. Louis, 75; monuments to, 36-37, *illus.*, 37; and pursuit of Governor Jackson, 69; *illus.*, 35
Lyon Park, 36-37, 40, 54

McClellan, George B., 6, 17, 93, 118, 122
McCulloch, Ben, 36
McCulloch, Robert, 114

MacDonald, Emmett, 55, 119, 123; *illus.*, 54
MacDonald, James Wilson Alexander, 102-3
McDougall, Charles, 146
McDowell, Drake, 79
McDowell, Joseph Nash, 79, 127; *illus.*, 127
McDowell, Max, 79
McDowell Medical College, 79-80, 127. *See also* Gratiot Street Prison
McGunnegle, Wilson, 130-31
McIntosh, Francis, 155
McLure, Margaret Parkinson, 85-86
McLure, William Parkinson, 86
McLure, William Raines, 85
McNeil, John, 45, 114
McNutt, John, 14
McPheeters, William M., 132
McPherson, James B., 153
McPike's Island, 153-54
Magoffin, Beriah, 80
Magoffin, Ebenezer, 153
Magruder, John, 116
Marine Hospital. *See* United States Marine Hospital
Marmaduke, John S., 95, 97, 119
Martin, Frank, 88
Mason, Margaret Hunter, 118
Mason, Richard B., 118
Medal of Honor, 114, 125, 126, 128, 129, 131, 139, 147, 150
Meigs, Montgomery C., 77
Memoirs of General W. T. Sherman by Himself, 18
Memorial to the Unknown Dead, Jefferson Barracks National Cemetery, 148
Menard, Alzire, 21-22
Menard, Pierre, 21
Mercantile Library, 25, 29-31; and the Civil War, 30, 82, 92
Meriwether, Minor, 110
Merritt, Wesley, 20
Mexican War: and Jefferson Barracks, 6; and the U.S. Arsenal at St. Louis, 38
Meyers, George F., 96
Miller, Bernard, 64
Miller, Charles C., 22
Miller, Madison, 132
Miller, Victor, 37
Milne, Henry, 51, 53
Minnekin, Charles W., 97, 150
Minnesota Monument (Jefferson Barracks National Cemetery), 147-48
Minute Men, 25, 31-33, 42, 44, 105
Missouri: and the Civil War, 4, 7, 27, 30, 36, 63, 68, 84-86, 95-96; and the 1860 election, 3-4; and John C. Frémont, 72, 142; and slavery, 3, 72, 83-85, 121, 142